WOMEN, ELECTIONS, and REPRESENTATION

WOMEN, ELECTIONS, and REPRESENTATION

R. Darcy,
Susan Welch, and
Janet Clark

Longman
New York & London

Senior Editor: David J. Estrin
Production Editor: Helen B. Ambrosio
Text Design: Steven A. Krastin
Production Supervisor: Eduardo Castillo
Compositor: Pine Tree Composition Inc.
Printer and Binder: Molloy Lithographing, Inc.

Women, Elections, and Representation

Longman Inc., 95 Church Street, White Plains, NY 10601

Associated companies: Longman Group Ltd., London; Longman Cheshire Pty., Melbourne; Longman Paul Pty., Auckland; Copp Clark Pitman, Toronto; Pitman Publishing Inc., New York

Library of Congress Cataloging-in-Publication Data

Darcy, Robert.
    Women, elections, and representation.

    Bibliography: p.
    Includes index.
    1. Women in politics—United States. 2. Women—Suffrage—United States. I. Welch, Susan. II. Clark, Janet, 1940-   . III. Title.
HQ1391.U5D37 1987   320'.088042   86-27621
ISBN 0-582-28536-4

87 88 89 90   9 8 7 6 5 4 3 2 1

CONTENTS

PREFACE

As public officeholders, women are the most underrepresented major social group in America. Why is this so? This is the question this book addresses.

For decades, women's role in politics was largely ignored by political scientists. Beginning in the early 1970s this situation changed, as at first a few and then a steady stream of articles and books about women and politics began to appear. But most of this research focused on mass political behavior or on the attitudes of women political officeholders rather than on why there were not more women in office.

As it became clear that in performing normal political chores—voting, campaigning, and talking about politics—women and men are very similar, the question of why women are underrepresented in public office began to be asked more frequently. After looking at pieces of this puzzle in our own research for several years, we decided to try to analyze the question more comprehensively.

With new research and a synthesis of old, we explore the numerous possible reasons for the dramatic underrepresentation of women. We examine the possible roadblocks to women: voter prejudice, the role of party leaders and other political elites in screening candidates, the influence of socialization and sex-role norms, and the impact of election structures, incumbency, and turnover.

We have tried to make our investigation wide-ranging and comprehensive. We explore the impediments to women in electoral politics using data from local, state, and national levels. We use information from surveys of public officials and of the public, from election returns, and from aggregate data on cities and other units of government. All can help us understand the problem of women's representation.

The answers are not complete, but we are led to recognize some changes that will open the doors wider for women. We also come to understand some of the reasons for the slow entrance of women into political office. In doing this, we learn more about the workings of our democracy.

We would like to thank the people who collaborated with us on the research of women and politics over the years: Sarah Slavin of the State University College at Buffalo, Tim Bledsoe of the University of South Carolina, James Choike of Oklahoma State University, Margery Ambrosius and Mark Daniels of Kansas State University, Lee Sigelman of the University of Kentucky, Sunhee Song of the Academy of Korean Studies, Albert K. Karnig of Arizona State University, Donley Studlar of Centre College of Kentucky, and Margaret Brewer and Judy Clay, former students at Oklahoma State University.

During the course of writing we had occasion to rely on the insights and knowledge of a number of scholars who freely shared their own thoughts and criticisms. In particular, we want to thank Bertil Hanson, Anne Schneider, and Bob England of

Oklahoma State University; Walter Kohn of Illinois State University; Robert Dinkin of California State University at Fresno; H. James Henderson, Glenna Matthews, and Carolyn Stefanco, all Oklahoma State University historians; John Gruhl of the University of Nebraska-Lincoln; Cassia Spohn of the University of Nebraska at Omaha; Charles D. Hadley of the University of New Orleans; Karen Beckwith of the College of Wooster in Ohio; Jarol Manheim of Virginia Polytechnic Institute and State University; Min C. Hyun of Kyunghee University; Janneke van der Ros of the University of Oslo; Kim Ok Sun and Kim Yung-Chung, members of the South Korean National Assembly.

Cindy Bear and Phil Outhier helped gather some of the data presented here.

R. Darcy
Susan Welch
Janet Clark

For our spouses, busy with their own academic writing:

Lynne C. Murnane

Alan Booth

Cal Clark

PART I

Women in Public Office:
Intellectual and Historical Background

This book is an inquiry into why so few women are elected to American public offices. To answer this question we must look into the workings of the American political system. Before doing this, however, we will examine the struggle for women's rights within this system as it gradually evolved. We will also discuss *why* the representation of women in American political life is an important question.

Our political system did not arise in a vacuum. Its origin was in the political life of England. When the English established colonies in North America, they brought with them the concepts of local, church, and national government to which they were accustomed. Ideas of political rights and who should enjoy them were also imported from England. Thus the English political experience is relevant to an understanding of our own system. The colonists did not simply transfer English politics to the New World, however; they adapted the familiar political forms to the different conditions of North America and to their own political views. This is where our inquiry begins, with the role of women in English and colonial political life.

The legal political role of women in colonial times was not clear at all. Political rights were based largely on birth and on property. Religion also played a part in determining who could and could not participate in politics. There was no consistent and universal *barrier* to the participation of women in political life, but few women voted in England and in the North American colonies, and few women participated in politics to the extent of exercising political influence. In fact, few women held any political office whatsoever in England, and no women can be identified as holding elective public office in the colonies.

It was not until the period of the American Revolution that newly drafted state constitutions explicitly and completely barred women from participation in political life. In the colonial period, custom and practice were somewhat

1

inconsistent and loose; the state constitutions, in contrast, specified political rights at the national and local level as well as at the state level. By barring women from participation in state politics, they barred women from national and local politics as well. Thus women were legally excluded from political life at the moment when political rights ceased to be based on custom and were instead derived from written state constitutions.

A female suffrage movement began in the early days of the new republic. In 1848 a convention for the purpose of advancing women's rights was held in Seneca Falls, New York. Among the rights advocated was the vote. What is clear from the activities and pronouncements of those advocating female suffrage, however, was that holding political office in large numbers was *not* a goal of the movement. For the suffragists, female political influence was going to derive from the vote in other ways than filling political offices with women. Indeed, after national suffrage was granted in 1920, very few of the suffragists entered into campaigns for elective office. That simply was not envisioned by those campaigning for the vote.

Strangely, political theorists, with a few significant exceptions, also have not envisioned political life in which women participate. The major exceptions are Plato, at the dawn of Western political thought, and John Stuart Mill, who lived recently enough to have participated actively in the women's suffrage movement. In the more than two millennia between these two thinkers one can scarcely find a single major figure who imagined a workable political system such as we have today, a political system in which women participate equally with men.

What we find in examining the thinking of the political theorists, the historical background of our present political system, and the female suffrage movement is that with certain exceptions, the idea that women would hold public office in any large numbers was simply not contemplated or envisioned. Not until the 1950s did the idea emerge, and not until the late 1960s did such ideas receive widespread attention and support. Thus the idea of women in public office is a relatively new one; it was not part of the political tradition of the West, it was explicitly denied as a possibility by the founders of our republic, and it was not a goal of the suffrage movement.

1

Women and Political Representation

"Her wings are clipped and it is found deplorable she does not fly."
Simone de Beauvoir

The argument of this book is that the representation of women in American political institutions is both a problem and a puzzle. It is a problem because women are poorly represented at a time when their participation in political decisions is most needed. It is a puzzle because it is not clear why women have such limited representation in our democratic institutions, nor is it clear what can be done to alter the situation.

How has it come about that our democracy so effectively limits the political role of women? To answer this question we will need to examine the period when our nation and its political practices began. Our ideas about the place of women in American politics are often shaped by short-term knowledge of women's exclusion from the national suffrage in the nineteenth century and their fight to win it in the early twentieth. Yet if we look back further, into the seventeenth and eighteenth centuries, we find not only that women, at some times and some places, had the right to vote but that a few even exercised a good deal of power as political decision makers. Rather than expanding the rights exercised by a few, however, the American Revolution resulted in a denial of political rights to all women.

Women and the Franchise from the 1500s to the 1700s

In England, and later in its American colonies, political rights, especially local political rights, were based largely on custom and usage. Where there were specifications as to who could exercise the franchise, these tended to be based on property, wealth, age, and religion. The right to political participation varied with place and situation. Although custom and usage implied that politics was for men, only occasionally was this specified in any formal way. Land ownership was considered a particularly important qualification for the franchise

3

in a number of places in England and its American colonies. Typically these freeholders were male, but circumstances existed in which freehold rights could be held by women. Daughters and widows could inherit; divorced women could leave a marriage with their property; women could even be granted freeholds in their own name, and many were.[1]

> By the late seventeenth century a widowed woman was listed among the top three landowners of Dedham, Massachusetts; more than a dozen women appeared in the top tax bracket of Jamaica, New York, at the turn of the century; and as the first generation of settlers grew to maturity, the female heirs assumed the direction of sizable estates in towns throughout the colonies.[2]

Property owners in England were typically few. Often an English borough had only one person able to exercise the franchise and, hence, to determine all local offices, including parliamentary representation. On more than one occasion this person was a woman, even as early as the reign of Elizabeth I.[3] Court decisions in the reign of James I both supported female parliamentary suffrage and provided evidence it was exercised.[4]

In England's American colonies it appears that similar conditions prevailed. A limited number of women not only had the right to the franchise but also exercised it, especially on matters relating to their property.

> Records from a few Massachusetts towns show that a number of widows who owned substantial property did exercise the franchise on occasion. Moreover, the *New York Gazette* reported in June, 1737, that at the recent Queens County election "two old Widdows tendred, and were admitted to vote."[5]

In Rhode Island, during an era when church and village affairs were not as distinct as today, Baptist women voted in church meetings and often formed the majority.[6] Quaker women in Rhode Island, eastern and western New Jersey, Pennsylvania, New York, Delaware, and Maryland served as ministers, participated in their own business meetings and meetings with men, served as church elders and overseers, and were selected by meetings for a variety of tasks that would be considered public today.[7]

Even in provinces that did not permit women to vote, women may have voted or attempted to vote in local elections because practices were often at variance with the provincial law.[8] At one point or another some provinces, including Pennsylvania, Delaware, Virginia, Georgia, New York, and South Carolina, limited the franchise explicitly to men.[9] At other times and in other provinces, at least some women did have the right to vote.

While women in England and its American colonies were able to exercise a franchise under certain conditions in a period when many men were not eligible, a limited number of women had the right to vote. But of those who had it, few exercised it. Colonial America was not a political golden age for women, but it did not bar them completely from political participation, either. That came about after the Revolution.

Colonial Women as Political Decision Makers

The political involvement of women was not limited to an occasional exercise of the franchise. In England, on a number of instances between 1641 and 1649, groups of women petitioned Parliament on political issues.[10] Colonial records tell of women participating in this way as well. In 1708 a woman signed a petition concerning a local dispute in Andover, Massachusetts,[11] and such female involvement in political petitions to legislatures was not isolated.[12] Women could also be political figures in their own right. In 1755 Catherine Payton addressed Pennsylvania's colonial assemblymen concerning political problems faced by Quakers,[13] and in 1742 Jane Hoskins selected and organized a slate of disaffected Quakers to contest Pennsylvania elections.[14] We also have reports of women campaigning politically for their husbands in the colonial elections of Virginia, Georgia, and Pennsylvania between 1732 and 1768.[15]

Women were prominent in a number of colonial disturbances in the period prior to the American Revolution. In 1676 in Virginia, Bacon's revolt broke out in reaction to the aristocratic government and political incompetence of Governor Berkeley. Berkeley, for example, refused to allow the raising of a militia to protect Virginia against Indians, even after massacres killed over 300 colonists. A recent study indicates that women led both the Berkeleyan and Baconian camps. Among the rebels, women organized public opinion and played a leading role in their deliberations.[16]

In the American provinces women were able to capitalize on control over property to exercise great local authority during the early period of proprietary government. In the seventeenth century Mary and Margaret Brent were given large grants of land in Maryland.

As owners of manorial estates, they had the right to hold courts-baron, where controversies relating to manor lands were tried and tenants did fealty for their lands, and courts-leet, where residents on their manors were tried for criminal offences.[17]

These women, then, were able to exercise feudal authority in at least local matters.

When Leonard Calvert, the governor of Maryland and brother to the proprietor Lord Baltimore, died in 1647, his will specified that Margaret Brent was to be his executrix. She was to "take all and pay all."[18] In this position she also acted with the power of attorney for Lord Baltimore and participated actively in the running and management of Maryland itself.

Margaret Brent was not the only woman to exercise wide power during the proprietary period. During the last years of his life William Penn was incapacitated by a stroke. Control over his affairs passed to his wife, Hannah. Between 1712 and 1726 it was she who exercised the rights of the proprietor in what is now Pennsylvania, Delaware, and parts of New Jersey. Until 1718 she acted as his wife and after that as the sole executrix of his estate. She sent William Keith, for example, to serve as the new governor of the province and, acting jointly with her stepson, subsequently replaced him with a new governor.[19] Other women were also able to exercise proprietary rights, although on a more limited scale than either Margaret Brent or Hannah Penn.[20]

In local affairs numerous colonial women are cited as among a town's leading and most influential citizens.[21] Elisabeth Dexter cites the remarkable Mary Starbuck of Nantucket (1645–1717): "She took an active part in town debates. . . . They would not do anything without her advice and consent therein."[22]

In England and in its American colonies prior to the nineteenth century, important local offices included the church wardens, the sexton, and the guardians of the poor. These were elected by parishioners, male and female. In England all these offices were held by women as well as men well into the nineteenth century.[23] As local government officials, the guardians of the poor were particularly interesting. Prior to the American Revolution one of the major functions of local government was to provide for the poor, orphans, and others unable to care for themselves. For this purpose a tax was collected. Subordinate to the guardians of the poor were the overseers of the poor, appointed to keep the roll of taxpayers. This list was also the electoral list, which determined who was and was not eligible to exercise the franchise. Both custom and court decisions in England held that women were permitted to hold this position.[24]

In the colonies we cannot document women being elected to local office. We do have, however, reports of local women in the colonies working as attorneys, founding and publishing newspapers, and serving a variety of local functions such as jailer and custodian of the poor.[25]

There are also instances of colonial women being appointed to a number of responsible public positions. In 1736 Anne Franklin was appointed printer to the Rhode Island Colony.[26] Clementina Rind was voted public printer for Virginia by the House of Burgesses,[27] and women served as public printers in Maryland and New York as well.[28] In 1715 the Pennsylvania Assembly voted to appoint Hannah Carpenter the tax collector.[29]

The American Revolution and the Loss of Political Rights for Women

As we have noted, prior to the American Revolution, the electoral franchise in Britain and the American colonies was often based on ownership of land, allowing some women as well as some men the *right* to participate in political life.

With the American Revolution the situation changed. State constitutions began to specify detailed qualifications for the franchise. These qualifications would apply at all levels of political life—local, national, and state. This was a process similar to what was happening in Britain at the same time. There, too, women with property had the right to participate in local politics and hold local offices, a right based on long community tradition. These local rights were lost, however, when national governments began to include local government within national political systems. This was done by first clearly specifying who had national (or state) political rights and then limiting local political participation to these persons.[30]

In the United States the result was a series of new state constitutions that specified a more relaxed property standard but a specifically male suffrage.[31] New Jersey was only a temporary exception to this process. That state's constitution of 1776 retained the old landowning basis of the suffrage, and its electoral law of 1790 specified "he or she" when referring to voters. Many women exercised this right. One observer reported that in the election of 1800, New Jersey Federalists "marched their wives, daughters, and other qualified 'females' to the polls."[32] In 1807, however, a new electoral law specifically excluded women.[33]

The American Revolution led to a general loss of status for women.[34] The reasons for this are complex, but two factors can be identified: the shift from custom, which permitted exceptions to an exclusively male political life, to written constitutions, which did not; and the shift away from a property basis of political life toward more universal manhood suffrage. The result was that

> Relative to men . . . women's political stature can be seen in decline after the American Revolution. For one thing, their disenfranchisement now stood out in bold contrast to almost universal white manhood suffrage. When young propertyless men went to the polls, leaving rich widows behind, sexual discrimination became a visible blemish on the republican complexion of the new nation.[35]

The Return of Women to Political Life

In Britain the process of removing women from local politics and their regaining that right was quite condensed. The Municipal Corporations Act of 1835 specified, for the first time, that the electoral franchise in municipal boroughs belonged to males only.[36] In nonmunicipal boroughs, however, local government was still conducted without reference to sex.

> As these cities enlarged and developed, they were admitted to the honor of municipal incorporation. But since the Municipal Corporations Act limited the franchise to men, it resulted that while the city which was promoted to the rank of municipal borough saw its rights increased, a part of its inhabitants—the women—saw theirs suppressed. This anomaly gave the advocates of women suffrage a chance to demand that the ballot be granted to women in the municipal boroughs. In 1869 Mr. Jacob Bright introduced such a measure in the House of Commons, and it was adopted almost without discussion.[37]

The disenfranchisement of women in English local government lasted from 1835 to 1869, only 34 years.

In the United States the process was far more complex because suffrage was controlled by the individual states and because of the distinctive electoral basis of various local governmental units. Nevertheless, the process of restoring and expanding the female franchise began with local government. Kentucky was the first state to reintroduce women to the electorate when in 1838 the right to vote for members of school boards was extended to widows.[38] Kansas granted school suffrage to all women in 1859, and a number of other states granted some form of local suffrage to women in the period before complete suffrage was gained. In Massachusetts women gained the school vote in 1879, beginning the process of regaining the rights lost 94 years earlier. Thus in the United States the period when no woman is known to have voted lasted only the 31 years, from 1807, when New Jersey withdrew suffrage, to 1838, when Kentucky granted it on a limited basis.

Between the 1870s and 1920 many women were exercising various forms of local suffrage in the states, even while full suffrage was denied. Further, women were being elected to local offices and appointed to other local positions in relatively large numbers—even in states where the local franchise was not available to women. In 1867 women were elected to the school committee in several small Massachusetts towns, and in 1874 two women were likewise elected in Boston, all before women could vote in such elections.[39] In the nonsuffrage states women were being elected to school-related positions in roughly the same proportions as in the suffrage states.[40] In 1906 women were elected to the position of county superintendent in 18 of 53 South Dakota counties, and in Illinois 9 of 102 county superintendents were women. Both of these were non-suffrage states at the time. Relatively large numbers of women were holding other local governmental positions as well, in both suffrage and nonsuffrage states.[41]

In Britain, and later in Britain's colonies, local government was one aspect of political life in which a few women at least were able to participate. These were women of property. With the change from property-based suffrage to manhood suffrage even these few women were excluded, at least temporarily, from local government. It was not long, however, before women began re-gaining the local franchise. Further, women began holding local elective offices again relatively quickly, even before the franchise was available. In this way local government is distinct from state and national politics, where women only began to participate in the latter part of the ninteenth century.

Women and the Style of Local Government

There are several reasons for the distinct history of women in local government. First, until relatively recently, local government at the village or commune level was considered to be part of the private rather than the public sphere. Where the franchise was based on ownership of property, the franchise was seen as an aspect of that private ownership. In exercising the right at the local level a woman was exercising a private right, not a public one. Therefore, the ideology by which women were excluded from public life also *included* an important private role for women, especially in the household. When for some reason or another a woman became the head of the household, there was no contradiction in her also exercising the local governmental rights that went along with that position.

A second reason for the participation of women in local politics is related to the first. It concerns the functions and activities of local government. These traditionally included caring for the poor and the management of the communal land and property. These certainly fit within the scope of activity traditionally expected of women. In more recent times local government activity expanded to include education, sanitation, and regulation of all manner of activities that affect the health and welfare of citizens. These newer activities can also easily be fit within the traditional role and concerns of women. In fact, one important justification for the ballot advanced by suffragists was the concern women had for protecting and advancing the health and welfare of their families.[42]

A third reason for the participation of women in local government, even while women were excluded from politics at other levels, was the locus of local government and its manner of conducting business. Most women have traditionally found themselves tied to a range of household and family obligations that permit only a limited amount of free time and force them to remain close to home. Men, especially those of the urban middle class of past centuries, had much more leisure. Their working hours were short and seasonal.[43] Local government could easily accommodate female time restrictions, especially in smaller villages and towns. There, local government was conducted close to home and involved only part-time commitments. Women could participate in the local government while at the same time fulfilling their other roles.

Further, the style of local government differed from that at other levels. It was voluntary, and decisions were typically reached through consensus rather than conflict.[44] In many ways, the style of village politics was a simple extension of personal relationships rather than the politics we have come to know from experiences at the national or even the state level. Given this style, women could participate in local government without being "politicians." Certainly politics in larger cities was quite different from that in the smaller villages. Nevertheless, the tradition of village politics still influences thinking about the municipal politics of even large urban areas. This has provided a basis for female participation even when such participation would be impossible at other governmental levels.

The Suffrage Movement and Women in Public Office

In 1920 the Nineteenth Amendment gave, and in some cases restored, the right of suffrage to women. Yet in the decades since that amendment, women moved only very slowly into public office. The suffragists wanted the ballot; they did not intend to seek public office. If anyone, it was the antisuffragists who brought up and discussed the possibility of women in elective office.[45]

Thus it was Mrs. Arthur Dodge, president of the National Association Opposed to Woman Suffrage, writing in 1914, who stressed the intimate connection between voting and serving in public office as an argument *against* female suffrage:

> Merely dropping a piece of paper in the ballot box is not a contribution to stable government unless that piece of paper be followed up by persistent and ofttimes aggressive activities in the field of political strife.[46]
>
> Woman will find her work as the educator who develops a trained and scientific opinion, not as the politician who must control votes.[47]

Similar arguments concerning the connection between suffrage and public officeholding were not made by those *favoring* suffrage. The advocates of suffrage in the United States used a number of arguments.[48] One argument, of course, was based on inalienable rights.[49] Another argument was that female suffrage would increase the weight of the "better" element in the electorate against the black and foreign-born.[50] The argument that won the day, however, was the housekeeping argument. The reasoning was that the traditional role of the woman gave her the responsibility for the moral, spiritual, and physical well-being of her family. In the modern industrial society, however, women could not exercise this responsibility solely from within the home itself. Municipal sanitation, food inspection, the regulation of working conditions, the control of drunkenness and all manner of vice—all these were relevant to her duties, and all were manageable only through political action. Women needed the ballot for reform so that women could better carry out their traditional responsibilities to their families.[51]

There is no mention in the arguments of the suffragists that the ballot will be used to elect women who will then in turn implement the desired reforms, the only exception being an interest in certain local offices. Instead, the ballot would facilitate two different strategies. First, with the ballot women would have more influence on male politicians and be able to lobby more effectively for needed reforms. Mary Beard wrote in 1914:

> Representative government is, to some extent at least, a government by petition, legislators responding to personal appeals from individuals and organizations when they are powerful enough to arouse interest or alarm . . .
>
> There can be no doubt that in cases of serious labor legislation affecting large employing interests women's weight has been almost negligible in many instances. Indeed, one of the New York legislators, in a very friendly and confidential talk with the representatives of the Women's Trade Union League, told them that the 35,000 voteless women whom they represented naturally could not carry the same weight as thirty-five voting men.[52]

The vote, then, would give women the ability to lobby male representatives more effectively.

Another way women would use their votes was through direct legislation. Between 1898 and 1919 some 18 states, largely in the West, where women had already gained the vote, permitted citizens to petition either to overrule legislative action or actually to initiate new legislation. The measures would be submitted to a direct vote of the people. Such direct democracy appealed to those with a distrust of politicians and a deep faith in democracy.[53] It appealed especially to women's groups desiring to avoid the seamy side of politics.[54] One area in which women employed referenda to gain their legislative ends was regulation of the liquor traffic. In 1914 Ella Stewart reported statewide prohibition referenda initiated by women in Colorado, California, Oregon, and Washington and numerous local referenda also initiated and supported by women.[55] Prohibition was not the only area in which women worked for direct legislation, although it remained the cause whose support was most disproportionately female.[56]

These were the reasons the suffrage movement wanted the ballot for women—either to influence or to bypass elected officials. No more telling indication of female indifference to officeholding are the statistics of women elected in the first election after gaining national suffrage. Women campaigned for and won offices in only 23 of the 48 states. In many states women gained no offices, and in states where women were elected, they were elected to only a very small proportion of the available offices. As far as public officeholding was concerned, there was little difference after national suffrage from the situation beforehand.[57] Eleanor Flexner described this process:

> No woman suffragist pushed herself aggressively forward as a candidate immediately after passage of the amendment in 1920. . . . The suffragists in 1920 were not only, many of them, weary of campaigning; they were confused. . . . planted firmly in the minds of a goodly number of politicians [was] the idea that ''the ladies'' were not really interested in politics—as politicians understood the term—but rather in ''reform,'' which was quite another matter.[58]

Thus it is not surprising that in 1929, only 122 women served in state legislatures[59] and that the number increased to only 140 by 1937.[60]

The Need for Female Political Representation

The still limited representation of women is of increasing concern to many people. Over the past century a number of arguments have been raised concerning the need for female participation in political decision making. Though some of these arguments have greater appeal and force than others, together they make a compelling case.

Ideological Advantage

The first of these arguments concerns the partisan or ideological advantages that will accrue to one side or another should the representation of women increase. This is a theme widely encountered during the suffrage movement.

Female suffrage was thought to be desirable (or undesirable) because it would increase the temperance vote[61] or add to the voting influence of the "better" social elements. The reasoning was that upper-class women would vote at greater rates and qualify themselves more readily than women of the other classes.[62] Today similar arguments are being made in favor of the representation of women. Now it is argued that feminist legislation is needed; and because women are more reliable feminists than men, the election of more women to public office is desirable.[63]

Anna Howard Shaw, then president of the National American Woman Suffrage Association, pointed out a weakness of this reasoning as it related to suffrage.

> Many women feel that the greatest good they can do with the ballot is to abolish commercialized vice, to prevent child labor, or to make effective their protest against war. This is perhaps true. We all agree that these evils must be abolished, and that women, unenfranchised, have not and will not be able to abolish them. But the evils themselves and the desire of women to right them do not constitute the reason women should be enfranchised. The reason would remain even though all the evils I have named, or could name, should be abolished at once. We and the women who come after us should have our political power to use in any way we think best. We cannot tell what it will be necessary to do; what women will want to do. All we know is that women must have the power to take part in the government of their country.[64]

Today feminists are working in a number of issue areas including the Equal Rights Amendment, affirmative action, abortion rights, and day care for children. Yet the need for female representation is not solely the concern of advocates of these policies. Opponents of the feminist agenda also have some stake in increasing female representation. For feminists, the need for female representation will not cease with the enactment of their agenda. The representation of women is more important than a specific issue agenda, momentary ideological gain, or partisan advantage.

Women's Expertise

A second argument for the participation of women in political decision making concerns women's expertise. This argument suggests that men and women have different spheres in society, and, as a consequence, women have knowledge and insights into some matters that men do not have.[65] Jane Addams, suffragist leader and social reformer, long ago pointed out that male legislators have made themselves "a little absurd" with uninformed discussions in the German Reichstag of infant mortality and naive debates in the English Parliament on infant clothing.[66] The modern state as it has developed over the past century increasingly concerns itself with such matters. It therefore needs the participation of women in formulating policies if these policies are to be intelligent and effective. Yet this reasoning, too, has its difficulty.

If women enter political institutions by virtue of their unique expertise, this can also provide the basis for keeping female representatives confined to a narrow sphere. There has been, in fact, a tendency for women, once elected to legislatures or selected to join governments, to be limited to functional areas associated with the traditional women's social role: education, social welfare, and children.[67] The other side of the coin of female expertise, then, is male expertise. This male expertise is thought to lie in the broad issues of politics, and economy, war and peace, morality, and general public policy.[68] Women's expertise, then, would seem to imply men's expertise as well, if not logically, then most certainly in practice. Surely justifying female participation in a way that simultaneously diminishes it is not very satisfactory.

Societal Benefits

A more persuasive argument for female officeholding involves the benefits that will accrue to a society from increased competition for public office. The idea that if the female half of the human race enters into political competition with the same intensity as has the male half, the quality of political leadership will necessarily increase due to the larger number of individuals involved. We will return to this argument in the discussion of John Stuart Mill later in this chapter.

Legitimizing the System

A final argument for the representation of women concerns the legitimacy of the political system itself. Our representative institutions have evolved in function and meaning over the centuries, but by the early part of the nineteenth century the notion took hold that representative bodies should include the various elements of a diverse society. John Adams, one of our founding fathers, wrote that representative assemblies ''should be an exact portrait, in miniature, of the people at large, as it should think, feel, reason and act like them.''[69] Hanna Pitkin notes that despite certain problems with the notion of representative bodies as a mirror of the nation, the idea that they *should* be so is widespread. One motive for designing our electoral institutions, in fact, was to ensure that outcome.[70] Pitkin quite rightly reminds us that though in one sense small farmers can be represented by a small farmer, in another sense small farmers might actually be better represented by a politician or a lawyer. Pitkin also reminds us that this ''mirror of the nation'' notion of representation may ignore the content of representation. Certainly *what* representatives do is as relevant to determining how representative they are as what they look like and where they come from.

Recognizing the great limitations of a representative body as a mirror of the nation, the idea does have an importance, especially with regard to our thinking about the representation of women. For one thing, women are not women by achievement; they are women by birth. One's sex says nothing about one's ability, potential, or achievements. Arguments that small farmers, for example, can be represented better by politicians than by other small farmers do not necessarily apply to the representation of women by men, especially in the absence of any convincing evidence on the matter. Women belong in the same category as racial, ethnic, religious, or linguistic groups, which in a just society are to be represented in political deliberations by able individuals of a like sort.

Our political system, like those of other democratic systems, has been designed to ensure such representation. In this regard the composition of governmental institutions serves as a legitimizing agency for political regimes. Today political decisions made by all-male or predominately male governmental processes can no longer serve this legitimizing function.[71]

From this last perspective the representation of women becomes a very important question—first, because the legitimacy of the political system is at stake and, second, because it becomes the test of the electoral mechanisms the political system has adopted to ensure representative assemblies.

Here is our puzzle. Political rights for women have grown rapidly since the late nineteenth century. Today most of us believe that women have the abilities and potential for political leadership, and we have been taught that our democratic institutions give to all the same opportunities for political influence. Why, then, are the numbers of women currently elected to public office so small that women can scarcely be said to be represented in the House of Representatives (5 percent), and even in lesser offices they are far from proportionately represented, holding, for example, only 14 percent of the state legislative seats. Why is the majority of the population confined to such minimal representation?

When we consider political affairs, it often helps to consult people who have examined important political questions over the centuries. Careful reading in those sources can help focus our questions and clarify our thoughts. What do such thinkers say about the political involvement of women? Why have women not achieved political equality with men?

Political Theory and the Representation of Women

Plato

As with many other questions, we can begin with Plato (born about 428 B.C.). Plato is a good starting point because he was the first thinker to look systematically at political questions.

In *The Republic* Plato reasoned that individuals differed in their abilities and that the well-ordered polity would recognize this and make use of these abilities. Of the three classes that Plato discussed, the workers who produce, the soldiers who fight, and the guardians who govern, our interest is in the last, the guardians. For Plato, one could become a member of the governing class only through natural political ability. The question, then, became whether or not women shared this ability. Women and men did differ in certain other aspects. Plato presented Socrates' reasoning:

> Then if the race of men and women seems to be different with regard to a particular craft or other pursuit we shall say that it is necessary to assign that craft to one or the other. But if it seems to differ in this only, that the female gives birth and the male mounts, we shall say that in no way has it been shown that a woman is different from a man concerning that about which we have been talking, but we shall still believe that it is necessary that our guardians and their women should engage in the same pursuits.[72]

For Plato, the order of his republic was a natural order; it grew out of the nature of man and the world. We can infer, then, that the well-documented *lack* of political influence on the part of women in contemporary Greek society[73] was, to Plato at least, not natural. Properly nurtured, Plato saw men and women as roughly equal in political ability and saw the ideal state as one governed in roughly equal proportions by men and women.[74] To quote Arlene Saxonhouse:

> The differences between male and female in the past were the result of different education, not of different natures. Socrates affirms that it is not nature that keeps women out of the public life of cities. It is custom. "We are not making laws which are impossible or similar to prayers, as if we set down a law which contradicted nature. Rather, those practices which exist now are in opposition to nature, as it seems."[75]

It took 22 centuries before a political thinker again suggested that a well-governed state have as its decision makers roughly equal proportions of men and women. Why did Plato's successors not follow his lead in this matter? The answer lies in the connection between the social and political systems. In Plato's thinking, the connection between the social system—the manner in which the young were educated, for example—and the nature of the political system was intimate. Plato's ideal state required a radical reconstruction of society from what was then prevalent in Greece. Property rights, marital relationships, and the family itself had to be radically changed or abolished altogether if his political order was to be possible. For the successors of Plato this was impossible. Plato became viewed as unrealistic.

Aristotle

The successor to Plato was Aristotle (died 322 B.C.). Aristotle approached the political role of women in several ways. As a biologist he viewed women as flawed beings, mutilated males. Since in the best political order the superior rule the inferior, the males should rule the females. Saxonhouse argues, however, that it is not primarily Aristotle's biological views that cause him to limit the political role of women. It is also the nature of political life itself. The civic life requires leisure, something not available to women. Their lives occupy them with childbirth, child rearing, household management. They do not have the

freedom political activity requires.[76] Another problem for Aristotle was that
he viewed women generally as controlled by their emotions, not by reason.
The political realm, for Aristotle, was a realm of reasoned discourse in which
women would be disruptive.[77] Thus when Aristotle seeks the role of the woman,
he turns to what we have come to call the traditional view:

> He finds it in her capacity within the structure of the family—a realm in which she
> not only gives birth but also gives stability, preserves and educates the young of the
> city. It is a realm in which she can demonstrate her unique virtue.[78]

Today we find Aristotle's discussion of the male and female soul flawed by
a lack of any real evidence concerning the emotionality of women and the
distinctive reasonableness of men. Likewise, while Aristotle recognizes that only
a small proportion of men will have the leisure requisite for the political life,
he fails to note that some women will also have this leisure.

On those rare occasions when ideas concerning the political role of women
are encountered in the thinking of political theorists between Aristotle and
John Stuart Mill in the mid-nineteenth century—just about the entirety of
Western political thought—they are disappointing. What emerges is not the
clarity, honesty, and boldness we expect from great minds. Instead, when
women are treated at all, we find evasion, confusion, and fear.

Two thinkers illustrate these tendencies well: John Locke (1632–1704), an
Englishman, and Niccolò Machiavelli (1469–1527), a Florentine.

Locke

To Locke, the political order is the result of free individuals freely making a
compact in which their original rights to life, freedom, and property remain
intact. Locke's logic starts with equality and freedom in a state of nature, equality and freedom that Locke makes clear women share as well as men. On this
point, consider, for example, Locke's discussion of marriage.

> This . . . leaves the wife in the full and free possession of what by contract is her
> peculiar right, and gives the husband no more power over her life than she has over
> his; the power of the husband being so far from that of an absolute monarch that
> the wife has in many cases a liberty to separate from him where natural right and
> contract allow it, whether that contract be made by themselves in the state of nature,
> or by the customs or laws of the country they live in.[79]

Locke somehow moves from a state of nature in which both men and women
enjoyed rights, property, and freedom and where both men and women entered freely into compacts to a state in which only men exercise political rights.
"When any number of men have so consented to make one community or
government, they are thereby presently incorporated and make one body pol-
itic wherein the majority have the right to act and conclude the rest."[80]

Nowhere in Locke is there any explanation for this slippage by which half of us have lost the political rights that by his own logic should belong to all.[81] Locke's failure to follow his premises to their conclusions cannot easily be attributed to oversight. Several commentators have noticed that Locke was vigorous in pointing out the failure of advocates of the divine rights of kings to account for the equally divine authority concerning the rights of women. These same commentators also point out that Locke's detractors challenged Locke to deny that by his logic women would have the same political rights as men.[82] Locke's evasions in this matter are certainly unsatisfactory.

Machiavelli

Machiavelli's concern is not with the moral foundation of the political order. The Italy of his day was weak and disunited, constantly being ravaged by more powerful and united nations. Pitkin argues that Machiavelli's goal can be seen as using politics to achieve autonomy both for the individual and for Italy as a whole.

> Machiavelli summons his contemporaries to *virtu* and to glory. In the cause of community welfare and political liberty, he tries to enlist their concern for manliness, their fear of dependence, their craving for sexual gratification. Machiavelli's ultimate challenge to his contemporaries is to shame them: stand up, and act like a man![83]

Pitkin shows us, however, that Machiavelli's misogyny, a theme that pervades his work, is not a surface phenomenon, a quirk that can be safely ignored by those concerned with his message.

> Machiavelli undermines the very teaching he wants to convey by appealing to his audience's desire for manliness and thereby also summoning up childishness: fantasies of huge engulfing mothers and rescuing fathers, relationships of domination and submission, an unstable combination of cynicism and exhortation, and misleading concepts of action, membership, judgment, and autonomy. The appeal to *machismo* can move men all right, particularly men troubled about their manliness, but it cannot make them free.[84]

Projecting onto women the feared parts of oneself, as Machiavelli does, is self-defeating.

> If such men move into public life, they do so in order to escape and deny their private selves, the vulnerabilities of the body and their troubling relations with women and children in the household. Fleeing their bodily and domestic selves, they march out to ravage "the sheepfolds of others." To the extent that they feel threatened by "inner" conflict, psychic or political, they will lack that capacity for limited struggle among peers that differentiates citizenship from civil war, political dispute from the factional disintegration of a community. . . . Theirs, in short will be a zero-sum world in which the only possible conception of public life is domination.[85]

For Pitkin, then, Machiavelli's misogyny is at the heart of his failure as a political thinker.

Men are not inherently more fit for citizenship than women and will appear so only in a society where women are confined to household and private affairs and denied access to public life. . . . Men who deny the humanity of women are bound to misunderstand their own.[86]

Where we found evasion in Locke's treatment of women, in Machiavelli we find confusion and fear.

Our brief look at some eminent political theorists between Plato and Mill is enough to reveal that a political order such as we find in the United States today and in other democratic states as well, a political order in which women and men may both participate, was either inconceivable or dismissed as an impossibility. Not until John Stuart Mill (1806–1873) do we find a thinker in the mainstream of political thought who carefully considers the role of women in the political order.[87]

John Stuart Mill

Beginning in 1848 with the famous meeting at Seneca Falls, New York, a growing number of men and women joined the struggle for women's political rights. John Stuart Mill was an early suffrage supporter and organizer in Britain. When elected to Parliament in 1865 he used the opportunity to advocate female suffrage and, in 1867, during the debate on a voting reform bill, moved to omit reference to sex, moving in effect to enfranchise women. In this he managed to gain the votes of seventy members, more than 10 percent. Mill was also one of the founders of the British women's suffrage movement.[88] The best presentation of Mill's views on the question of political rights for women is contained in his book *On the Subjection of Women,* published in 1869. What is interesting is not only that Mill argues for the suffrage and for full legal, economic, and political rights for women but that he also argues that it is important that women participate in government at every level, top to bottom, on the basis of complete equality.

His reasoning is founded on two arguments, the first against forbidding women to enter Parliament and the second in favor of the political abilities of women. In the first case Mill argues that if women's nature renders them unfit for public office, it is superfluous to forbid them such offices, for they are unlikely to seek that for which their nature renders them unfit. If they are unfit and yet seek these offices, the competition will serve to exclude them. If some unfit women still manage to be elected to Parliament, well, that is still no calamity for it is obvious that unfit males are already being elected in large numbers. On the other hand, if there are women who do have a special capacity for political life, it would be a disservice to fail to benefit from their ability.

Is there so great superfluity of men fit for high duties, that society can afford to reject the service of any competent person? Are we so certain of always finding a man made to our hands for any duty of function of social importance which falls vacant, that we lose nothing by putting a ban upon one-half of mankind, and refusing before-hand to make their faculties available, however distinguished they may be?[89]

Mill's next point is that of all the range of occupations available, women have *most* distinguished themselves in political life, the one area forbidden them.

Now it is a curious consideration, that the only things which the existing law excludes women from doing, are the things which they have proved that they are able to do. There is no law to prevent a woman from having written all the plays of Shakespeare, or composed all the operas of Mozart. But Queen Elizabeth or Queen Victoria, had they not inherited the throne, could not have been intrusted with the smallest of the political duties, of which the former showed herself equal to the greatest. . . . If anything conclusive could be inferred from experience . . . it would be that the things which women are not allowed to do are the very ones for which they are peculiarly qualified; since their vocation for government has made its way, and become conspicuous, through the very few opportunities which have been given. . . .

Exactly where and in proportion as women's capacities for government have been tried, in that proportion have they been found adequate.[90]

Conclusions: The Problem and the Puzzle

With the passage of the suffrage amendment, the energy seemed to go out of the movement for women's political rights. We satisfied ourselves that women *could* enter public office with regular reminders of Senator Margaret Chase Smith or United States Representative Jeannette Rankin. We measured and celebrated progress with a series of "firsts": Rebecca Latimer Felton, first woman senator; Frances Perkins, first woman member of a president's cabinet; Patience Latting of Oklahoma City, first woman mayor of a major American city; Sandra Day O'Connor, first woman member of the Supreme Court; Geraldine Ferraro, first woman nominated for the vice-presidency by a major political party. These all received widespread publicity and reminded us that the right to office was there and that "progress" was being made. What we have failed to see is that there has been a lack of fundamental change in the political situation of women, with regard to gaining elective office, since gaining the vote in 1920. This failure is particularly disappointing as it is now clear to all but the most naive that the strategy of lobbying and the initiative petition has not been as effective an alternative as was once hoped.[91]

We began this chapter with a problem, the need for more equitable rep-resentation of women in American public offices, and a puzzle, the reason for the failure of our democratic institutions to incorporate more women. The problem remains, and it is a real one that can only be solved in the actual practice of politics. But part of the answer to the puzzle has been identified. With the exception of Plato and Mill, there is no tradition of envisioning women as active in public life.

The suffrage movement, where visions of political equality might be expected to project women doing more than voting and acting as interested citizens, also shunned considerations of women holding office. Suffrage was not thought of as the first step in shifting the composition of American officialdom toward greater female representation. Neither in political theory nor in the ideas of the suffrage movement was there much basis for such a vision.

It is not until 1955, when Maurice Duverger published *The Political Role of Women*, that the problem of the lack of female representation in political bodies came to be seen as a puzzle. In contrast to the emphasis on "progress" encountered in previous work documenting a series of women "firsts,"[92] Duverger stresses the almost complete absence of women from public life. To explain this absence, he developed the basic explanatory theory that will be the focus of our subsequent chapters. What makes Duverger's work important is that it was the first to focus serious attention on the problem of female representation. Before Duverger the concern with women in politics was the vote and how women voted. It was Duverger who shifted our attention to officeholding.

Duverger suggested that women may encounter three sorts of barriers when trying to gain public office. Voter hostility is one. Voters may, for one reason or another, prefer to be represented by a male rather than a female. The male conspiracy is a second. In this notion the political parties are dominated by males who will resist new groups such as women who challenge their control.[93] The third barrier is the electoral arrangements themselves. Duverger argues that some electoral systems are more conducive to the election of women than others.

Duverger's basic ideas are still worthy ones to begin a consideration of barriers to American women in electoral politics. We will use them as we review the now quite large literature on women as candidates and officeholders.

Notes

1. See Mary P. Ryan, *Womanhood in America: From Colonial Times to the Present*, 3d ed. (New York: Franklin Watts, 1983): 21, 24; Sumner Chilton Powell, *Puritan Village: The Formation of a New England Town* (Middletown, Conn.: Wesleyan University Press, 1963); and Elisabeth Anthony Dexter, *Colonial Women of Affairs: Women in Business and the Professions in America before 1776* (Boston: Houghton Mifflin, 1931).
2. Ryan, *Womanhood in America*, 24.
3. Antonia Fraser, *The Weaker Vessel* (New York: Random House, 1985), 231; Edward Porritt, *The Unreformed House of Commons: Parliamentary Representation before 1832*, vol. 1 (Cambridge: Cambridge University Press, 1903), 40, 377; and Esther Cope, "Women from the Nobility and Gentry in Politics," unpublished paper, Department of History, University of Nebraska, 1985.
4. See Fraser, *The Weaker Vessel*, 231.

5. Robert J. Dinkin, *Voting in Provincial America: A Study of Elections in the Thirteen Colonies, 1689-1776* (Westport, Conn.: Greenwood, 1977), 30; see also Elizabeth Cady Stanton, Susan B. Anthony, and Matilda Gage, eds., *History of Woman Suffrage*, vol. 1 (Rochester, N.Y.: Charles Mann, 1887), 208.

6. Sidney James, *Colonial Rhode Island: A History* (New York: Scribner, 1975), 248.

7. J. William Frost, *The Quaker Family in Colonial America: A Portrait of the Society of Friends* (New York: St. Martin's Press, 1973); Kenneth Carroll, *Quakerism on the Eastern Shore* (Baltimore: Maryland Historical Society, 1970).

8. Ryan, *Womanhood in America*, 53; Dinkin, *Voting in Provincial America*, 30; Chilton Williamson, *American Suffrage: From Property to Democracy, 1760-1860* (Princeton, N.J.: Princeton University Press, 1960), 16.

9. Dinkin, *Voting in Provincial America*, 30; Williamson, *American Suffrage*, 15; Michael K. Kammen, *Colonial New York: A History* (New York: Scribner, 1975), 207.

10. Fraser, *The Weaker Vessel*, 220-239; Esther Cope, "Some Women's Thoughts about War in Early Stuart England," paper presented at the North American Conference on British Studies, Houston, November 1985.

11. Edward M. Cook, *The Fathers of the Towns: Leadership and Community Structure in Eighteenth Century New England* (Baltimore: Johns Hopkins University Press, 1976), 217.

12. See Hugh Lefler and William Powell, *Colonial North Carolina: A History* (New York: Scribner, 1973); Dexter, *Colonial Women of Affairs*, 37.

13. Alan Tully, *William Penn's Legacy: Politics and Social Structure in Provincial Pennsylvania, 1726-1755* (Baltimore: Johns Hopkins University Press, 1977), 244.

14. Ibid., 32.

15. Dinkin, *Voting in Provincial America*, 101.

16. Stephen Saunders Webb, *1676: The End of American Independence* (Cambridge, Mass.: Harvard University Press, 1985), 5.

17. Julia Cherry Spruill, *Women's Life and Work in the Southern Colonies* (New York: Norton, 1972), 237.

18. Ibid., 238.

19. See John A. Munroe, *Colonial Delaware* (Milwood, N.Y.: KTO Press, 1978); Joseph Illik, *Colonial Pennsylvania: A History* (New York: Scribner, 1976); Tully, *William Penn's Legacy*.

20. See Dexter, *Colonial Women of Affairs*.

21. See Kenneth A. Lockridge, *A New England Town, the First Hundred Years: Dedham, Massachusetts, 1636-1736* (New York: Norton, 1970), 144; Carroll, *Quakerism on the Eastern Shore*, p. 40; Dexter, *Colonial Women of Affairs*, 101; Cook, *The Fathers of the Towns*, 24; Edward Countryman, *A People in Revolution: The American Revolution and Political Society in New York, 1760-1790* (Baltimore: Johns Hopkins University Press, 1981), 22; Tully, *William Penn's Legacy*, 195.

22. Dexter, *Colonial Women of Affairs*, 210.

23. Moisei Ostrogorski, "Women Suffrage in Local Self-government," *Political Science Quarterly* 6 (December 1891): 677-710; Moisei Ostrogorski, *The Rights of Women: A Comparative Study in History and Legislation* (London: Swan Sonnenschein, 1893).

24. Ostrogorski, "Women Suffrage," 687.

25. Linda K. Kerber, *Women of the Republic: Intellect and Ideology in Revolutionary America* (Chapel Hill: University of North Carolina Press, 1980), 153; Ryan, *Womanhood in America*, 34.
26. Dexter, *Colonial Women of Affairs.*
27. Robert E. Brown and Katherine Brown, *Virginia, 1705-1786: Democracy or Aristocracy?* (East Lansing: Michigan State University Press, 1964), 55.
28. Dexter, *Colonial Women of Affairs.*
29. Joseph J. Kelley, *Pennsylvania: The Colonial Years, 1681-1776* (Garden City, N.Y.: Doubleday, 1980), 143.
30. Ostrogorski, "Women Suffrage"; Ostrogorski, *The Rights of Women.*
31. Williamson, *American Suffrage*, 115.
32. James MacGregor Burns, *The Vineyard of Liberty* (New York: Knopf, 1981), 148.
33. Stanton et al., *History of Woman Suffrage*, 447–451; Robert J. Dinkin, *Voting in Revolutionary America* (Westport, Conn.: Greenwood, 1982), 42.
34. Gerda Lerner, "The Lady and the Mill Girl: Changes in the Status of Women in the Age of Jackson," *Midcontinent American Studies Journal* 10 (Spring 1969): 5–14.
35. Ryan, *Womanhood in America*, 70.
36. Ostrogorski, "Women Suffrage," 688.
37. Ibid., 688–689.
38. Stanton et al., *History of Woman Suffrage*, 670; Helen L. Sumner, *Equal Suffrage* (New York: Harper, 1909).
39. Stanton et al., *History of Woman Suffrage*, vol. 2, 289.
40. Sumner, *Equal Suffrage.*
41. Ibid.
42. See Aileen Kraditor, *The Ideas of the Woman Suffrage Movement, 1890-1920* (New York: Norton, 1981).
43. James, *Colonial Rhode Island*, 250.
44. See Clarence Stone, Robert Whelan, and William Murin, *Urban Policy and Politics in a Bureaucratic Age* (Englewood Cliffs, N.J.: Prentice-Hall, 1979), 42; Powell, *Puritan Village.*
45. See Ryan, *Womanhood in America*, 186. Curiously, it was the antisuffragists who elected the first woman to the House of Representatives after suffrage: Alice Robertson of Oklahoma, elected in 1920. See Sophonisba P. Breckinridge, *Women in the Twentieth Century* (New York: McGraw-Hill, 1933), 296.
46. Mrs. Arthur Dodge, "Women's Suffrage Opposed to Woman's Rights," *Annals of the American Academy of Political and Social Science* 56 (November 1914): 101.
47. Ibid., 103.
48. Of course suffrists did more than develop arguments. They organized politically, demonstrated, and did other practical things to force the suffrage amendment through to ratification.
49. See Kraditor, *Ideas.*
50. See Fred W. Eckert, "Effects of Woman's Suffrage on the Political Situation in the City of Chicago," *Political Science Quarterly* 31 (March 1916): 105–121; Kraditor, *Ideas.*
51. See Kraditor, *Ideas;* Nancy E. McGlen and Karen O'Connor, *Women's Rights: The Struggle for Equality in the 19th and 20th Centuries* (New York: Praeger, 1983).

52. Mary Beard, "The Legislative Influence of Unenfranchised Women," *Annals of the American Academy of Political and Social Science* 56 (November 1914): 56, 60.

53. V. O. Key and Winston W. Crouch, *The Initiative and Referendum in California* (Berkeley: University of California Press, 1939).

54. See Kraditor, *Ideas.*

55. Ella Seass Stewart, "Woman Suffrage and the Liquor Traffic," *Annals of the American Academy of Political and Social Science* 56 (November 1914): 134–152.

56. Stewart, "Woman Suffrage and the Liquor Traffic"; William F. Ogburn and Inez Goltra, "How Women Vote: A Study of an Election in Portland, Oregon," *Political Science Quarterly* 34 (September 1919): 413–433.

57. See J. Stanley Lemons, *The Woman Citizen: Social Feminism in the 1920's* (Urbana: University of Illinois Press, 1973), 68; Bella Abzug with Mim Kelber, *Gender Gap* (Boston: Houghton Mifflin, 1984), 108.

58. Eleanor Flexner, *Century of Struggle: the Woman's Rights Movement in the United States,* rev. ed. (Cambridge, Mass.: Harvard University Press, 1975), 339–340. There were exceptions, however. In 1922 two well-known suffrage leaders were nominated by their party for the House of Representatives but lost: Mrs. Anna Dickie Oleson, Democrat of Minnesota, and Mrs. Jessie Jack Hooper, Democrat of Wisconsin. See Breckinridge, *Women in the Twentieth Century,* 301.

59. Dorothy Moncure, "Women in Political Life," *Current History* 29 (January 1929): 639–643.

60. National League of Women Voters, *A Survey of Women in Public Office* (Washington, D.C., 1937).

61. See Stewart, "Woman Suffrage and the Liquor Traffic"; Ogburn and Goltra, "How Women Vote."

62. See Eckert, "The Effects of Woman's Suffrage"; Kraditor, *Ideas.*

63. See Virginia Sapiro, "Research Frontier Essay: When Are Interests Interesting? The Problem of Political Representation of Women," *American Political Science Review* 75 (September 1981): 701–716.

64. Anna Howard Shaw, "Equal Suffrage: A Problem of Political Justice," *Annals of the American Academy of Political and Social Science* 56 (November 1914): 97.

65. See Irene Diamond and Nancy Hartstock, "Beyond Interests in Politics: A Comment on Virginia Sapiro's 'When Are Interests Interesting? The Problem of Political Representation of Women,' " *American Political Science Review* 75 (September 1981): 717–721.

66. Jane Addams, "The Larger Aspects of the Woman's Suffrage Movement," *Annals of the American Academy of Political and Social Science* 56 (November 1914): 5.

67. Maurice Duverger, *The Political Role of Women* (Paris: UNESCO, 1955); Elina Haavio-Mannila et al., *Det Uferdige Demokratiet: Kvinner i Nordisk Politikk* (Oslo: Nordisk Ministerrad, 1983); R. Darcy and Sunhee Song, "Men and Women in the Korean National Assembly: Social Barriers to Representational Roles," *Asian Survey* 26 (June 1986): 670–687; Susan Carroll, "Women Candidates and Support for Women's Issues: Closet Feminists," *Western Political Quarterly* 37 (June 1984): 307–323; Susan Gluck Mezey, "Does Sex Make a Difference? A Case Study of Women in Politics," *Western Political Quarterly* 31 (December 1978): 492–501; Susan Gluck Mezey, "Support for Women's Rights Policy: An Analysis of Local

Politicians," *American Politics Quarterly* 6 (October 1978): 485–497; Elizabeth Vallance, *Women in the House: A Study of Women Members of Parliament* (London: Athlone, 1979).

68. See Darcy and Song, "Korean National Assembly."

69. Quoted in Hanna Fenichel Pitkin, *The Concept of Representation* (Berkeley: University of California Press, 1967), 60.

70. See James Madison, "Factions: Their Cause and Control," in Alexander Hamilton, John Jay, and James Madison, *The Federalist Papers,* ed. Andrew Hacker (New York: Pocket Books, 1964), 16–24; Pitkin, *The Concept of Representation;* Dieter Nohlen, "Two Incompatible Principles of Representation," in Arend Lijphart and Bernard Grofman, eds., *Choosing an Electoral System: Issues and Alternatives* (New York: Praeger, 1984), 83–89.

71. Kenneth J. Meier, "Representative Bureaucracy: An Empirical Analysis," *American Political Science Review* 69 (June 1975): 526–542; Donald R. Matthews, "Legislative Recruitment and Legislative Careers," *Legislative Studies Quarterly* 9 (November 1984): 547–585.

72. Quoted in Arlene W. Saxonhouse, *Women in the History of Political Thought: Ancient Greece to Machiavelli* (New York: Praeger, 1985), 43.

73. See Philip E. Slater, *The Glory of Hera* (Boston: Beacon Press, 1968).

74. See Ernest Barker, *Greek Political Theory* (London: Methuen, 1918); Ernest Barker, *The Political Thought of Plato and Aristotle* (New York: Dover, 1959); Susan Moller Okin, *Women in Western Political Thought* (Princeton, N.J.: Princeton University Press, 1979); Jean Bethke Elshtain, *Public Man, Private Woman* (Princeton, N.J.: Princeton University Press, 1981); Saxonhouse, *Women in Political Thought.*

75. Ibid., 43.

76. Ibid., 88.

77. Ibid., 73, 88.

78. Ibid., 90–91.

79. John Locke, *The Second Treatise of Government* (Indianapolis: Bobbs–Merrill, 1952), 46.

80. Ibid., 54–55.

81. See Melissa Butler, "Early Liberal Roots of Liberal Feminism: John Locke and the Attack on Patriarchy," *American Political Science Review* 72 (March 1978): 135–150; Okin, *Women in Western Political Thought,* 199–200; Elshtain, *Public Man, Private Woman.*

82. See Butler, "Early Liberal Roots."

83. Hanna Fenichel Pitkin, *Fortune Is a Woman: Gender and Politics in the Thought of Niccolò Machiavelli* (Berkeley: University of California Press, 1984), 293.

84. Ibid., 294.

85. Ibid., 305.

86. Ibid., 306.

87. There are some exceptions, for example, the Marquis de Condorcet (1743–1794) and Charles Fourier (1772–1837).

88. See Anne P. Robson, "The Founding of the National Society for Woman's Suffrage," *Canadian Journal of History* 8 (March 1983): 1–22.

89. John Stuart Mill, *Collected Works,* vol. 21, *Essays on Equality, Law and Education* (Toronto: University of Toronto Press, 1984), 300.

90. Ibid., 302, 304.

91. See Bertil L. Hanson, "Oklahoma's Experiment with Direct Legislation," *Southwest Social Science Quarterly* 27 (December 1966): 262–273.

92. See Bernice van de Vries, "Housekeeping in the Legislature," *State Government* 21 (June 1948): 127–128; but also see Hans Beyer, *Die Frau in der politischen Entscheidung: Eine Untersuchung über Frauenwahlrecht in Deutschland* (Stuttgart: F. Enke, 1933).

93. See also Flexner, *Century of Struggle,* 340.

PART II

Women Candidates:
Local, State, and National

One explanation offered for the paucity of women in American public office is that some voters are hostile toward women candidates. Another suggestion is that political elites, rather than facilitating the entrance of women into political life, have made things more difficult. On the surface, these explanations seem plausible. After all, ours is a society in which women, until quite recently, have been excluded from all sorts of positions. Wage and job discrimination is still widely encountered. Thus it is not unreasonable to suggest that women in politics are finding the same difficulties women find in the medical or legal professions or in corporate life.

Further, there is a great deal of anecdotal evidence in favor of this argument. There are numerous reports of political leaders making disparaging remarks about women. There are many accounts of women who have tried to enter active political life and have been mistreated by male political elites. Many surveys indicate that some voters are not ready to vote for women candidates, even if they are of the voter's own party and otherwise qualified for the position. One cannot overlook all of this evidence.

Nevertheless, many women candidates are being encouraged, indeed assisted in every way, by male political elites. There are many cases dating back well into the nineteenth century where women candidates have run successfully for office, have led their tickets, and have been reelected for as many times as they have chosen to run. Instances of women being elected to office before they had the vote are not rare.

Thus anecdotal accounts of the treatment of women candidates tell two very different stories: on the one hand, hostility, on the other, enthusiasm. Political scientists certainly cannot ignore these accounts. But anecdotal evidence has serious weaknesses. For example, it would be easy to gather accounts from men candidates who were discouraged and frustrated by political elites. Obviously, there is also no shortage of men who have been rejected decisively by the voters.

In the face of these anecdotes, the political scientists must try to establish more systematically whether or not the gender of the candidate has anything to do with how voters and political elites react to that candidate. We cannot just collect stories about women who have been given a difficult time by politicians. We need to look at all candidates, over a large number of elections, for a great variety of political offices, male and female. This we shall do. Our questions will be these:

Overall, is there any difference in the vote for male and female candidates?
Overall, is there any difference in how political elites treat male and female candidates?
Overall, are there any differences in the ability of male and female candidates to wage effective campaigns?

To answer these questions we have gathered a great deal of information from thousands of elections since the early 1970s. We have also carefully examined surveys of voters conducted at different times and in various places.

We deal with each level of government—local, state, and national—separately because there are great differences among elections at each level. Further, the nature of the evidence available varies with the level of government. For example, surveys are available concerning congressional elections but not in any usable form for city council or state legislative races. We have a uniform system of electing representatives to Congress, but members of city councils and other local boards are selected in a great variety of ways. All this means that we will need to examine carefully each level of government individually.

When trying to determine the effect of a candidate's gender on things such as money available for campaigns, it is important to compare *similar* male and female candidates. That will mean different things at the different levels of government. At the local level, for example, that might mean comparing female candidates running in nonpartisan races with men running in nonpartisan races. We would get misleading results should we compare male candidates in races for partisan offices with female candidates for nonpartisan offices, or vice versa.

In the three chapters of Part Two we will examine men and women candidates in a great variety of circumstances: women candidates in local elections in Chapter 2, in state legislative elections in Chapter 3, and in congressional elections in Chapter 4. What we shall find after very extensive analysis is that women candidates are treated no differently than men by either voters or by party or other elites. In one sense, then, this section will produce little by way of explanation for the small numbers of women elected to public office. On the other hand, we will show that contrary to how things may appear on the surface, women candidates are not discriminated against by voters or party elites. Women candidates suffer no barriers not encountered by men candidates as well. This is important because it removes a major discouragement to women who are thinking of running for office. As for the question of why women are so underrepresented in American political office, we will return to that in the third section of the book.

2

Electing Women to Local Government

Most women who hold public office in the United States do so at the local level, as members of city councils, school boards, county commissions, and other elected groups governing our cities, counties, and other local entities.[1] Twenty times more women hold local office than hold state or federal office combined.[2] It is only at the local level that there are *any* legislatures where women are a majority. Furthermore, many women who hold state and national office started their careers as elected local officials. For example, eight women members of Congress first held local office, including Senator Nancy Kassebaum (R, Kansas), who was a member of the Maize school board, Mary Rose Oakar (D, Ohio), who served on the Cleveland city council, and Barbara Boxer (D, California), who was a member of the Marin County board of supervisors.

Because there are tens of thousands of local governments across the United States—cities and counties, townships, school boards, special districts established to operate parks, libraries, sewage systems, and many other specialized services—it is difficult to study systematically the success of women in being elected to local governmental offices. There are no centralized, comprehensive records that provide information about who was elected to city governing boards, let alone those of other local units.

For this reason it is not easy to chart the progress of women in winning election to local offices. Hardly anyone has studied the election of women to county positions or those in special districts or townships.[3] A few have studied school boards;[4] most have focused on city councils and mayoral positions.[5] Even examinations of city governments, however, have few common threads. Various scholars have examined various sets of cities, differing in size and region. Some have studied cities and their characteristics as predictors of women's success in being elected; others have focused on candidates and their characteristics.

With these limitations in mind, we will review the evidence about the election of women to local government.

The Increase in Women City Officeholders

There is no disputing the evidence that the number of women in local public office has grown enormously since the mid-1970s. Between 1975 and 1982, the number serving in county offices tripled.[6] The number of women mayors of cities increased from 566 to 1,670 during that time, and the number of women members of town and local councils more than doubled, from 5,365 to 12,903. Women have been elected, and in some cases reelected, mayors in major cities such as Houston (Kathy Whitmire), San Francisco (Dianne Feinstein), Chicago (Jane Byrne), Oklahoma City (Patience Ladding), San Antonio (Lila Cockrell), and San Jose (Janet Gray Hayes). The growing number of women mayors was reflected in the election of Helen Boosalis, then mayor of Lincoln, Nebraska, to the presidency of the U.S. Conference of Mayors in 1983.

The increasing number of women mayors in large cities gives us some confidence that the overall growth of women in local office has not occurred only in small towns. Further, though figures are not exactly comparable over time, we know that there has definitely been growth in the *proportion* of city councillors who are women. As Figure 2.1 illustrates, in 1983, about 20 percent of council members in cities from 50,000 to 1 million were women. This is almost double the 10 percent proportion of women city councillors in 1975–1976 in cities of over 25,000. Fitting into the upward trend is the fact that in 1978 women served on about 13 percent of the city councils of these same cities of 25,000 and over.[7]

Additional confirmatory evidence of the increase of women in city offices is provided by examining the years in which men and women currently serving on city councils were elected. For example, in a national survey of council members in 1983, of the 113 members elected before 1974, fully 88 percent were men. But of those elected since 1974, only 75 percent were men, and that proportion was fairly constant for each year (71 to 77 percent). Of course, it is possible that men and women councillors have different attrition rates and that these comparisons of ''survivors'' are therefore not totally accurate. Nevertheless, these data point again to the rather dramatic growth in the proportions of local councillors who are women.[8]

Even with these increases, women are still clearly underrepresented in local government offices. If they are 20 percent of council members, they are still represented at only about 40 percent of their population proportions. And if they are less than 10 percent of all mayors, they are underrepresented in that office by a factor of 5. Even more indicative of their underrepresentation is that only in rare cases do they comprise majorities of legislative bodies, even at the local level. In 1978, for example, there were only six city councils with majorities of women among 264 cities with populations of 25,000 and more. Though that number may have since increased, it has not done so by much. A 1985 study of Santa Clara County in California pointed out that it was a rare county because it had a female majority on its county board of supervisors and a woman mayor and council majority in its largest city.[9]

Still, women are better represented at the local than at the state or national level of government. Only 5 percent of the members of the House of Representatives are women, for example, and only 2 percent of the Senate. It is of

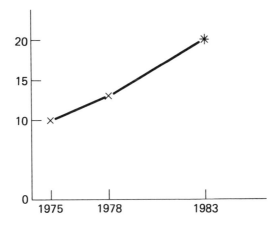

× Cities 25,000 and over

✳ Cities 50,000 to 1,000,000

Figure 2.1 Estimated increase in women city councillors. (Data for 1975 from Albert Karning and B. Oliver Walter, "Election of Women to City Councils," *Social Science Quarterly* 56 [March 1976]: 605–613, and from Susan MacManus, *Determinants of the Equitability of Female Representation on 243 City Councils,* paper presented at the meeting of the American Political Science Association, Chicago, August, 1976; data for 1978 from Susan Welch and Albert Karnig, "Correlates of Female Office Holding in City Politics," *Journal of Politics* 41 [May 1979]: 478–491; data for 1982 from Susan Welch and Timothy Bledsoe, "Differences in Campaign Support for Male and Female Candidates," in Glenna Spitze and Gwen Moore, eds., *Research in Politics and Society,* Greenwich, Conn.: JAI Press, 1985).

some interest to note that this pattern is not universal. In some nations, women do as well at being elected to the highest national legislative body as at the local level. In the Scandinavian nations, local and national governments have about the same proportion of women. In Britain, the representation of women at the district level is nearly identical with that at the next higher level, the county.[10] In the United States, by contrast, there is a clear pattern: The higher one goes, the fewer women one finds in public office.

Nevertheless, as at every other level of government, we find women substantially underrepresented in local government. We now turn to the question of why. Researchers examining women in local government have largely turned their attention to two aspects of that question: the support that women candidates get in elections and the city environments that seem to be conducive to women being elected.

Campaign Support

Campaigning is crucial in winning elections. Through a campaign, a candidate first seeks to become known to the voters. Along with sparking name recognition, the candidate also tries to project a positive image.

In partisan races, candidates can start from a base of loyal Democrats or Republicans, focusing first on arousing their partisan loyalties and support. Candidates of each party can also expect support from allied groups; Democrats often seek support from labor groups and sympathetic businesses, while Republicans can usually obtain hefty financial support from the business community.

In a nonpartisan race, a candidate must build on other networks of friends, fellow workers, and associates in civic, religious, and other organizations. Party organizations may help, but a partisan appeal to voters cannot readily be made.

The success of a campaign depends on how well a candidate can mobilize support, first from close associates, then from a larger group of supporters, and finally from the voters. If a candidate cannot get money and volunteer time from a loyal cadre of friends, associates, and like-minded people, attempts to reach the larger public will fail.

The Importance of Organizational Support in Campaigns

Sometimes it is suggested that women do not do as well in winning office because they are less successful in gaining the necessary support. Perhaps women are less able than men to call on associates in their work or civic activities for help. This could inhibit women in two ways. It could prevent women candidates from being elected, and it could discourage potential female candidates from even running. For example, perhaps organized labor is less supportive of potential female Democratic candidates than of male Democrats. Networks of business support for Republican candidates may be less for women than men. Or organized ethnic groups may encourage ethnic males but not females to run. In other words, perhaps women suffer from discrimination in the early stages of recruitment where potential candidates are screened and encouraged and in the campaign stage where candidates are given varying degrees of financial, organizational, and volunteer support by organized groups.

In partisan races, parties can be crucial. But do party leaders and activists discriminate against women in giving campaign support? There is a belief that party leaders are most apt to slate women as "sacrificial lambs," supporting them most often when the race is a hopeless cause and ignoring them when the party has a real chance of winning,[11] but the evidence is not persuasive that party leaders currently do so. On the one hand, a study of local candidates for office in suburban Cook County, Illinois, showed that men were more often recruited by party and interest group leaders than were women.[12] A survey of southern state legislators recently showed that 47 percent of the men and 75 percent of the women agreed that men in party organizations keep women out of leadership roles (though they did not ask specifically about candidate slating).[13]

On the other hand, interviews with a large group of women candidates from all over the United States provided evidence that party support is higher for women than men running for mayor and about the same for those running for council.[14] Several studies have found that women officeholders are more likely to have been active in the party than men.[15] And a multistate study of candidates for local office found that women were at least as likely as men to be recruited by parties and interest group leaders.[16]

The evidence regarding support by other organizations is even clearer. A common finding has been that women local officeholders have a history of civic activity, including, for example, leadership roles in the PTA and the League of Women Voters.[17] This kind of activity has several useful functions. It gets women involved in and informed about public issues. It provides contacts they can call upon to staff and finance a campaign. Male candidates often use contacts made in business groups such as the Chamber of Commerce or service organizations such as Rotary or Kiwanis, and women do the same with contacts from their own civic involvement.

Recent evidence indicates that this civic activity, in particular, activity in women's organizations, also translates into a significant political base. A national study of women officeholders indicates that fully 40 percent belong to a woman's or feminist organization.[18] The most common such organization is the League of Women Voters, but Business and Professional Women and the American Association of University Women are also powerful springboards into office. In the national survey, encouragement by women's organization was given as the most important reason for women to run. And compared to men in this sample, women were more likely to say that organizational support was important to their try for office.

Surveys of candidates, both losers and winners, have shown that women were *more* likely than men to be actively involved in civic activities, many of them women's organizations.[19] Having civic organizational experience seemed to increase a woman's chances of winning; those who won were more likely than those who lost to have such experience.[20] However, activity in civic organizations is not the same as support by them. Whether or not women were formally recruited by a political party or civic group seemed to make no difference whether they won or lost. For men, winning was strongly related to being recruited by a party or civic group; a history of general civic involvement had no impact on their success. Thus it appears that women candidates are more successful coming from a background of volunteer activity, such as the League of Women Voters, neighborhood organizations, or the PTA; this may compensate for their lack of professional careers.

An examination of the women officeholders of Santa Clara County revealed this rich background of civic activity.[21] Mayor Hayes was active in PTA, the

League of Women Voters, the American Association of University Women, and neighborhood organizations. Her first appearance before the city council was as a mother protesting the lack of traffic signs in her neighborhood. A woman county supervisor was a member of the League and the National Woman's Political Caucus, and other women officeholders were active in neighborhood groups, the League, and a variety of statewide groups.

The career of Helen Boosalis, the first woman president of the U.S. Conference of Mayors, also illustrates the importance of civic activity. Boosalis became active in politics through several years of membership in the League of Women Voters. After serving as League president involved in fighting for changes in the city charter, she ran for city council. After four terms as a council member, she was twice elected mayor of Lincoln. In 1986 she defeated six primary election opponents to become the Democratic nominee for governor of Nebraska. Although she has built a diverse network of support throughout the state, some of her most loyal supporters and volunteers are women who first worked with her in the League. Though this support did not win her victory in the general election in this predominantly Republican state, she lost to another woman, Republican Kay Orr. The race made history because it was the first gubernatorial race in the United States in which both major party candidates were women.

Recent Evidence on Organizational Support for Council Members' Campaigns

Case studies can provide insight, but we also need a firmer basis for generalization about the support that women candidates receive in election campaigns. In an attempt to determine the relative support given to women candidates by a variety of groups, an analysis was done on a 1983 national sample of nearly 1,000 male and female city council members.[22] Members were asked to rate the importance of a series of reasons why they ran for office. One reason was "persuaded by party," another "issue concern." Council members also rated a number of groups, such as political parties, labor, business, neighborhood groups, race or ethnic groups, and issue groups as to their importance in the member's last campaign. The rating was done on a 3-point scale: important, somewhat important, and not very important.[23]

These items and their associations with the gender of the candidate are listed in Table 2.1. There are some differences in perceived campaign support offered for men and women council candidates in their campaigns. While party, labor, business, and ethnic groups were perceived by males and females as equally supportive of their campaigns, neighborhood groups and issue organizations were seen by women as more supportive than by men. Almost twice as many women as men (25 to 13 percent) thought that issue groups were important to their campaigns, and over 45 percent of the women but only 31 percent of the men believed neighborhood organizations to be important.

Table 2.1   Differences Between Men and Women in Sources of Campaign Support

	Male-Female Differences[a]	
	No Controls	Controls[b]
Reason for Running		
Party persuasion	0	0
Issue concern	W	W
Source of Support		
Political party	0	0
Labor	0	0
Business	0	0
Neighborhood organization	W	W
Race or ethnic group	0	0
Single-issue group	W	W

[a]0 = no significant difference between men and women; W = women significantly more likely to run for that reason or significantly more likely to get support from that source.

[b]Controlling for partisan or nonpartisan election, district or at-large election, region, and party identification of candidate.

To what extent are these differences explainable by the differing party loy-alties or electoral arenas of males and females? Table 2.1 shows the relationship between gender and campaign support when factors such as region, party, and election structures are taken into account. These factors reduce, but do not eliminate, significant gender differences. Thus while no gender differences ex-ist in support from political parties, labor, and business, some differences are still apparent in support from neighborhood organizations and some issue groups. Overall, whatever significant differences do exist in support and en-couragement for candidates favor women, not men, in local politics.

Table 2.1 also indicates that party encouragement was a factor affecting equally the decision of men and women to run for office. Consonant with the finding that women report greater issue-group support in their campaigns, more women than men report running for office out of a concern for issues. These relationships are only slightly diminished when controls for partisanship and election structure are taken into account.

As we might expect, in addition to the differences in the frequency with which men and women cited support from issue groups, there was a substantial difference in the type of issue group giving its support. For candidates indi-cating support from a single-issue group, we asked for information as to what kind of group it was. Men were slightly more likely to cite support from what might be broadly defined as right-of-center groups (prodevelopment, tax re-duction, anti–rent control, antiabortion, anti–public housing) than more lib-eral groups such as those supporting funding for education, tenants' rights, controlled development, and feminist issues. Women cited left-of-center groups at over six times the rate they cited right-of-center groups. In fact, only a handful of women respondents mentioned right-of-center group support in this open-ended question.

It is reasonable to assume that the gender-perceived support linkage may vary with the kind of city or the partisan identity of the candidate. We therefore examined these links separately in partisan and nonpartisan cities, cities where members are elected by districts and those where they are elected at large, cities of the North and the South, cities of different sizes, and for Democratic and Republican council members.

Our overall relationships are remarkably stable under these varying conditions, but a few exceptions need to be noted. For example, only in at-large systems do male candidates report higher levels of business support than do females. This, of course, is the system in which ties to the business community are thought to be especially important because of the necessity of citywide name recognition and the funds to achieve it. In at-large systems, therefore, greater business support engendered by men may offset the greater neighborhood support going to women. Parties are apparently a bit more supportive of women in partisan systems. This bears out the accumulating recent wisdom that parties are not now antiwomen, on the whole.

The size of the city seems to make some difference in electoral support for men and women. The perceived support of neighborhood groups for women is strongest in smaller cities, evident (but not significant) in the medium-sized cities, and disappears entirely in the largest cities. In medium-sized cities, business support is significantly more likely to go to men, while in the other cities the relationships are small and not significant. In these same medium-sized cities, however, women are more likely than men to have perceived that party leaders were persuading them to run.

Given the variety of conditions we examined, overall our findings are remarkably clear. Under all conditions women are more likely than men to perceive support from issue organizations. Under most conditions the same is true of neighborhood groups. The major exception is in the largest cities, where no significant relationship is found, and the direction of the relationships points to more support for men. In partisan systems and in medium-sized cities, women perceive more party support than do men; under other conditions and overall, no significant gender differences exist. There seem to be no significant differences in perceived support from labor or ethnic groups under any conditions. Finally, though overall business support appears not to favor one gender or the other, under two important conditions it is perceived to favor men: in at-large systems and in medium-sized cities.

The Outcomes of Support

Do the differences in support we have found have any consequences? Overall, men and women perceive almost identical levels of campaign competition, indicating that differences in sources of support do not result in different outcomes (Table 2.2). Over 61 percent of each sex say they ran unopposed or won by a large margin, and only 14 percent of the men and 13 percent of the women indicated theirs was a "close contest."

The outcomes of the races also result in an equal proportion of Democrats and Republicans among each sex. About 30 percent of each sex are Republicans, 45 percent Democrats, and the rest independents or "leaners." However, women are considerably more likely than men to consider themselves "liberal": Only 26 percent of the men but 42 percent of the women describe themselves as such. On three specific issues these women council members also show themselves to be more "liberal": They are significantly more likely to favor tax increases rather than service cuts, to oppose unlimited growth, and to be

Table 2.2 *Outcomes of Support: Marginality, Political Identification, and Ideology*

	Men %	Women %
Margin of Victory		
Unopposed	9.9	8.6
Won by large margin	52.1	53.2
Won by moderate margin	24.0	25.5
Won in close contest	14.0	12.7
Ideology[a]		
Very conservative	7.9	3.8
Conservative	28.9	18.7
Slightly conservative	17.8	13.3
Middle of the road	19.2	22.2
Slightly liberal	14.2	18.4
Liberal	9.5	16.5
Very liberal	2.4	7.0
Party Identification		
Strong Democrat	30.0	31.7
Weak Democrat	15.1	13.7
Leaning Democrat	10.2	13.9
Independent	6.3	4.6
Leaning Republican	8.1	7.2
Weak Republican	9.6	12.6
Strong Republican	20.6	16.3
Issue Stance		
Prefer increased taxes to service cutbacks[a]	38.7	47.2
Believe that public employee unionization is damaging[a]	45.9	34.1
Support unlimited development[a]	43.4	30.5

[a]Significant at ≤ .001.

sympathetic to public employee unions. Perhaps these differences are due to the stimulation of female candidacies by women's issues or by reform-oriented groups such as the League of Women Voters. Certainly the differences between men and women council members in their sources of campaign support reflect greater liberalism on the part of these women. The greater liberalism of women officeholders also mirrors the gender gap in the public. The expression ''gender gap'' refers to the greater tendency of women to be Democrats, to consider themselves liberal, to support spending for the poor, elderly, and disabled, to oppose increased military spending, and to support environmental protection.[24]

Organizational Support: Some Conclusions

In searching for reasons why women do not run for office as often as men, we speculated that women do not receive the same levels of support from institutionalized political groups such as political parties, labor, business, ethnic and neighborhood groups, and others. Such lack of support would deter potential female candidates from running and diminish the chances that female candidates would win even primary elections. We have found, though, both in our own studies and in reviewing the numerous studies of other observers of the local scene, that women do not suffer from a lack of organizational support. Under most circumstances women may receive more support than men from such groups as neighborhood organizations, single-issue groups, and women's organizations. Political party leaders, traditionally thought to be important barriers to women seeking office, no longer appear to be so, at least at the local level. The only source of support where women sometimes seem to fare worse is that of business, but even there the evidence is mixed.

More research on campaign support is needed. The research we have examined focuses either only on winning or losing candidates. It does not examine the support for the pool of *potential* candidates. Yet at some initial stage of the recruitment process, even before the primary election, some potential candidates are discouraged while others are encouraged. Are potential women candidates more likely than potential male candidates to be discouraged? Studying potential candidates is very difficult, and no one has devised a reasonable way to isolate this rather abstract group. How might we define potential candidates in a way that makes comparisons between men and women potential candidates possible? Because women are still a minority in local government, however, we can be fairly confident that our political system is not bringing in potential women as efficiently as men candidates.

But for the moment, we can be fairly confident that, at least at the local level, when they become candidates, women do not have to jump large hurdles that men do not. The overwhelming majority of the evidence indicates that their sources of support are just as firm and widespread as those of men.

In What Kinds of Cities Are Women Elected?

Another way of gaining a perspective on women's electability to local office is to consider the kinds of cities in which women officeholders are found most often. Examinations of this question have largely focused on the assumption that women will win office more often when the office is less desirable.[25] It seems to be true that the higher the level and the less power the office shares with others, the less likely a woman is to be elected, at least in the United States.

City Characteristics and the Election of Women to Local Office

Comparing the electability of women at one particular level of government, such as local, and in one type of office, such as council, we might distinguish more and less desirable offices by factors such as the salary of the position, the size of the council, the length of the term, and the number of people being elected to the same office at the same time (in other words, is the member elected in a single-member or at-large district?). We might suppose that council seats that pay more, are fewer in number, have longer terms, and have single-member district elections might be more desirable than those with the opposite characteristics.[26]

Competition from other groups might also influence whether women are going to be successful in winning office. For example, in cities where minority populations are large and well organized, white women may not do as well in winning election. In a study of employment in state and local government, women were found to hold more jobs in places where minority hiring was least proportional.[27] It is possible the same relationship holds in elective office. Having large and well-organized minority populations might seem to facilitate the election of minority women, but it does not. For example, the relationship of black and Mexican-American population proportions to the proportion of black and Mexican-American men elected to councils is quite strong; on the other hand, this relationship to population proportions is quite modest for black women, and for Mexican-American women it is nonexistent.[28] Further, minority women are elected at a lower ratio in comparison to minority men than white women are to white men.

The legal partisanship of cities might influence the success of women. We have already seen that women in partisan cities perceive that they get more support from political parties than do men. There are no such perceived differences in nonpartisan cities. However, an earlier study of women council members found a slight tendency for more women to be candidates in nonpartisan systems.[29]

The general affluence of a community might also affect women's chances to win election.[30] Better-educated individuals, with higher income, are somewhat more sympathetic to women's rights than others.[31] Further, more affluent and better-educated communities are likely to have proportionally more women available for officeholding, given that candidates are recruited from just those classes.[32] In blue-collar towns, for example, most women might be tied down to jobs paying hourly wages from which they could not conveniently take time off.

We would also expect more women to be elected to office in the North than the more traditional South. And we would predict that women would be more likely to be elected in larger rather than smaller towns. There are two reasons for this. One is that larger communities tend to be more cosmopolitan and less traditional, thus perhaps more open to women officeholders. The other reason is that in larger towns, there are more likely to be groups such as the League of Women Voters, the National Women's Political Caucus, and the American Association of University Women that would give support to women candidates. However, two previous studies have found that factors such as education and income levels of city populations were only slightly related to female representation on councils.[33]

Some Evidence

Data from 264 U.S. cities over 25,000 in population provided some evidence for these arguments.[34] The proportion of women on the council and whether or not a woman was serving as mayor were compared with the relevant city characteristics. Overall, none of these characteristics was strongly related to whether women got elected to either the mayor's office or the council (Table 2.3). Women were somewhat more likely to be elected mayor, as predicted, in cities with low mayoral salaries and in the larger cities. They were also more likely to be elected in cities where the council elects one of its own as mayor than where the mayor was popularly elected. This relationship is not significant, however.

We can predict only a little better the cities where women are more frequently elected to city councils. This is somewhat more likely in cities with at-large elections and larger populations. Why this is so is not clear.[35] They are a little likelier to be elected when council salaries are low, but that relationship is not statistically significant. These findings provide only weak support for the idea that women do better when the office is less desirable.

On the whole, none of the competition explanations were supported. Women tend to be elected in places where minorities are large in number and well represented just as much as, but no more than, in places where minorities are small in number and not well represented.

The economic status of city residents has the largest single impact on council elections; women are, as expected, more likely to be elected in higher-income cities. It is somewhat contradictory, however, that they are also more likely to be elected where there are fewer owner-occupied homes. Perhaps this reflects

Table 2.3   *Predictors of Women Holding Local Office in 1978*

	Male-Female Differences[a]	
	No Controls	Controls
Political Structure		
Nonpartisanship	0	0
At-large elections	—	W
Length of term of office	0	0
How the mayor is chosen	0	0
Ratio of council seats to population	—	0
Veto power of mayor	0	—
Higher salary	M	0
Community Demographic Characteristics		
Percent black in community	0	0
Percent Hispanic in community	0	0
Southern locale	0	0
Size of the community	W	W
Percent who are college-educated women	0	0
Percent who live in owner-occupied homes	0	M
Median educational level	0	0
Percent families with over $10,000 annual income	0	W
Equitability of Minority Representation		
Proportionality of black council representation	—	0
Proportionality of Hispanic council representation	—	0

[a]0 = has no effect on the proportion of women serving; W = characteristic favors the election of women; M = characteristic favors the election of men; — = not appropriate. All relationships noted with a W or M are significant when controlling for the other factors listed, though even these relationships are modest in size.

the greater success of women in university towns, which tend to have high proportions of rental units.

Women were slightly more likely to be elected to the council in partisan than nonpartisan cities. However, this impact was not significant.

Some Conclusions

The fact that characteristics of cities are so weakly related to whether or not women are elected presents a "good news, bad news" message. The bad news is that such weak relationships make it difficult to determine the particular impediments to women being elected to local office. If city income, for example, had a strong impact, we would understand better why so few women are in local councils or mayoral offices. The fact that all the relationships were

weak means that we cannot really predict where or why women will fare well
in seeking local office.

However, this may be more "good news" than "bad news." It indicates
that no particular demographic or political characteristics of cities seem to bar
women from office. Women do about the same in all types of cities. Only a
bit of the difference in the proportion of women in office in various cities can
be explained by the characteristics that we have examined. Women do a little
worse in running for the more desirable offices, but not a lot worse. This suggests that women are found in only slightly less proportions in full-time, well-
paid councils as in part-time, poorly paid ones.

It also seems to be good news that the election of women to office is not
related to the presence of well-represented, large minority groups. White
women, it would appear, are not being elected at the expense of male or female
members of minority groups.

The Future of Women in Local Government

These findings suggest some optimism for the continued increase in the power
of women in city politics and probably more generally at the local level. In
contrast to the national and state levels (see Chapters 3 and 4), the trends in
the numbers and proportions of women being elected to local office are clearly
in the upward direction. More women are being elected to local offices of all
sorts, from mayor to county boards. This growth seems to have been fairly
steady since the early 1970s and continues in the mid-1980s. While we are far
from having equitable representation of women at the local level, we are much
closer to it there than at either of the two higher levels.

These general upward trends are buttressed by the evidence we have examined concerning campaign support for women. While undoubtedly there
are many exceptions, on the whole women seem to be able to generate the
kind of community support necessary to win elections in about the same proportions as men. The bases of support for women appear to be slightly different: They are more likely to have support from women's groups, neighborhood groups, and single-issue groups, but they have also been successful
in winning support from political parties and other traditional groups. They
may be less successful than men, under some conditions, in winning business
support, and in some communities this could be fatal.

Though U.S. communities differ in about every way possible, these differences are not very helpful in predicting women's success in being elected to
office. The presence of women in local government appears to be evident in
all types of cities, not just the larger, more cosmopolitan ones. There are some
types of cities where women are slightly more likely to be elected (larger cities
and those with higher incomes), but these differences are not very substantial.

One would suppose that to the extent that women are establishing themselves as competent officeholders at the grass-roots, local level, the prospects for more women in state and national elective office increase, for local government provides a training ground for many who would like to go further in elective office. To what extent are we already seeing an increase in women in state and national government? This is the question to which we turn next.

Notes

1. This chapter incorporates some analyses presented earlier in Susan Welch and Timothy Bledsoe, "Differences in Campaign Support for Male and Female Candidates," in Glenna Spitze and Gwen Moore, eds., *Research in Politics and Society* (Greenwich, Conn.: JAI Press, 1985); and Susan Welch and Albert Karnig, "Correlates of Female Office Holding in City Politics," *Journal of Politics* 41 (May 1979): 478–491.

2. Center for the American Woman and Politics (CAWP), *Women in Elective Office, 1975–1980* (New Brunswick, N.J.: Rutgers University, CAWP, 1981). See also Denise Antolini, "Women in Local Government: An Overview," in Janet Flammang, ed., *Political Women* (Beverly Hills, Calif.: Sage, 1984).

3. But see Janet Flammang, "Female Officials in the Feminist Capital: The Case of Santa Clara County," *Western Political Quarterly* 38 (March 1985): 94–118.

4. Trudy Bers, "Local Political Elites: Men and Women on Boards of Education," *Western Political Quarterly* 31 (September 1978): 381–391.

5. Sharyne Merritt, "Winners and Losers: Sex Differences in Municipal Elections," *American Journal of Political Science* 21 (November 1977): 731–744; Sharyne Merritt, "Recruitment of Women to Suburban City Councils: *Higgins* v. *Chevalier*," in Debra Stewart, ed., *Women in Local Politics* (Metuchen, N.J.: Scarecrow Press, 1980), 86–105; Susan Gluck Mezey, "The Effects of Sex on Recruitment: Connecticut Local Offices," in Stewart, *Women in Local Politics,* 61–85; Welch and Karnig, "Correlates"; Albert Karnig and B. Oliver Walter, "Election of Women to City Councils," *Social Science Quarterly* 56 (March 1976): 605–613; Susan MacManus, "Determinants of the Equitability of Female Representation on 243 City Councils," paper presented at the meeting of the American Political Science Association, Chicago, August 1976.

6. *Statistical Abstracts of the United States* (Washington, D.C.: Government Printing Office, 1985), tab. 420.

7. The sources cited in Figure 2.1 and others reflect growth in the percentage of women officeholders at the local level. See also Susan Carroll and Wendy Strimling, *Women's Routes to Elective Office* (New Brunswick, N.J.: Rutgers University, CAWP, 1983).

8. Welch and Bledsoe, "Differences in Campaign Support."

9. Flammang, "Female Officials."

10. Stephen Bristow, "Women Councillors: An Explanation of the Underrepresentation of Women in Local Government," *Local Government Studies* 6 (May-June 1980): 73–90.

11. Susan Tolchin and Martin Tolchin, *Clout: Womanpower and Politics* (New York: Coward, McCann & Geoghegan, 1973); Mary Cornelia Porter and Ann B. Matasar,

"The Role and Status of Women in the Daley Organization," in Jane Jaquette, ed., *Women in Politics* (New York: Wiley, 1974), 85–108.

12. Merritt, "Winners and Losers."

13. Eleanor C. Main, Gerard S. Gryski, and Beth Schapiro, "Different Perspectives: Southern State Legislators' Attitudes about Women in Politics," *Social Science Journal* 21 (January 1984): 21–28.

14. Carroll and Strimling, *Women's Routes to Elective Office.*

15. Mezey, "Effects of Sex on Recruitment"; Merritt, "Recruitment of Women."

16. Lawrence Miller, "Winners and Losers: Another Look at Sex Differences in Municipal Elections," paper presented at the meeting of the Southern Political Science Association, Memphis, November 1981.

17. Merritt, "Winners and Losers"; Merritt, "Recruitment of Women"; Miller, "Winners and Losers"; Lawrence Miller, "Political Recruitment and Electoral Success: A Look at Sex Differences in Municipal Elections," paper presented at the meeting of the Southwestern Political Science Association, Fort Worth, April 1984; Lawrence Miller and Lillian Noyes, "Winners and Losers: Women Candidates for Municipal Elections Revisited," paper prepared for the annual meeting of the Midwest Political Science Association, Chicago, April 1980; Janet Flammang, "Filling the Party Vacuum: Women at the Grassroots Level in Local Politics," in Flammang, *Political Women,* 87–113; Nicki Van Hightower, "The Recruitment of Women for Public Office," *American Politics Quarterly* 5 (July 1977): 301–314.

18. Carroll and Strimling, *Women's Routes to Elective Office,* 87. For a similar finding from local women officeholders in suburban Cook County, Illinois, see Merritt, "Recruitment of Women."

19. Merritt, "Winners and Losers."

20. Ibid.; Miller, "Winners and Losers"; Miller, "Political Recruitment and Electoral Success."

21. Flammang, "Female Officials."

22. The initial sampling unit was the city. An interest in having as many respondents elected by district as at-large mandated the oversampling of district and mixed cities. All cities in the specified population category that were identified as having district or mixed systems by the *Municipal Yearbook* (Washington, D.C.: International City Managers Association, 1978) were included in the sample. The more numerous at-large cities were sampled at approximately a .64 ratio. Names and addresses of council members were obtained by contacting the city clerks in each community. A maximum of 10 council members were sampled in any city. Where there were more than that number, 10 were selected randomly. A response rate of 61 percent was achieved. For further details on the survey, see Timothy Bledsoe and Susan Welch, "The Effect of Political Structures on the Socioeconomic Characteristics of Urban City Council Members," *American Politics Quarterly* 13 (October 1985): 467–484.

23. The question wording was "How important were each of the following in your last campaign in terms of giving money, helping in your campaign in some way, or giving other kinds of support?" Options offered were "your political party, organized labor, business, neighborhood organizations, organized racial or ethnic groups, groups organized over a single issue."

24. A survey of men's and women's attitudes is found in "Opinion Roundup," *Public Opinion Magazine,* April-May 1982.

25. See Irene Diamond, *Sex Roles in the State House* (New Haven, Conn.: Yale University Press, 1977).
26. Richard Engstrom, Michael McDonald, and Chou Bir-Er, "The Election of Women to Central City Councils in the United States: A Note on the Desirability and Compatibility Explanations," paper presented at the meeting of the International Society of Political Psychology, Toronto, June 1984.
27. Lee Sigelman, "The Curious Case of Women in State and Local Government," *Social Science Quarterly* 57 (March 1976): 591–604.
28. Susan Welch and Albert Karnig, "Sex and Ethnic Differences in Municipal Representation," *Social Science Quarterly* 60 (December 1979): 465–481.
29. Karnig and Walter, "Election of Women."
30. Flammang, "Female Officials."
31. Susan Welch and Lee Sigelman, "Changes in Public Attitudes toward Women in Politics," *Social Science Quarterly* 63 (June 1982): 312–322.
32. Flammang, "Female Officials," provides examples.
33. Karnig and Walter, "Election of Women"; MacManus, "Equitability of Female Representation."
34. See Welch and Karnig, "Correlates."
35. G. W. A. Bush, "Voters in a Multi-member Constituency: The 1977 Auckland Election," *Electoral Studies* 4 (December 1985): 241–254.

3

Women as State Legislative Candidates

American state legislatures have a special importance to women. Many of the issues that concern women, such as the Equal Rights Amendment,[1] wife abuse and crimes of violence against women,[2] comparable worth and equal pay for men and women,[3] aid to dependent children, and the rights of wives to the joint property of the marriage are decided by state legislatures. The fact that as recently as 1985 only 14 percent of the nation's state legislators were female[4] means that matters of great importance to women are decided with only minimal input from them.

State legislatures are also crucial to women because they are key entry points to higher elective office.[5] Many congressional and gubernatorial candidates begin in the legislatures. Governors and members of Congress, in turn, provide a number of successful Senate candidates. It is from these groups that candidates for president and vice-president are drawn.[6] Jimmy Carter was the most recent president to begin public service in the state legislature; Franklin D. Roosevelt was another. Barriers to women entering state legislatures will effectively limit the recruitment of female candidates for higher office as well.

Impediments to women entering state legislatures are therefore of concern both to those interested in bringing women into state government and to those puzzled by the scarcity of women in higher office. We will explore some explanations for the rarity of women state legislators.

Patterns of Female Representation among the States

Figure 3.1 shows the female proportion of the state legislative membership for each of the states and the change over the decade 1975–1985. We can see that female representation is quite low in all the states. Colorado, Wyoming, Ver-

Figure 3.1 Female percentage of state legislatures in 1985 and change in female legislative percentage, 1975–1985. (Author's calculations from Chrisman, et al, *Women in Public Office: A Biographical Directory and Statistical Analysis*, New York, 1976, and National Women's Political Caucus, *National Directory of Women Elected Officials, 1985*, Washington, D.C., 1985.)

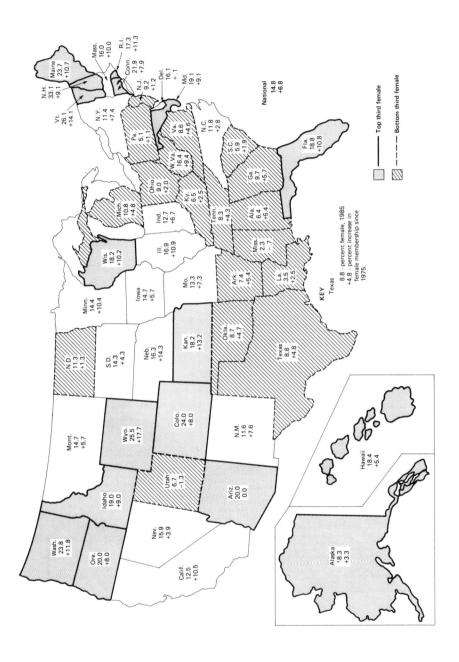

N.H.
33.1
+9.1

Maine
23.7
+10.7

Mass.
16.0
+10.0

R.I.
17.3
+11.3

Conn.
21.9
+7.9

N.J.
9.2
+1.2

Del.
16.1
+.1

Md.
19.1
+9.1

National
14.8
+6.8

Vt.
26.1
+14.1

N.Y.
11.4
+7.4

Pa.
5.1
+1.1

Va.
8.6
+4.6

N.C.
11.8
+2.8

S.C.
5.9
+1.9

Fla.
18.8
+10.8

W.Va.
16.4
+9.4

Ohio
9.0
+2.0

Ky.
6.5
+2.5

Ga.
9.7
+5.7

Mich.
10.8
+4.8

Ind.
12.7
+6.7

Tenn.
8.3
+4.3

Ala.
6.4
+5.4

Wis.
18.2
+10.2

Ill.
16.9
+10.9

Mo.
13.3
+7.3

Miss.
2.3
−.7

La.
3.5
+2.5

Minn.
14.4
+10.4

Iowa
14.7
+5.7

Ark.
7.4
+5.4

Texas

KEY

8.8 - percent female, 1985
+4.8 - percent increase in
female membership since
1975.

N.D.
11.3
+1.3

S.D.
14.3
+4.3

Neb.
16.3
+14.3

Kan.
18.2
+13.2

Okla.
8.7
+4.7

Texas
8.8
+4.8

Mont.
14.7
+5.7

Wyo.
25.5
+17.7

Colo.
24.0
+8.0

N.M.
11.6
+7.6

Idaho
19.0
+9.0

Utah
6.7
−1.3

Ariz.
20.0
0.0

Hawaii
18.4
+5.4

Wash.
23.8
+11.8

Ore.
20.0
+8.0

Nev.
15.9
+3.9

Calif.
12.5
+10.5

Alaska
18.3
+3.3

———— Top third female

– – – – Bottom third female

mont, and New Hampshire stand out as impressive in their proportions of women legislatures until we remember that the female majority in those states holds less than a third of the seats. The male minority is still elected to two-thirds or more of the positions. These states, then, stand out only in contrast to the even poorer performance of their neighbors.

We can also observe that there has been very little change during the decade 1975–1985. In this period of intense activity on the part of women and women's groups, female state legislative membership rose only 6 percent, an average of *less than 1 percent per year*. We can also note that this growth trend in female representation in the states is not an irreversible process. While in the nation as a whole slow but uniform growth occurred each year during the decade, in many states the trend was up and down. Exactly half the states, as a matter of fact, had at least one year when the proportion of women in the legislature *dropped*. The situation is even more dismal when viewed over a slightly longer time: *More women served in the legislatures in 1963 than in 1972.*[7] Even between 1975 and 1985, two states, Utah and Mississippi, experienced a net drop in female representation.

Scholarly notice of the fact that women were better represented in some legislatures than in others came several decades ago.[8] Explanations offered then are still being asserted by scholars today.

1. *Hostility.* People in some states are less ready than people in other states to see women moving into what is seen as the male political world. Political elites will inhibit the candidacies of women in these states, and voters will be reluctant to support women candidates.

2. *Competition.* In some states competition for legislative seats is more fierce than in other states. Women are not able to wage and win tough, hard-fought campaigns. Women will be more likely to be elected in states where legislative campaigns are less difficult.

3. *Traditional Roles.* While men traditionally could devote their full time and energies to politics, women are required to split their efforts between domestic and public activities. Women will be elected to legislatures in states where a dual domestic-public role is facilitated.

Scholars have studied state characteristics to test these explanations. They have tried to tie these explanations, either individually or in combination, to characteristics of states that can be easily measured and analyzed. If we can find out what kinds of states have more women legislators or fewer, the basic mechanisms keeping women out of state political life will be identified, and strategies for change can be developed. Unfortunately, a lot of slippage has occurred between the explanations and the state characteristics analyzed. As we will see, political culture, the size of legislative districts, and other state characteristics correspond at best only tangentially to the explanations advanced for certain states' having more or less female representation. Consequently, this kind of analysis still leaves us considerably in the dark. So let us follow a second strategy as well: Let us examine actual election contests in which women and men seek legislative office. This will prove more fruitful than looking at state characteristics.

State Environments and Female Legislative Representation

Hostility: Political Culture, Regionalism, and Party

Several scholars have examined the impact of political subcultures on a state's female legislative representation. Typically they use some variant of Daniel Elazar's seminal classification of states as traditionalistic, individualistic, or moralistic.[9] Hostility toward women's political activity and the level of competition in politics are expected to be different in each subculture.

The traditionalistic political subculture, confined to the southern states, places its emphasis on the continuity of elite control of social, economic, and political affairs. The role of government is to maintain the existing social order.

> It functions to confine real political power to a small and self-perpetuating group drawn from an established elite who often inherit their "right" to govern through family title or social position. . . . At the same time, those who do not have a definite role to play in politics are not expected to be even minimally active as citizens.[10]

Since women represent a new group entering the political system, people in the traditional political culture are expected to be hostile to them.

People in the individualistic political culture will be more or less indifferent to women in politics. In this subculture, found in states as varied as Pennsylvania, Missouri, and Wyoming, politics is simply a way of getting ahead, as in any other business or career. Individuals seek political power for personal benefits. People in this political subculture do not oppose a political role for women per se. People will not resist women competing on an equal footing with males for the rewards of political power. But because of these rewards, competition for public office is intense. A number of researchers feel that women are less able than men to meet this competition. Thus competition, rather than hostility toward women, will inhibit the emergence of female political elites in the individualistic political culture.[11]

The moralistic political subculture, found in many western and northwestern states—Minnesota, Iowa, Kansas, and Oregon, for example—is expected to be the most favorable toward women candidates.[12] Politics is viewed as a means by which the public good is advanced. The political elite emphasize honesty, selflessness, and commitment. Amateur participation in politics is encouraged. Unlike the traditionalistic political culture, where the entrance of female political elites will be opposed, or the individualistic political culture, where women political candidates will be greeted with neutrality, in the moralistic political culture women would be attracted and welcomed to the political elite for the contributions they would bring to civic life.

A number of different measures of political culture have been developed to account for the interstate variation in female representation. The results have been mixed. Two studies find that traditionalistic and moralistic political cultures differ in the proportion of women serving in state legislatures[13] and that cultural variations explain regional differences in female representation *within* at least one state (Florida) as well,[14] but other studies have found political culture less important.[15] One problem with these analyses is that with most measures of political subculture, the traditional political subculture is almost completely confined to the South and typifies all but perhaps one of these states.[16] Traditionalistic political subculture, then, may be just another way of saying southern regionalism. Southern states *are* lagging behind the rest of the nation in female legislative representation, but we learn little as to why by saying this is caused by "southernism" or by the traditionalistic political subculture, which in this context is the same thing.

Political culture and southern regionalism are only one possible cultural source of the interstate differences in female legislative representation. Wilma Rule proposed that historical tradition may also affect contemporary patterns of female representation.[17] She measured the "non-egalitarian political heritage" of the states by whether or not the women's suffrage amendment (Nineteenth) was ratified before it became part of the Constitution in 1920. This heritage was, however, unrelated to women's current representation. Ratification of the Equal Rights Amendment, on the other hand, *is* associated with election of women to state legislatures in the 1980s,[18] but the presence of women in legislatures should have increased the likelihood of ERA passage, not vice versa.[19] When David Hill tried to measure the climate in a state toward women's advancement with the ratio of female to male professional incomes, reasoning that "cultures which evidence support for such discrimination are also apt to discriminate against women who seek public office," he found no significant relationships when other factors were held constant.[20]

Some of the earliest research on women in state legislatures pointed out that women were more likely to be elected to legislatures in traditionally Republican states than in states dominated by the Democratic party.[21] It is not entirely clear why this might be so. Of course, traditional Democratic states were located largely, but not entirely, in the South. Studies of local party organizations suggest that outside the South, the Democratic party is controlled by eastern and southern European ethnics and is characteristically blue-collar in orientation. Ethnics and blue-collar milieus, in turn, are male-dominated, with only limited roles for women.[22] Another explanation is that women, until recently, have not been a salient political bloc to which the coalition-oriented Democrats needed to cater.

Democratic dominance used to be the strongest predictor of diminished recruitment of women legislators.[23] However, by the 1980s, the negative relationship between Democratic dominance and the election of women to the legislature had become minuscule and insignificant when the heavily Democratic southern states were excluded.[24] This change may be due to the emergence of women as a politically relevant group in the 1970s and the Democratic party's attempts to capitalize on the gender gap.[25] In any case, the historical relationship between Democratic dominance and the election of women to state legislatures has diminished.

We have looked at the results of a number of investigations into the relationship between the political culture and tradition in a state and the election of women to the legislature. A number of indirect but seemingly reasonable measures have been proposed—political culture, partisan leanings, historical traditions. Yet few consistent conclusions emerge. Even when there are fairly clear conclusions—for example, that women fare less well in southern states— it remains unclear exactly *how* women are being kept out of the legislature. If the eventual goal is to *do* something about getting more women into legislatures, we need to know more than that some states are doing better than others. We need to know *why*.

Competition: Urbanization, Constituency Size, and Legislative Compensation

Female representation in the states generally considered to be urban is lower than in more rural states.[26] Some theorists suggest that this is because political campaigns in urban areas are more expensive and more difficult than in rural areas. In urban districts the mass media, for example, span dozens of legislative districts, greatly limiting news coverage of any one of them.[27] Further, advertising rates for media are prohibitive in the large urban areas. On the surface this relationship seems valid. The larger the district in population, the more difficult and competitive the campaign. If women cannot raise funds in campaigns as effectively as men, they will be more disadvantaged in the urban districts. Some people have inferred that this ineffectiveness must be true because the average constituency size of a district does seem to be related to women's representation.[28] And the more populous the state, the fewer the women elected.[29]

All this suggests that women do have difficulty in urban areas. However, these findings do not stand up to close scrutiny. The specific problems faced by women in states with large constituencies remain unspecified.[30] If women are having a harder time getting elected from populous or urban districts, is it because of hostility on the part of elites, difficulties in raising money, lack of ability to wage professional and aggressive campaigns, the strength of the male opposition, or some other reasons? Then, too, there is also evidence that women do better in the urban, not rural, areas of states.[31] As Carol Nechemias concluded, "the image of women politicians as non-competitive, as securing election to state legislatures where men do not want the job, is inconsistent with women's record in large, urban centers."[32]

The desirability of legislative seats has also been used as a measure of legislative competitiveness. Service in some state legislatures is less desirable than in others. Where seats are less desirable, women candidates presumably will have weaker opposition than for more desirable seats and will gain election in greater numbers. Where legislative service is desirable, women candidates will face stronger opposition and be elected in diminished numbers.

One measure of legislative service desirability is salary. States that pay more may attract more and better candidates than states that pay less. Legislative salaries, by this reasoning, should be associated with the proportion of women in a state legislature. Contrary to expectations, the attractiveness of legislative service has nothing to do with the numbers of women elected.[33] Legislative compensation has, at most, a weak effect on female legislative membership, once other factors are taken into account.

The competitiveness of legislative seats has been indirectly measured in different ways: the urban or rural locale of the district, its size, and the salary of the legislator. None of these factors, however, stands up as an important predictor of women's election to office.

Traditional Roles: Legislative Sessions and the Location of State Capitals

We will examine one more explanation for interstate differences in the number of women elected to legislatures. It involves the compatibility of domestic and legislative roles. Where legislative service is incompatible with traditional domestic roles, particularly child-care responsibilities, so this reasoning runs, women will be forced to make choices between the two. The result will be fewer women serving.

If child-care responsibilities and other domestic commitments do deter women from legislative service, we would expect that they would be most inhibited when that legislative service is a full-time job. Where the legislative session is short and the job of the legislator is considered to be only part-time, perhaps fewer conflicts for women would emerge. However, the length of the legislative session does not, in fact, account for any of the interstate variation in women in the legislatures.[34]

Another possibility is that the distance a member has to travel in order to attend a legislative session may affect the willingness of women to serve. Service close to home may disrupt family responsibilities less than if long distances, especially involving an overnight stay, must be traveled. In a study of 16 state legislatures in 1981, Carol Nechemias found that in 13 of these states, the distance the average woman member traveled was less than that traveled by the average man.[35] In the 16 states she studied, women traveled less than three-quarters the distance the average male did. We need to be cautious in interpreting these findings, but it does appear that closeness to the state capital does facilitate female legislative membership. More research will be needed to connect this to child care and other traditional female roles, however.

Variation across the States: Conclusions

We have reviewed attempts to account for interstate differences in female legislative representation. With few exceptions, this research has failed to provide any clear guide either as to the reasons female legislative representation varies among the states or why it is generally low. Patterns have emerged but, as Irene Diamond has reminded us, our goal is to isolate the specific aspects of the state environment that inhibit the election of women.[36] In this light the measures we examined turned out to be merely suggestive and indirect, not actual causal agents. Thus political subculture and the state's position on the Equal Rights Amendment or the suffrage amendment were used as indicators of likely hostility to women candidates; they did not actually document that hostility. Further, as these factors tend to cluster in particular states, it is difficult to determine which factor, if any, is actually affecting female representation. On the whole, then, research comparing state characteristics has not gotten us very far in explaining why so few women are state legislators.

Now we will try a different strategy. We will directly examine the conditions under which men and women run for the state legislature, and what happens when they do. By examining actual races, the problems encountered with indirect indicators can be avoided. This approach will allow us to say something more concrete about whether voters or political elites discriminate against women candidates.

Women as Legislative Candidates

An examination of legislative races may not tell us why women choose to run, but it does tell us how women candidates fare compared with men running under similar conditions. Such an examination allows us to look more directly at voter reaction to and elite support for women candidates.

Our purpose here is to look at current patterns across a number of states. We will examine the races of 6,339 male and female candidates running for the state legislature in six states: Iowa, Missouri, Nebraska, New Mexico, Oklahoma, and Wyoming. Except for Nebraska, which has a unicameral (single-house) legislature, we will focus on lower house contests only.

For New Mexico, Nebraska, Oklahoma, and Wyoming, data on all candidates filing for the lower house (or unicameral legislature in the case of Nebraska) in elections between 1974 and 1980 were gathered. For Missouri and Iowa a different procedure was followed. Information concerning the candidates in all districts in which a female filed were gathered for these same years. In addition, data were collected from a random sample of districts in which only male candidates filed.

Although these states form a contiguous band, they also exhibit quite a bit of diversity. For example, the proportion of women in the legislature ranges from 8.7 percent in Oklahoma to 25.5 percent in Wyoming. Oklahoma and

New Mexico are below the national average; Missouri, Nebraska, and Iowa are close to the national average; and Wyoming is considerably above it. The political and cultural traditions of these states also vary. This is important for our study because, as we have seen, some researchers feel that hostility to women candidates is due to the southern traditionalistic political subculture, a tradition of nonequality, or to Democratic party domination. Urbanization was also suggested as a source of difficulty for women candidates. Our diverse group of six states allows us to look at these suppositions more directly.

Oklahoma has the traditionalistic political subculture found in the South,[37] and though not part of the original Confederacy (it did not become a state until 1907), it supplied fighting units to the southern cause, retained segregation into the 1950s, and politically identifies itself with the South.[38] Its politics is considered largely Democratic.[39] If political culture, Democratic dominance, and southern tradition produce hostility toward women candidates on the part of the electorate, this certainly should be manifested in Oklahoma. Iowa, by contrast, is a northern state with a moralistic political culture. At the state and local level it is a two-party state tilting toward the Republicans.[40] Voter hostility toward women candidates should be minimal in that state. Missouri, Nebraska, and New Mexico should be somewhere between Iowa and Oklahoma in hostility toward women candidates. Nebraska is a northern two-party state with an individualistic political subculture. New Mexico and Missouri also have individualistic political subcultures and are classified politically as largely Democratic.[41] Missouri is a border state, and New Mexico is in the Southwest. We will postpone looking at Wyoming for the moment. Its method of selecting a legislature is sufficiently different from that used in the other states to merit a special discussion. We will return to Wyoming in Chapter 6.

It is well known that two major forces that determine the outcome of state legislative races are party and incumbency. In some states Republican candidates generally have an edge, and in other states Democratic candidates have the advantage. No matter what their party, incumbents generally do substantially better than challengers or candidates running for an open seat. Up to 90 percent of legislative incumbents can be reelected, depending on the state. Thus to compare male and female candidates, their party and incumbency status must be taken into account.

Voter Hostility

Earlier we indicated that one explanation for the small number of women in the legislature may be voters' hostility toward women taking on political roles. It was further suggested that this hostility might be manifested more in some areas than in others. One comparison of the success of women and men candidates in three states during the 1950s, 1960s, and early 1970s showed that women received about 13 percent fewer votes than men.[42] We will try to discover if that hostility manifests itself today when women enter legislative races.

Our interest at this point is voter reaction to new male and female candidates aspiring to seats in the legislature. Some of these entered races against incumbents; others were running for open seats. Table 3.1 presents the mean proportion of the vote received by similar new male and female candidates in each of the five states. This average vote is then adjusted to take into account party and opponent's incumbency to make male and female candidates more comparable.[43]

There were no significant differences between the male and female candidates in general elections after party and opponent incumbency were controlled. Except for Nebraska, in no state did the difference between male and female candidates exceed 2 percent. Women actually did better than men in the traditionalistic political culture of Oklahoma, and they fared worst in the individualistic political subculture of Nebraska. By the mid-1970s, then, no evidence of voter hostility toward women candidates was being registered in these states.

Thus in general elections the voter reluctance to support female candidates, as observed in the 1950s and 1960s, had all but disappeared by the mid-1970s. The expected pattern of voter hostility due to political culture, party domination, and region also failed to emerge. Voters were consistently *more* favorable to women candidates in the traditional political culture of Oklahoma than in the moralistic political subculture of Iowa or the individualistic political subcultures of the other three states. Women candidates had the most difficult time in Nebraska. Because Nebraska's legislature is selected in nonpartisan

Table 3.1   Vote in Contested General Elections for New Men and Women Candidates, 1974-1980

State	Candidate (number)	Mean Vote (%)	Mean Vote Adjusted for Party and Opponent Incumbency (%)
New Mexico	Men (172)	42	42
	Women (37)	41	41
Nebraska	Men (95)	46	46
	Women (14)	40	42
Iowa	Men (125)	42	42
	Women (55)	41	41
Missouri	Men (152)	39	38
	Women (52)	36	37
Oklahoma	Men (159)	42	42
	Women (30)	46	44

Source: Data from election material supplied by the states.

Notes: Nebraska results are not adjusted for party because the legislature is nonpartisan. None of the relationships are statistically significant (p ranges from .19 for Nebraska to .59 for Oklahoma).

elections it was not possible to control for candidate party. This nonpartisanship may have had something to do with the appearance of female disadvantage there. But, again, even this disadvantage was statistically insignificant. Nevertheless, the lack of a party label may somehow heighten the salience of other candidate characteristics, including gender, to the disadvantage of women candidates.[44]

If women are disadvantaged in nonpartisan elections, they might also be disadvantaged in primaries where party label does not differentiate among the candidates for the party nomination. It is possible that women candidates are eliminated disproportionately in the primaries even though they suffer no disadvantage in general elections. The result would be few women gaining legislative seats. With these considerations in mind we examined how new women candidates fared in primaries compared with similar male candidates. The results are presented in Table 3.2.

Contrary to expectation, there were fewer differences between the typical female candidate and similar male candidates in primaries than in the general elections. All the differences were small and statistically insignificant. Again, women candidates in the traditionalistic political culture of Oklahoma did *better* than their male counterparts. As was the case in general elections, women did worst in Nebraska's primaries. But again, the nonpartisan legislature in that state makes the primary there unique.

We have examined—and rejected—the hypothesis that voter hostility keeps women from being elected to state legislatures. Women candidates are getting

Table 3.2   *Vote in Contested Primaries for New Men and Women Candidates, 1974-1980*

State	Candidate (number)	Mean Vote (%)	Mean Vote Adjusted for Party and Opponent Incumbency (%)
New Mexico	Men (147)	37	37
	Women (22)	39	38
Nebraska	Men (127)	26	26
	Women (24)	21	21
Iowa	Men (77)	42	42
	Women (30)	41	41
Missouri	Men (210)	33	33
	Women (62)	32	32
Oklahoma	Men (334)	32	32
	Women (30)	34	34

Source: Data from election material supplied by the states.

Notes: Nebraska results are not adjusted for party because the legislature is nonpartisan. None of the relationships are statistically significant (*p* ranges from .12 for Nebraska to .87 for New Mexico).

the same voter support as similar male candidates in *both* primaries and general elections. There is some interstate variation in how women perform, but this is limited and not in the direction predicted by political subculture, region, or party. Voter hostility cannot account for the lack of female representation in state legislatures today in these five diverse states.

Candidate Targeting

The notion that women candidates would meet with greater hostility in some states than in others or that women candidates would be greeted with hostility at all, for that matter, did not specify the source of the hostility and in fact implied that the hostility might be general. We have demonstrated that voters are not reacting any differently to similar male and female candidates either in primaries or in the general election. It may be that whatever cultural hostility remains toward female candidates is carried not by the voters at all but by the political, social, and economic elites. Maurice Duverger, the French sociologist, labeled this argument the "male conspiracy."[45] Jeane Kirkpatrick described the idea in this way: "This explanation of women's non-participation in power sees women as oppressed, barred from power by a ruling class bent on maintaining its hegemony."[46] The idea goes back to another era. At the final meeting of the National Woman Suffrage Association in 1920, Carrie Chapman Catt warned the newly enfranchised women:

> If you . . . move around enough, keeping your eyes open, you will discover a little . . . group, which we might call the umbra of the political party. You won't be so welcome there. Those are the people who are planning the platforms and picking out the candidates, and doing the work which you and the men voters will be expected to sanction at the polls. You won't be so welcome there, but that is the place to be. And if you stay there long enough and are active enough, you will see something else—the real thing in the center, with the door locked tight, and you will have a long hard fight before you get behind that door, for there is the engine that moves the wheels of your party machinery.[47]

There are several possible mechanisms by which women candidates may have their chances of election reduced. While nomination is typically through primaries and women do well when they enter primaries, political elites could subtly discourage women candidates from running or steer them toward unwinnable races. Several observers have noted that women find it more difficult to gain their party's nomination than to get elected.[48] Others have charged that the parties nominate women only when the race is hopeless and the situation calls for a "sacrificial lamb."[49] In the 1960s John Bailey, Democratic National Committee chairman and head of the Democratic party in Connecticut, remarked that "the only time to run a woman . . . is when things look so bad that your only chance is to do something dramatic."[50] Failure to encourage women candidates or nominating them only in hopeless races, then, are two ways political elites can prevent the election of women legislators despite the public's willingness to vote for them.

If women candidates are nominated for races they have a good chance of winning, political, social, or economic elites can still hurt their chances of election by withholding campaign support. A number of commentators have pointed out that women candidates seem to have greater difficulty in raising the funds necessary to wage the most effective campaign.[51]

However, political scientists are not unanimous in their belief that there really is a male conspiracy of political elites against women candidates. Jeane Kirkpatrick, for example, treats it only as a hypothesis and not as an established finding. Two studies of local party officials, in fact, fail to document any hostility on the part of male political elites toward female candidates.[52] One study does document *perceptions* of discrimination on the part of southern party leaders,[53] but little evidence of this can be found in practice.[54] Conspiracies take place privately, behind closed doors. In fact, they might not actually involve planning and coordination at all if, for example, a general prejudice against women candidates is shared among a significant portion of the political elite. Therefore, even if there were a male conspiracy, it would be very difficult to document directly.

It can be tested indirectly, however, in two ways. If a greater tendency for women candidates to be slated in difficult-to-win races can be proved, it would constitute one kind of evidence for an elite conspircy. If women candidates are funded at lower levels than male candidates running under similar conditions, this would be a second kind of evidence for a male elite conspiracy. Put another way, finding that women candidates are *not* discriminated against in slating and in fund-raising would be evidence *against* the male conspiracy theory.

Evidence of the first sort is shown in Table 3.3, which displays the races entered by nonincumbent male and female legislative candidates in Okla-

Table 3.3   Types of Primaries and General Elections Faced by New Men and Women Candidates, 1974–1980

Candidate (number)	Against Incumbent (%)	Open Seat (%)	Unopposed (%)	Total (%)
Primary				
Men (2,053)	35	40	25	100
Women (449)	31	37	32	100
General				
Men (1,129)	61	33	6	100
Women (275)	66	31	3	100

Source: Data from election material supplied by the states.

Note: For the primary elections the relationship is significant ($p < .008$), but for the general elections it is not ($p < .13$).

homa, Iowa, New Mexico, and Missouri. (Nebraska and Wyoming are excluded because their unique electoral systems make comparisons with them misleading.) In primaries, new women candidates are significantly advantaged over new male candidates because they are less likely than nonincumbent males to have an opponent and less likely to face an incumbent. To some degree this is due to the fact that new women candidates are still disproportionately Republican (although this is less pronounced today), and Republicans are less likely than Democrats to have primary contests or to challenge incumbents in primaries. In any case, there is no evidence that new women candidates face more difficult primary races than new male candidates. To the contrary, men have the more difficult primary races.

Turning to general elections, there are no significant differences between new male and female candidates. Women are slightly more likely to face an incumbent and somewhat less likely to run unopposed or for an open seat than a new male candidate, but these differences are relatively small and insignificant. However, given the overwhelming success rate of incumbents, if women ran for the same kinds of seats as men, we could expect at least a few more women to be elected. In any case, these differences do not explain why so few women are being elected to legislatures. By and large, when women are legislative candidates, they run the same sort of races as men.

Another aspect of slating that can be examined concerns party. If women run disproportionately as candidates of the state's minority party, they will be disadvantaged, even if party slating is done without any bias. Table 3.4 examines the party label under which new legislative candidates ran. Although there were no significant differences between the party labels of the new male and female candidates, a pattern did emerge. In the Republican state (Wyoming), women ran disproportionately as Democrats, while in the Democratic states (Missouri, Oklahoma, and New Mexico), new women candidates ran disproportionately as Republicans. Thus in states dominated by one party, women were more likely than men to be the candidates of the weaker party. This will certainly hurt the chances of these women getting elected, though again, the differences (which range from 3 to 7 percent) are small and insignificant. Further, when we examine *where* in the state the women run, it turns out that in the Republican state of Wyoming, for example, the new women Democratic candidates run in counties where Democrats have the advantage. Table 3.4 also shows that the female proportion of new candidates is still low. Party differences cannot account for the small proportions of women running and serving in the legislatures.

Candidate Funding

As noted, common wisdom holds that women face a major obstacle in raising money for their campaigns. Several assumptions underlie this belief. One is that although women have quite a bit of experience raising money for other

Table 3.4   New Candidates for Lower House Seats, 1974-1980

State	Candidate (number)	Republicans (% of gender)	Democrats (% of gender)	Percentage of New Candidates
States Strongly Democratic				
New Mexico	Men (330)	44	56	83
	Women (68)	48	52	17
Missouri	Men (473)	38	62	—
	Women (130)	45	55	—
Oklahoma	Men (526)	29	71	90
	Women (61)	36	64	10
State Leaning Republican				
Wyoming	Men (339)	49	51	83
	Women (67)	45	55	17
Two-Party State				
Iowa	Men (251)	46	54	—
	Women (102)	49	51	—

Source: Data from election material supplied by the states.

Notes: None of the relationships between candidate gender and party were statistically significant (*p* ranges from .23 for Oklahoma to .63 for Iowa). Due to the sampling used for Iowa and Missouri, the proportions among all candidates could not be calculated.

causes, they are not accustomed to raising it for themselves. Bella Abzug, who even as a child raised money on the streets, conveys this image when she expressed difficulty in participating in the fund-raising efforts of her own campaign.

> I flew back to New York for the "Ball for Bella" fund-raiser at Katz's, which I approached with a great deal of reluctance. I feel very self-conscious appearing at a function where money is being raised for me. I find it a terrible chore. We still have that campaign deficit."[55]

Another argument is that women do not give to women's campaigns and that males withhold their financial support from women, restricting their donations to men within their social, business, and political circles. The parties too, so the argument runs, are reluctant to support female candidates. One woman fund-raiser, Lilly Spitz of the Sacramento Women's Campaign Fund, suggests that since women cannot compete in fund-raising with men, they should work to limit campaign expenses: "One of the things we need to think about is political reform, because there's no way women are going to be able to compete at the spending levels we're talking about."[56]

While it is clear that women candidates have had problems raising money, without comparable evidence from male candidates the argument is inconclusive. Male candidates too find fund-raising difficult and often unpleasant. Thus the fund-raising and campaign spending of comparable male and female candidates need to be examined.

Not all states require candidates to report spending, and for those that do, getting access to these reports is often no simple matter. However, Oklahoma requires all candidates in contested elections to file reports of campaign receipts and expenditures. These are available to the public. Data for 1978 and 1980 were collected and examined.[57] Table 3.5 compares the fund-raising ability of comparable male and female candidates in Oklahoma.

In the traditionalistic political culture of Oklahoma, one would expect to find that women experience difficulty in raising money. The evidence is clearly in the other direction. For every incumbency and party category, women candidates raised and spent considerably *more* than their male counterparts. This evidence is from only one state, but a similar examination of legislative campaign fund-raising in Pennsylvania also found that women candidates did not have unusual problems raising money.[58]

Conclusions

We have examined several factors thought to restrict the election of women to state legislatures. First we explored interstate differences to determine if these could account for women's being better represented in some places than in others. The results were inconclusive. Characteristics of the states themselves were largely unable to account for the legislative representation of women.

We then examined voter reactions, slating of women candidates, and campaign funding in legislative races. The findings here were clearer. We found

Table 3.5 Campaign Funds Raised by Candidates in Contested Oklahoma Lower House Races, 1978 and 1980

Candidate Party	Candidate (number)	Mean Funds Raised by Candidate ($)
Not Incumbent		
Republican	Men (69)	5,158.81
	Women (12)	6,617.68
Democrat	Men (177)	3,010.14
	Women (27)	5,989.51
Incumbent		
Republican	Men (18)	6,495.55
	Women (3)	14,138.33
Democrat	Men (72)	6,422.37
	Women (2)	29,445.50

Source: Data from Oklahoma State Board of Elections.

that voters were *not* discriminating against female candidates. There was little difference in the voters' reactions to male and female candidates of similar party and incumbency status. We found only slight, largely insignificant differences in the slating of male and female candidates. These differences were not of a magnitude to justify concluding the existence of a male conspiracy against women candidates. Nor can the magnitude of these differences account for the low representation of women. We also found little evidence that women are being underfinanced in their campaigns. Instead, reports from two states indicate that women state legislative candidates are being funded at the rate of similar men candidates, and often at higher rates.

Thus the political system and cultural milieu no longer present the barriers to women state legislative candidates they may once have. If more women run, more women will be elected. And as more women begin gaining tenure in legislatures, the pool of women candidates for higher office will also increase. The problem remains, however, as to why the process has been so slow. We will return to this question in Part Three.

Notes

1. See Janet Boles, *The Politics of the Equal Rights Amendment* (White Plains, N.Y.: Longman, 1979); Mark Daniels, R. Darcy, and Joseph Westphal, "The ERA Won— At Least in the Polls," *PS* 15 (Fall 1982): 578–584; Mark Daniels and R. Darcy, "As Time Goes By: The Arrested Diffusion of the Equal Rights Amendment," *Publius* 15 (Fall 1985): 51–60.
2. See Mark Daniels and R. Darcy, "Notes on the Use and Interpretation of Discriminant Analysis," *American Journal of Political Science* 27 (May 1983): 359–381.
3. See Elaine Johansen, *Comparable Worth* (Boulder, Colo.: Westview, 1984).
4. National Women's Political Caucus, *National Directory of Women Elected Officials* (Washington, D.C.: National Women's Political Caucus, 1981, 1983, 1985).
5. See Joseph Schlesinger, *Ambition and Politics: Political Careers in the United States* (Chicago: Rand McNally, 1966).
6. See Gary Jacobson and Samuel Kernell, *Strategy and Choice in Congressional Elections* (New Haven, Conn.: Yale University Press, 1981); Roderick Kiewiet, "The Rationality of Candidates Who Challenge Incumbents in Congressional Elections," Social Science Working Paper No. 436 (Pasadena: Division of Humanities and Social Sciences, California Institute of Technology, 1982).
7. Carol Nechemias, "Women's Success in Capturing State Legislative Seats: Stability and Instability of Empirical Relationships over Time," paper presented at the meeting of the Midwest Political Science Association, Chicago, April 1985.
8. See Emmy Werner, "Women in the State Legislatures," *Western Political Quarterly* 21 (March 1968): 40–50; Maurice Duverger, *The Political Role of Women* (Paris: UNESCO, 1955); see also Dorothy Moncure, "Women in Political Life," *Current History* 29 (January 1929): 639–643; Marion Martin and Bernice van de Vries, "Women in State Capitols," *State Government* 10 (October 1937): 213–215; Marion Martin, "Fair Play in Maine: Down East Women Legislators Given Equal Footing," *State Government* 10 (October 1937): 212–213.

9. Daniel J. Elazar, *American Federalism: A View from the States* (New York: Crowell, 1966).

10. Ibid., 93.

11. Irene Diamond, *Sex Roles in the State House* (New Haven, Conn.: Yale University Press, 1977); David Hill, "Political Culture and Female Political Representation," *Journal of Politics* 43 (February 1981): 159–168.

12. See Jeane Kirkpatrick, *Political Woman* (New York: Basic Books, 1974); Diamond, *Sex Roles;* Wilma Rule, "Why Women Don't Run: The Critical Contextual Factors in Women's Legislative Recruitment," *Western Political Quarterly* 34 (March 1981): 60–77; Hill, "Political Culture"; Woodrow Jones and Albert Nelson, "Correlates of Women's Representation in Lower State Legislative Chambers," *Social Behavior and Personality* 9 (1981): 9–15.

13. Hill, "Political Culture"; Nechemias, "Women's Success"; Carol Nechemias, "Geographic Mobility and Women's Access to State Legislatures," *Western Political Quarterly* 38 (March 1985): 119–131.

14. Joan Carver, "Women in Florida," *Journal of Politics* 41 (August 1979): 941–955.

15. Jones and Nelson, "Correlates of Women's Representation."

16. See Elazar, *American Federalism;* Charles Johnson, "Political Culture in American States: Elazar's Formulation Examined," *American Journal of Political Science* 20 (August 1976): 491–509.

17. Rule, "Why Women Don't Run."

18. Nechemias, "Women's Success."

19. See David Hill, "Women State Legislators and Party Voting on the ERA," *Social Science Quarterly* 63 (June 1982): 318–326; David Hill, "Female State Senators as Cue Givers: ERA Roll-Call Voting, 1972–1979," in Janet Flammang, ed., *Political Women: Current Roles in State and Local Government* (Beverly Hills, Calif.: Sage, 1984), 177–190.

20. Hill, "Political Culture," 164; see also David Hill, "A Time Series Analysis of Female Representation in the Legislatures," paper presented at the meeting of the Midwest Political Science Association, Chicago, April 1980.

21. Werner, "Women in the State Legislatures," *Western Political Quarterly* 21 (March 1968): 40–50.

22. See Edmond Costantini and Kenneth H. Craik, "Women as Politicians: The Social Background, Personality, and Political Careers of Female Party Leaders," in Marianne Githens and Jewell Prestage, eds., *A Portrait of Marginality: The Political Behavior of American Women* (New York: McKay, 1977), 221–240; Mary C. Porter and Ann B. Matasar, "The Role and Status of Women in the Daley Organization," in Jane Jaquette, ed., *Women in Politics* (New York: Wiley, 1974), 85–109; and Diamond, *Sex Roles.*

23. Rule, "Why Women Don't Run."

24. Nechemias, "Women's Success."

25. Ibid.

26. Werner, "Women in the State Legislatures."

27. William C. Adams, "Local Television News Coverage and the Central City," *Journal of Broadcasting* 24 (Spring 1980): 253–265.

28. Diamond, *Sex Roles;* Hill, "Time Series of Female Representation"; Hill, "Political Culture"; Nechemias, "Women's Success."

29. Rule, "Why Women Don't Run."

30. Nechemias, "Geographic Mobility."

31. Elizabeth King, "Women in Iowa Legislative Politics," in Githens and Prestage, *Portrait of Marginality,* 284–303; Carver, "Women in Florida"; Susan Welch, Margery Ambrosius, Janet Clark, and R. Darcy, "The Effect of Candidate Gender on Election Outcomes in State Legislative Races," *Western Political Quarterly* 38 (September 1985): 464–475; Janet Clark, R. Darcy, Susan Welch, and Margery Ambrosius, "Women as Legislative Candidates in Six States," in Flammang, *Political Women,* 141–155.

32. Nechemias, "Geographic Mobility," 127.

33. Diamond, *Sex Roles;* Hill, "Political Culture"; Rule, "Why Women Don't Run"; Nechemias, "Geographic Mobility."

34. Hill, "Political Culture."

35. Nechemias, "Geographic Mobility." The binomial formula indicates that this is very unlikely to have happened by chance ($n = 16$, $p = .5$, $k = 0, 1, 2, 3$; probability $= .01$).

36. Diamond, *Sex Roles,* 25.

37. R. Darcy, Margaret Brewer, and Judy Clay, "Women in the Oklahoma Political System: State Legislative Elections," *Social Science Journal* 21 (January 1984): 67–78.

38. Oklahoma is part of the southern regional primary and the Southern Governor's Conference, for example.

39. Austin Ranney, "Parties in State Politics," in Herbert Jacob and Kenneth Vines, eds., *Politics in the American States: A Comparative Analysis,* 3d ed. (Boston: Little, Brown, 1976), 51–92.

40. Ibid.

41. Ibid.

42. Margery Ambrosius and Susan Welch, "Women and Politics at the Grassroots: Women Candidates for State Office in Three States, 1950–1978," *Social Science Journal* 21 (January 1984): 29–42.

43. The method used was the MCA technique, which has the effect of adjusting categories of one independent variable such that other independent variables are equally distributed among the categories of that independent variable.

44. See John E. Mueller, "Choosing among 133 Candidates," *Public Opinion Quarterly* 34 (Fall 1970): 395–402; Gary Byrne and J. Kristian Pueschel, "But Who Should I Vote for for County Coroner?" *Journal of Politics* 36 (August 1974): 778–784; Jonathan Kelley and Ian McAllister, "Ballot Paper Cues and the Vote in Australia and Britain: Alphabetic Voting, Sex, and Title," *Public Opinion Quarterly* 48 (Summer 1984): 452–466.

45. Duverger, *Political Role of Women.*

46. Kirkpatrick, *Political Woman,* 19.

47. Quoted in Eleanor Flexner, *Century of Struggle: The Women's Rights Movement in the United States,* rev. ed. (Cambridge, Mass.: Harvard University Press, 1975), 340.

48. Bernice van de Vries, "Housekeeping in the Legislature," *State Government* 21 (June 1948): 127–128; Duverger, *Political Role of Women;* Frank Sorauf, *Party and Representation: Legislative Politics in Pennsylvania* (New York: Atherton, 1963); Werner, "Women in the State Legislatures"; Susan Tolchin and Martin Tolchin,

Clout: Womanpower and Politics (New York: Coward, McCann & Geohegan, 1973), 62; Rule, "Why Women Don't Run"; Susan G. Mezey, "Does Sex Make a Difference? A Case Study of Women in Politics," *Western Political Quarterly* 31 (December 1978): 492–501.

49. See Lester Seligman, "Political Recruitment and Party Structures: A Case Study," *American Political Science Review* 60 (March 1961): 77–86; M. Kent Jennings and Norman Thomas, "Men and Women in Party Elites: Sex Roles and Political Resources," *Midwest Journal of Political Science* 12 (November 1966): 469–492; Peggy Lamson, *Few Are Chosen* (Boston: Houghton Mifflin, 1968); Naomi Lynn, "Women in American Politics: An Overview," in Jo Freeman, ed., *Women: A Feminist Perspective* (Palo Alto, Calif.: Mayfield, 1975), 264–285; Susan Carroll, "Women Candidates and State Legislative Elections, 1976: Limitations in the Political Opportunity Structure and Their Effects on Electoral Participation and Success," paper presented at the meeting of the American Political Science Association, Washington, D.C., August 1977; King, "Women in Iowa Legislative Politics." Sophonisba P. Breckinridge quotes an editorial in the *Woman Citizen* of November 1922:

First of all it is clear that the barriers in the way of women being elected to any political office are almost insurmountable. The dominant political parties do not nominate women for political office if there is any chance of winning. Political offices are the assets of the political machine. In general, they are too valuable to be given to women. They are used to pay political debts or to strengthen the party, and so far as the parties are not greatly in debt to women, and it has not been shown that it strengthens a party to nominate them. (*Women in the Twentieth Century,* 302).

50. Quoted in Lamson, *Few Are Chosen,* xxiii.
51. See Werner, "Women in the State Legislatures"; Tolchin and Tolchin, *Clout;* Carroll, "Women Candidates and State Legislative Elections"; Sandra Baxter and Marjorie Lansing, *Women and Politics: The Invisible Majority* (Ann Arbor: University of Michigan Press, 1980).
52. See Janet Clark, "Party Leaders and Women's Entry into the Political Elites," paper presented at the meeting of the Southwestern Political Science Association, Fort Worth, April 1979; Jean Graves McDonald and Vickey Howell Pierson, "'Female County Party Leaders and the Perception of Discrimination: A Test of the Male Conspiracy Theory," *Social Science Journal* 21 (January 1984): 13–20.
53. Eleanor Main, Gerard Gryski, and Beth Schapiro, "Different Perspectives: Southern State Legislators' Attitudes about Women in Politics," *Social Science Journal* 21 (January 1984): 21–28.
54. See R. Darcy, Charles D. Hadley, and Janet Clark, "The Changing Roles of Southern Women in State Party Politics," paper presented at the Citadel Symposium on Southern Politics, Charleston, S.C., March 1986.
55. Bella Abzug, *Bella!* (New York: Saturday Review Press, 1972), 89; see also Virginia Currey, "Campaign Theory and Practice: The Gender Variable," in Githens and Prestage, *Portrait of Marginality,* 162; Kirkpatrick, *Political Woman,* 90.
56. Quoted in Katherine E. Kleeman, *Women's PACs* (New Brunswick, N.J.: Eagleton Institute of Politics, 1983), 24.

57. Darcy et al., "Women in the Oklahoma Political System."
58. Robert O'Connor, "Parties, PACs, and Political Recruitment: The Freshman Class of the Pennsylvania House of Representatives," paper presented at the meeting of the Midwest Political Science Association, Chicago, April 1984; Robert O'Connor, "Party Political Recruitment: Access to the Pennsylvania House of Representatives," paper presented at the meeting of the Midwest Political Science Association, Chicago, April 1985.

4

Women as Congressional Candidates

We know quite a bit about congressional elections. We know that the outcomes of congressional elections are cyclical and linked to the state of the economy and the performance of the president[1] and that party and incumbency are major determinants of a voter's choice.[2] These powerful influences leave only a limited scope for individual candidates to affect election outcomes. Yet candidates can and do influence voters. But of this we know less. Little is known about the effect of individual candidate characteristics or their efforts on the electoral outcome.[3] This becomes particularly relevant when we consider women candidates for the House of Representatives.

Since 1920 women have composed at least half of the eligible voters while making up only a minute fraction of those elected to the U.S. House of Representatives. Although there continue to be minuscule increases in the number of women serving, women still comprise only about 5 percent of the total membership. This is now far out of line with female proportions in most democratic national legislatures, where women comprise up to 34 percent of the members.[4] Figure 4.1 compares the proportion of women in the U.S. House of Representatives with the legislatures in Canada and several European nations. The figures represent the highest percentage of women members reached in each of the nine decades of this century. Only the U.S. Senate and Great Britain's Parliament have a poorer record than the U.S. House of Representatives.

The experience of other countries helps dispel myths about the electability of women. First, the decade-by-decade growth of female representation in Scandinavia and elsewhere in Europe belies the notion that the United States has not had enough time to incorporate women fully into the political system.[5] This steady growth found elsewhere has not occurred here.

The European experience also demonstrates that long periods of transition are not necessary in order to attain gender equality in legislatures. In Germany and Austria rapid growth was achieved after World War II, and in Switzerland, after women achieved suffrage in 1970. In Iceland the proportion of women tripled in a single election. Growth has been apparent almost everywhere in the 1970s and the 1980s, except in the United States and Great Britain.

Finally, the belief that it takes a great crisis to force political systems to relax

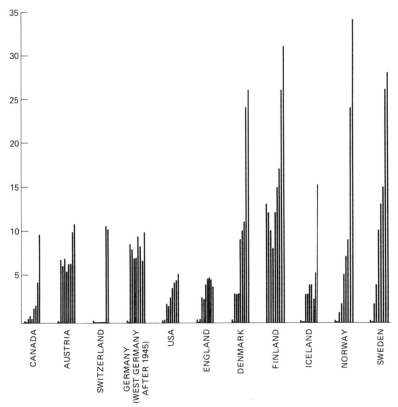

Figure 4.1 Female proportion of national legislatures (lower house) by decade in 11 nations, 1900–1985. (Data for Canada, Austria, Switzerland, Germany, and Great Britain from Walter Kohn, *Women in National Legislatures,* New York: Praeger, 1980, and from information supplied by national embassies; data for the United States from Barbara Schwemle, *Women in the United States Congress,* Washington, D.C.: Congressional Research Service, 1983; data for Denmark, Finland, Iceland, Norway, and Sweden from Elina Haavio-Mannila et al., *Det Uferdige Demokratiet: Kvinner i Nordisk Politikk,* Oslo: Nordisk Ministerrad, 1983)

barriers against women[6] is also not supported. The three major crises of this century were the two world wars and the Great Depression. But unusual growth in female representation took place in the 1920s, in the late 1940s, and in the 1970s and 1980s—before or after these crises, not during them. If there is any pattern it is one of female representational growth during periods of relative tranquility.

The American House of Representatives, then, is an anomaly; it has had neither a steady rise nor rapid jumps in female representation. Only a Pollyanna would consider the half-century gain from 2 percent in 1929 to 5 percent today progress. The U.S. House of Representatives has been largely immune to the increases in female representation that have taken place around the nation. Three broad explanations for this paucity of women in the House have been suggested—voter hostility, the inadequacies of women congressional candidates, and a conspiracy of male political elites. Let us examine each.

Voters and Congressional Candidates

There is some reason to think that female candidates for Congress have more to overcome than their male counterparts. Although women have formally achieved political equality in this country, the Nineteenth Amendment did not end the tradition that politics was essentially a male domain. Gallup asked Americans on three occasions whether they would vote for a qualified woman of their own party for Congress; although there was a decline from the 13 percent who said no in 1970, as late as 1984 some 6 percent still would not vote for a qualified woman (see Table 4.1).

Six percent may seem few, but in the highly competitive world of congressional elections such a disadvantage would pose an almost insurmountable barrier to women candidates. Yet this 6 percent may be an *underestimate* of the proportion of Americans looking at women candidates with a jaundiced eye. Even though most Americans are now willing to vote for a qualified woman, women may have more difficulty than men establishing themselves as qualified. The National Opinion Research Center (NORC) at the University of Chicago has asked on six occasions in their General Social Survey if most men are more suited emotionally for politics than most women. As Table 4.2 indicates, well over a third of the respondents still feel that most women are emotionally less suited for politics than men. Although this represents a decline over the past decade, it is a surprisingly strong antifemale bias for a system professing equality for over 60 years.

Survey results, then, indicate a residual hostility on the part of voters toward

Table 4.1   Attitude toward Women Congressional Candidates

If your party nominated a woman to run for Congress in your district, would you vote for her if she were qualified for the job?

Date	Yes (%)	No (%)	No Opinion (%)	Total (%)
1970	84	13	3	100
1975	88	9	3	100
1984	91	6	3	100

Sources: Gallup Opinion Index 228–229 (August-September 1984): 13; Gallup, *The Gallup Poll* (New York: Random House, 1972), 2261.

Table 4.2   Attitudes toward the Qualifications of Women for Politics

Tell me if you agree or disagree with this statement: Most men are better suited emotionally for politics than are most women.

Year	Agree (%)	Disagree (%)	Not Sure (%)	Total (%)	Number of Respondents
1974	44	49	7	100	752
1975	48	48	4	100	1,488
1977	47	48	5	100	1,529
1978	42	54	4	100	1,530
1982	35	59	6	100	743
1983	34	62	4	100	1,589

Source: Data from the General Social Survey, 1972–1984, made available through the Roper Center and the Inter-University Consortium for Political and Social Research.

women candidates. But does this bias actually manifest itself in elections? The evidence from other nations is mixed. Kelley and McAllister reported that women candidates in national parliamentary elections in Great Britain and Australia suffer an electoral disadvantage.[7] But contrary findings from these countries are also available.[8] These studies find little voter discrimination against women in national legislative elections.

In any case, there are a number of reasons for distinguishing American congressional elections from the parliamentary elections held elsewhere. In Great Britain, for example, national elections have only one race, for Parliament, and, until recently, ballots did not indicate party, only the names of the candidates. In Australia voting is accomplished by a ranking system, and nonvoting is minimized through a system of fines. These and many other differences suggest that findings from other political systems should be applied to the American situation cautiously.

Even if voters are hesitant about women as political leaders, their bias may not translate into votes against female candidates. Most voters cannot name the congressional candidates running in their districts, and only a little over half the voters even know the name of the congressional candidate for whom they voted.[9] Other research demonstrates the importance of name recognition and party as determinants of the vote.[10] This gives an advantage to incumbents and others who have made themselves prominent.

Since much less than half the electorate (38 percent in 1982) can be expected to participate in an off-year congressional election, and just about half in a presidential election year, it is the orientation of the voters, not the nonvoters, that is crucial. It is possible that nonvoters will be disproportionately hostile to female candidates,[11] but this does not seem to be the case. Table 4.3 shows that there is absolutely no difference in attitudes toward women in politics between people who voted in presidential elections and people who did not.

Table 4.3   Attitude toward Women in Politics among Voters and Nonvoters in the Previous Presidential Election, 1974–1983

Tell me if you agree or disagree with this statement: Most men are better suited emotionally for politics than are most women.

Vote	Agree (%)	Disagree (%)	Not Sure (%)
Voted	66	66	66
Did not vote	34	34	34
Total (number)	100 (3,216)	100 (4,123)	100 (353)

$\chi^2 = .625$; DF = 2; $p < .73$ (not significant).

A factor minimizing electoral outcomes hostile to women is that some portion of the electorate is biased *in favor* of women candidates. The *Washington Post,* for example, quoted Representative Martha Keys of Kansas: "Women are perceived as not being part of the power structure . . . not part of what happened in the past—and that's good."[12] Women are still not yet associated with the negative aspects of politics. The General Social Survey found on two occasions (1974 and 1982) that 5 percent of the respondents considered women emotionally *better* suited for politics than men. Although this is not nearly the proportion of those questioning the political qualifications of female candidates, it does offset the disadvantage somewhat.

Probably the best reason for not expecting an antifemale bias to manifest itself in election results is that this bias, where it exists, must compete with other voter tendencies. The most important of these are a candidate's party and incumbency status. Also important are a candidate's name recognition and popular image. Other factors only rarely enter into the electorate's voting decision. Even charges of corruption reduce a representative's share of the vote by as little as 6 percent.[13] Given the impact of such a well-publicized factor, the sex of the candidate would seem to have even less impact in a campaign.

While it has been established that there is a great deal of inertia in the vote for congressional candidates, it is also clear that an effective campaign can make a difference. It is through the campaign that a candidate can achieve recognition and overcome disadvantages.

The Congressional Campaigns of Women and Men

A number of studies have confirmed that candidates' campaigns can have an impact. The goals of a campaign are, first, to achieve recognition for the candidate and, second, to establish a favorable image. An effective campaign increases voter recognition and awareness of the candidate, and that in turn affects the vote.[14]

A number of factors are important to a successful campaign. Candidate credibility is primary. The candidates most likely to be taken seriously are those who have either held or are holding public office.[15] Individuals who have previously run strong but losing races can also establish their credibility as candidates.[16] Those who have run for office previously are more likely to develop effective campaign organizations, and a well-organized campaign is more effective in reaching voters.[17]

The ability to attract media coverage increases voter awareness of the candidate and influences the vote.[18] This media attention is essential for candidates challenging well-known and established incumbents. The vigor and energy a candidate brings to the campaign is therefore important because these characteristics attract the media. Several studies document successful candidates whose energy overcame difficult electoral situations. Thomas Mann, for example, describes the great variability in candidate recognition among candidates in similar electoral situations.[19]

While some people have argued that women candidates, rarities by virtue of their being women, can gain immediate recognition and electoral advantage,[20] a number of others point to a possible weakness in women congressional candidates. Robert Bernstein marshals provocative evidence for this premise.[21] Arguing that an ambitious and energetic candidate has the advantage, all things being equal, Bernstein draws on a number of studies to document the lack of political ambition of female political elites.[22] He reasons that this lack of ambition will make women less aggressive candidates than men.

Others have characterized women candidates as reluctant competitors or as "sacrificial lambs" running with a sense of party loyalty and not intent on winning.[23] This suggests that women will be less effective as candidates than their male counterparts.

Studies have documented that first-time women candidates are typically older than beginning male candidates.[24] This, too, is associated with less effective candidates, at least in the minds of some observers.[25] Bernstein suggests that the older women candidates will be less ambitious than their younger male competition and that this will be reflected in their campaigns. Women candidates, so this reasoning runs, will be less likely than men to wage the aggressive campaign necessary to overcome partisan and incumbency disadvantages.

Though these arguments have a certain surface plausibility, discouraging as they might seem, they are indirect. In fact, there is no concrete evidence that women candidates are less effective campaigners than men. Many anecdotal accounts of female political campaigns have been published,[26] but little systematic evidence on this point has been presented.

Campaign Contacts

One way the effectiveness of women compared to men congressional candidates can be gauged is through the 1982 Survey Research Center's National Election

Study. This survey, conducted in 173 congressional districts, examined respondents' attitudes toward and reactions to the campaigns of the congressional candidates. There were 22 women candidates running with major party endorsements in the districts sampled. By comparing voter reaction to these women candidates to voter reactions to men candidates in similar situations, direct evidence concerning the effectiveness of female campaigners could be obtained.

Several researchers found that the ability of candidates to make contact with voters is related to their electoral success. Contact includes being seen on television, heard on the radio, read about in a newspaper or magazine, met in person, or even brought to the voters' attention through a public speech or mailed campaign literature.[27] Table 4.4 shows the campaign contacts recalled by respondents for men and women congressional candidates.

As might be expected, given the advantages possessed by incumbent candidates, their campaigns are the most effective in making contact with voters. Challengers and those contesting open seats are somewhat less successful. Because almost all incumbents are male, while women are more likely to be challengers or to run for an open seat, the performance of male and female candidates cannot be compared without first adjusting for the kinds of races the candidates contest. For Tables 4.4 through 4.6 this is done by weighing respondents so that the proportion in districts having male or female incum-

Table 4.4 Candidate Contact by Type of Race and by Candidate Sex, with Type of Race Held Constant, 1982

	Contact by Campaign[a] (%)	No Contact by Campaign[a] (%)	Total (%)	Number of Respondents
Type of Race[b]				
Incumbent	79	21	100	1,715
Challenger	45	55	100	975
Open seat	56	44	100	298
Candidate[c]				
Men	65	35	100	2,812
Women	75	25	100	176

Source: Data from the 1982 CPS American National Election Study Post-Election File made available through the Inter-University Consortium for Political and Social Research.

[a] Contact was determined from respondents' answers to the following item: "There are many ways in which U.S. Representatives (or candidates) can have contact with people in their district. On this page are some of these ways. Think of (name of candidate) . . . have you . . . met him or her . . . attended a meeting or gathering where he or she spoke . . . talked to a member of his or her staff . . . received something in the mail . . . read about him or her in a newspaper or magazine . . . heard him or her on the radio . . . saw him or her on television . . . other contacts not mentioned above?"

[b] $\chi^2 = 327.74$; DF = 2; $p < .001$.

[c] $\chi^2 = 7.18$; DF = 1; $p < .01$.

bents, male or female challengers, or males or females running for open seats is the same proportion as in the entire sample. This has the effect of controlling for candidate and opponent incumbency.

When male and female candidates are compared after adjusting for incumbency, no evidence is found for the notion that women somehow wage less effective campaigns. To the contrary, respondents report significantly more campaign contacts from women than men candidates. Clearly the women candidates are not running as passive sacrificial lambs in contrast to more aggressive male colleagues.

Candidate Recognition

Candidates who are unknown are unlikely to overcome any disadvantages associated with party and incumbency and unlikely to overcome advantages possessed by better-known candidates.[28] But the measurement of the degree to which a candidate is well known is subject to some dispute. Surveys have long asked respondents to name the congressional candidates running in their districts, and most voters cannot.[29] Other researchers have argued, however, that the ability to recall the name of the candidate is not the best gauge of candidate recognition. Instead, the ability to *recognize* the name of the candidate, they argue, is what is important, for that is what they will find on the ballot when they vote.[30] Not surprisingly, recognition levels are considerably higher than name-recall levels.

Table 4.5 compares name-recall levels for similar male and female major

Table 4.5 *Ability to Name Men and Women Candidates by Type of Race and by Candidate Sex, Holding Type of Race Constant, 1982*

	Cannot Name[a] (%)	Can Name[a] (%)	Total (%)	Number of Respondents
Type of Race[b]				
Incumbent	65	35	100	1,224
Challenger	82	18	100	988
Open seat	81	19	100	298
Candidate[c]				
Men	74	26	100	2,353
Women	69	31	100	157

Source: Data from 1982 CPS American National Election Study Post-Election Survey made available through the Inter-University Consortium for Political and Social Research.

[a]Respondents were asked, "Do you happen to remember the names of the candidates for Congress—that is, the House of Representatives in Washington—that ran in your district this November? . . . Who were they?"

[b]$\chi^2 = 93.13$; DF = 2; $p < .001$

[c]$\chi^2 = 1.91$; DF = 1, $p < .20$ (not significant).

party candidates in the 173 congressional districts studied by the Survey Research Center in 1982. As might be expected, about twice as many respondents can name the incumbent candidate than can name either the challenger or the candidates for an open seat. Only about one-third of the respondents can even name the incumbent. Comparing men and women candidates, however, we find no significant differences in recall of male or female candidates. Whatever differences exist in the sample favor the female candidate, not the male.

Turning to candidate recognition, Table 4.6 indicates, again as expected, that recognition levels are much higher than name recall levels. While less than half of the respondents can name the incumbent, about 90 percent can recognize the incumbent's name. The ability to recognize candidates challenging incumbents and candidates in open-seat contests is about three times the level of the ability to name these same candidates.

As with the ability to name candidates, no significant differences between respondents' ability to recognize male and female candidates were found, and whatever differences exist between male and female candidates in name recognition favor the female candidate, not the male candidate.

Reactions to Candidates

We can now examine how respondents react to women candidates. If voters stereotype women candidates or apply the reservations they express in the abstract concerning women candidates, recognition will work against rather than in favor of the woman candidate.

Two methods were used to gauge reactions to women candidates. First, the survey asked respondents to indicate things they liked and then things they

Table 4.6 *Recognition of Candidate Names by Type of Race and by Candidate Sex, Holding Type of Race Constant, 1982*

	Recognizes Name[a] (%)	Does Not Recognize Name[a] (%)	Total (%)	Number of Respondents
Type of Race[b]				
Incumbent	90	10	100	1,215
Challenger	64	36	100	970
Open seat	70	30	100	298
Candidate[c]				
Men	77	23	100	2,329
Women	83	17	100	154

Source: Data from the 1982 American National Election Study, Post-Election Survey, made available through the Inter-University Consortium for Political and Social Research.

[a] Name recognition was derived from the CPS feeling thermometer items.

[b] $\chi^2 = 216.20$; DF = 2; $p < .001$.

[c] $\chi^2 = 2.41$; DF = 1; $p < .20$ (not significant).

disliked about each candidate. Up to four responses were recorded for each question. By subtracting the number of negative references from the number of positive references made by each respondent, we created a measure of how favorably the respondent viewed a candidate. A second measure of favorability toward a candidate was the feeling thermometer. Respondents are shown a drawing of a thermometer in which 100 degrees indicates very favorable feelings toward a candidate, 50 degrees neutral feelings, and 0 degrees very unfavorable feelings. Respondents were asked to indicate in degrees how they feel about each candidate running in their district. Table 4.7 presents the analysis of these measures.

The net favorable minus unfavorable references and the thermometer ratings were averaged for male and female candidates of each party. Analyses of variance were performed and the means adjusted[31] to take into account the type of race (incumbent, challenger, open seat).

Although the differences are not significant, women Democratic candidates in the sample netted more favorable mentions than men and had higher thermometer scores after the type of race was adjusted. Among the Republican candidates, women netted significantly *more* favorable references than men and gained significantly *higher* thermometer ratings after adjusting for type of race. Whatever differences exist between men and women candidates, then,

Table 4.7   Reactions to Men and Women Congressional Candidates, 1982

Constituent Response	Candidate	Unadjusted Mean	Mean Adjusted for Type of Race	Number of Respondents
Democratic Candidate				
Number of favorable	Men	.45	.43	1,282
minus unfavorable	Women	.31	.52	91
references[a]				
Feeling thermometer[b]	Men	63	62	809
	Women	61	67	53
Republican Candidate				
Number of favorable	Men	.28	.28	1,307
minus unfavorable	Women	.74	.65	66
references[c]				
Feeling thermometer[d]	Men	58	58	713
	Women	68	66	44

Source: Data from 1982 American National Election Study made available through the Inter-University Consortium for Political and Social Research.

[a]F (partial for sex) $= .399$; DF $= 1/1,365$; $p < .52$ (not significant).

[b]F (partial for sex) $= 2.02$; DF $= 1/855$; $p < .15$ (not significant).

[c]F (partial for sex) $= 7.52$; DF $= 1/1,365$; $p < .006$.

[d]F (partial for sex) $= 4.72$; DF $= 1/750$; $p < .030$.

benefit the women, not the men. Voters are at least as favorable toward women candidates as toward similar men candidates.

Issue Congruence

One final aspect of reactions to men and women candidates concerns ideology and issues. Are women candidates being stereotyped by an electorate unaware of their positions?

Most political scientists feel that issues are not generally important in individual congressional campaigns.[32] This is because information concerning candidate positions is quite minimal in the electorate. Further, there is quite a bit of indecision on the part of voters themselves concerning their own issue positions.[33] Still, it is possible that voter perception of women's stands on issues could work to the detriment of women candidates.

The 1982 survey asked respondents to rate themselves on six attitudes ranging from liberalism or conservatism to increasing or decreasing defense spending. On each of these scales one extreme was indicated by a score of 1 and the other extreme by 7. Respondents were asked where they would place themselves on the scale. They were then asked where they would place their congressional candidates on the same scale. By measuring the difference (in absolute value) between the respondents' own positions and their perceptions of the candidate, a measure of how close the respondent is to the candidate was obtained. The average distance between the respondent and men and women Republican and Democratic candidates could then be determined. Table 4.8 presents the results.

To determine if there were significant differences in the closeness of men and women candidates to voters on the issues, each item and the *pattern* of differences across all the items were studied. When the six items were examined individually, no significant differences between men and women candidates were found. Women candidates were not seen to be farther from the voter on issues and ideology than men candidates. In fact, the differences indicate that the women candidates, not the men, are perceived as closer to the voter.

We examined six items for Republican and Democratic candidates. That allowed for 12 comparisons. In 9 of the 12 instances respondents, on the average, felt closer to the woman than the man candidate.[34] There is no evidence that voters are stereotyping women candidates in a way negative to their campaigns. On the contrary, the limited evidence available indicates that voters see themselves as closer to the women than the men candidates of the same party.

Voting Patterns and Women Candidates

At this point we can examine how voters react to women candidates in actual congressional elections. A study of 1,099 races from 1970 to 1974 found that after adjusting for party and for whether or not a candidate was an incumbent,

Table 4.8 Closeness of Constituents to Men and Women Candidates on Political Issues and Political Ideology, 1982

Issue	Candidate	Democratic		Republican	
		Mean	Number	Mean	Number
Liberal (1)–Conservative (7)[a]	Men	1.47	460	1.31	379
	Women	1.41	32	1.40	21
Greatly increase (1)–Greatly decrease (7) defense spending[b]	Men	1.26	443	1.47	347
	Women	1.58	18	.91	21
Government should help minority groups (1)–Minority groups should help themselves (7)[c]	Men	1.52	478	1.50	367
	Women	1.91	22	1.67	24
Government should see to a job and a good standard of living (1)–Government should let each person get ahead on his own (7)[d]	Men	1.60	508	1.47	378
	Women	1.52	21	1.32	31
Men and women should have an equal role (1)–Woman's place is in the home (7)[e]	Men	1.51	489	1.79	376
	Women	1.23	35	1.52	29
Government should provide many fewer services, reduce spending a lot (1)–Government should provide many more services, increase spending a lot (7)[f]	Men	1.60	479	1.53	352
	Women	1.42	26	1.50	24

Source: Data from the 1982 CPS National Election Study Post-Election Survey, made available through the Inter-University Consortium for Political and Social Research.

[a] Democrats: $F = .09$; DF = 1/490; $p < .76$. Republicans: $F = .08$; DF = 1/398; $p < .77$.

[b] Democrats: $F = 1.13$; DF = 1/459; $p < .28$. Republicans: $F = 3.30$; DF = 1/366; $p < .07$.

[c] Democrats: $F = 1.65$; DF = 1/498; $p < .19$. Republicans: $F = .34$; DF = 1/389; $p < .56$.

[d] Democrats: $F = .05$; DF = 1/527; $p < .80$. Republicans: $F = .39$; DF = 1/407; $p < .53$.

[e] Democrats: $F = 1.20$; DF = 1/522; $p < .26$. Republicans: $F = 1.93$; DF = 1/394; $p < .38$.

[f] Democrats: $F = .339$; DF = 1/503; $p < .56$. Republicans: $F = .01$; DF = 1/374; $p < .90$.

a challenger to an incumbent, or running for an open seat, men and women candidates performed equally well.[35] Voters were not differentiating congressional candidates on the basis of their sex. We need to update these findings, however, because there has been a change in the nature of women congressional candidates since 1974 and because there are now many more women candidates.

In the years 1916–1940 some 56 percent of the women elected to the House of Representatives were widows of congressmen who had served in that district. Between 1941 and 1964 this figure declined to 40 percent, and between 1965 and 1974 the figure was 30 percent. The proportion of congressional widows among the women elected to Congress has continued to drop since then. In the first two elections of the 1980s (1980 and 1982), only 9 percent of the women elected were congressional widows. Perhaps a symbol of changing times is that the first congressional *widower* emerged in 1980, the husband of Representative Gladys Spellman. Representative Spellman was reelected in 1980 but was unable to be seated due to illness. When the seat was declared vacant in February 1981, her husband became a candidate to succeed her.

Congressional widows such as Lindy Boggs of Louisiana, Margaret Chase Smith of Maine, and Cardiss Collins of Illinois have a number of campaign advantages not available to other women candidates. They have the sympathy of an electorate often asked to choose a successor for their deceased representative soon after his death. They inherit the name recognition of the previous representative and whatever goodwill he had. Often they also inherit his successful personal campaign organization and the loyalty of his old staff. The widows had often campaigned with their husbands, and many had managed or run their husbands' campaign organizations. Typically, they were familiar to both voters and local political elites. With these advantages they were quite unlike other candidates running for an open seat, male or female. Instead, they had many of the advantages of an incumbent candidate. The presence of large numbers of these congressional widows in past elections, then, is likely to yield a distorted picture of the vote-getting performance of new women candidates.[36]

There are other reasons for wanting more recent information on voter reactions to male and female congressional candidates. When women candidates were still relatively rare, in the early 1970s, they were able to attract valuable attention and recognition simply by virtue of their being candidates. This is less so today. Finally, the greater number of women candidates today makes for a better evaluation of the comparative performance of male and female candidates.

Table 4.9 compares male and female candidates running in the congressional elections of 1982 and 1984. Only major party candidates are included. Those who did not have a major party opponent were not included. This left 1,490 congressional candidates. The unadjusted mean vote shows the average proportion of the vote gained by candidates in various groups. As expected, Re-

Table 4.9 *Vote for Men and Women Candidates in Contested Elections,*
1982-1984

	Unadjusted Mean Vote (%)	Mean Vote Adjusted for All Other Factors (%)	Number of Candidates
Party[a]			
Republican	47	49	745
Democratic	53	51	745
Type of Race[b]			
Incumbent	65	65	667
Challenger	35	35	657
Open seat	50	50	166
Candidate[c]			
Men	50	50	1,391
Women	45	50	99

Source: Data from *Congressional Quarterly Weekly Reports,* various issues.
[a]F (adjusted) = 18.59; DF = 1/1,485; $p < .001$.
[b]F (adjusted) = 1,195.80; DF = 1/1,485; $p < .001$.
[c]F (adjusted) = .054; DF = 1/1,485; $p < .816$ (not significant).

publicans, on the average, did not do as well as Democrats, and incumbents did much better than challengers. Women candidates, on the average, got about 5 percent of the vote *less* than men candidates. These results, however, do not take into account that most Republican candidates, for example, are running as challengers and most Democratic and male candidates are running as incumbents. The apparent advantage of the Democrats or the males may be due to their disproportionate status as incumbents and not to their being Democrats.

Once the type of race and the sex of the candidate are controlled for, there is very little difference between the performance of the average Democratic and Republican candidate (about 2.5 percent). This difference, however, remains significant. The differences between the performance of incumbents, challengers, and those competing for open seats remains large and quite significant. Finally, the difference between male and female candidates, after adjusting for party and type of race, becomes minute (about .2 percent, on the average) and insignificant. The difference observed initially between the average male and female candidates was due to the greater likelihood of women to run as slightly disadvantaged Republicans or as greatly disadvantaged challengers. As in the 1970s, there is currently no disadvantage to being a woman candidate.

We have looked at women and men congressional candidates in a number of ways. While we find that respondents in surveys persist in questioning the qualifications of women for public office, we find *absolutely no evidence* that these reservations are being applied to actual women candidates in congressional elections. Where there are differences between men and women candidates, women candidates have the advantage.

As measured by campaign contacts, women run the same campaigns as similar men candidates or better ones. As measured by ability to name or to recognize the name of congressional candidates, women candidates have done as well as or better than men campaigners in reaching the voters. As measured by favorable references and by feeling thermometers, women candidates are regarded as favorably as or even significantly more favorably than similar men candidates. On issues and on political ideology, constituents see themselves as closer to women than to men candidates. Finally, when it comes to voting, women candidates get the same proportion of votes as similar men candidates. From all angles, women candidates in congressional races are as effective and do as well as similar men candidates. In terms of voter reactions, sex is not relevant to congressional elections.

There is some disquiet in one aspect of these findings, however. Before party and type of race are adjusted for, the average woman candidate in the 1980s is not doing as well as the average man candidate. This is not because of the voters' reaction to her sex. Instead, as Table 4.9 indicates, it is because women candidates are running in different sorts of races than the typical male candidate. It is to this aspect of congressional elections that we now turn.

Congressional Candidates and the Male Conspiracy

In Chapter 3 we found no evidence that women state legislative candidates were being slated in more difficult situations or were failing to get the campaign support and financing similar men candidates were getting. In like manner, no evidence was found to support the proposition that women candidates at the local level were not getting the support enjoyed by men candidates (see Chapter 2). Races at the congressional level, however, have important differences from state and legislative races, and findings concerning women candidates there may not hold for contests at this level.

While many races for local and legislative offices are of short duration, entail limited organizational effort, and involve relatively moderate campaign expenses, congressional campaigns are of a different order. Both national parties play a role in recruiting congressional candidates.[37] These campaigns can last for up to two years,[38] are usually competitive, involve mobilizing substantial organizational support,[39] and are very expensive. Under these circumstances congressional candidates are more dependent on political and economic elites for support than are candidates at the local and legislative level.

Candidate Slating

Several studies have argued that under these circumstances, women congressional candidates are, in fact, victims of the male conspiracy. One study presents evidence from a number of Pennsylvania congressional elections that
women candidates were drafted only in hopeless districts.[40] Another study suggests that women candidates are more likely than men to run in "hopeless"
congressional contests.[41] Evidence from other countries indicates that Canadian,[42] British,[43] and Australian[44] party elites are reluctant to nominate women
candidates for the national legislature or do so only where the race is difficult.

However, the role of the party in recruiting congressional candidates has
declined quite a bit in recent years,[45] and the primary system, unavailable in
Great Britain, Canada, and Australia, permits American candidates to challenge the decisions of party elites. The primaries, however, may not prove as
advantageous to women candidates as expected. Bernstein argues that when
faced with aggressive and youthful male competition, as is likely when the
nomination is desirable, women candidates will not be as competitive.[46] Con-
ceivably primaries, in this view, may actually work against behind-the-scenes
party efforts to recruit women congressional candidates for desirable races.

It is almost impossible to determine directly the nature of the behind-the-
scenes maneuvering that goes on before congressional nominations are decided.
Anecdotal evidence from a few cases may not be generalizable to the thousands
of such nominations made each decade. Here we will employ an indirect
method to determine party or elite bias in slating women congressional candidates. Earlier studies defined "hopeless" races in terms of the performance of
previous candidates in a district.[47] The problem with this method is that the
situation in a district changes drastically when the incumbent is no longer a
candidate.[48] A district can very quickly change from hopeless to competitive
when an incumbent retires. Here we will look at nomination patterns the way
we did for legislative candidates. Our concern will be the sorts of races in which
new (nonincumbent) men and women candidates are running. Table 4.10 presents the results for the period 1970–1984.

There has been only a small increase in the proportion of women among the
new congressional candidates. Six percent of new candidates in the early 1970s
were women; 8 percent in the four elections between 1978 and 1984 were
women. But the proportion of incumbents contesting seats also increased during this period. Only 20 percent of the new candidates ran in open seats in
recent elections, a drop of 3 percent from the early 1970s. Looking at male
and female candidates, however, no significant difference in the proportion
slated in open-seat races can be observed in either period or overall. In the
early part of the 1970s there was an insignificant advantage for women in gaining nominations for open seats rather than the more difficult races against
incumbents; in more recent elections men had an insignificant advantage in
that respect.

Table 4.10   Types of Elections Faced by New Men and Women Candidates

Period	Candidate	Against Incumbent (%)	Open Seat (%)	Total (%)	Number of Candidates
1970–1976[a]	Men	77	23	100	1,563
	Women	76	24	100	100
1978–1984[b]	Men	79	21	100	1,550
	Women	82	18	100	143

Source: Data from *Congressional Quarterly Weekly Reports,* various issues.
[a]$\chi^2 = .07$; DF = 1; $p < .70$ (not significant).
[b]$\chi^2 = .56$; DF = 1; $p < .30$ (not significant).

In slating new congressional candidates, therefore, there is no evidence that women candidates are being systematically recruited for hopeless or sacrificial-lamb races. Likewise, there is no evidence that they are being systematically denied nomination for the winnable open seats. Instead, we find that the sex of the candidate makes no difference in slating. Most new candidates wind up facing incumbents. That is because incumbents contest over 80 percent of the seats. New candidates of both sexes are being recruited to contest these difficult-to-win seats.

Campaign Funding

One additional aspect of the male conspiracy hypothesis remains to be examined. When we analyzed legislative contests, we found that in at least one state, women candidates were raising and spending more money than similar men candidates (see Chapter 3). These legislative races, however, involved relatively small amounts, and there was some question as to whether women candidates would be as competitive in races where substantial funding was required.[49]

Recently several studies of the congressional fund-raising abilities of men and women candidates have been completed. Two studies examined *close* races between 1974 and 1982 and found that women did as well as men in raising money.[50] An examination of *all* races between 1972 and 1982 uncovered little difference in fund-raising between men and women candidates once the type of race was controlled for.[51] A fourth in-depth analysis of candidates in the 1980 congressional elections determined that except for a small advantage among certain women incumbents, the sex of the candidate made no significant difference in the amounts raised.[52]

There is some evidence that a candidate's fund-raising represents a response to opponent fund-raising.[53] Politically this relative fund-raising is crucial. Which candidate in a particular race raises the most money is what counts, not the amounts compared to national averages. Large campaign funds can be dwarfed by the larger campaign funds of an opponent. Small amounts can outspend an opponent's even smaller amounts. From this viewpoint the total amount raised is less relevant than the candidate's fund-raising relative to that of the opponent. When the funds raised by candidates relative to those raised by opponents in the 1980 election were compared, here, too, women did well: "In terms of relative receipts women seem to have suffered no direct, gender-based disadvantage."[54] The authors of this study also examined the source and amounts of individual donations going to candidates. They found that women candidates were no more likely to gain their funds through small donations than men. The image of women raising money in small trickles through bake sales and teas is not borne out. Compared to men, women candidates were as well supported by the PACs or supported even better. Thus there is little evidence that party leaders are withholding campaign funds as a means of discouraging women candidates.[55]

This is confirmed by an examination of amounts and sources of campaign funds for congressional candidates between 1976 and 1982. In these four elections, women's congressional campaigns were not underfinanced in comparison with those of similar men. Instead, women candidates raised and spent money at about the rates of similar men candidates.[56] Table 4.11 presents these findings for 1982 races, broken down by party and type of campaign. In that year the average woman raised 111 percent as much as the average man candidate once safe incumbents were excluded.[57] With regard to the source of funding,

Table 4.11   Funds Raised by Congressional Candidates, 1982

Type of Race	Candidate Party	Candidate	Campaign Funds Raised by Candidate (mean)	Number of Candidates
Incumbent	Democrat	Men	$277,353	205
		Women	187,054	9
	Republican	Men	311,962	159
		Women	333,679	8
Challenger	Democrat	Men	134,401	149
		Women	131,378	12
	Republican	Men	148,343	156
		Women	131,378	14
Open seat	Democrat	Men	274,068	46
		Women	212,758	6
	Republican	Men	349,516	47
		Women	458,279	6

Source: Adapted from Jody Newman, Carrie Costantin, Julie Goetz, and Amy Glosser, *Perception and Reality: A Study of Women Candidates and Fund-raising* (Washington, D.C.: Women's Campaign Research Fund, 1984).

the authors of this study found that the Republican party gave more, on the average, to women than men candidates in every category of race in 1982, while the Democratic party, which contributed substantially less to candidates in general, averaged more support for women candidates only when they were contesting open seats. There were no differences in 1982 between women and men in raising money from individuals in small amounts, from individuals in large amounts ($500 and over), or from political action groups (PACs).

The available evidence confirms the pattern already observed in state legislative races. Whatever problems women candidates have in raising money are faced also by similar men. Women candidates are not running underfinanced campaigns compared to those of similar men candidates.

We have looked at the male conspiracy from two perspectives, that of candidate slating and campaign financing. In each case we have found no evidence that women candidates suffer any disadvantage when compared with similar men. Women are no more likely than men to face difficult-to-defeat incumbents when they run. The congressional campaigns of women candidates are as well financed and supported as those of similar men.

Conclusions

It is clear that the explanation for the persistent failure of more women to enter Congress is not due to the inability of women to wage effective and aggressive campaigns. Women candidates are known and recognized as much as, or more than, similar men candidates. Voters like women candidates and feel closer to them than to men running under similar conditions. Women receive their share of desirable nominations as well as their share of difficult ones. Women candidates are able to raise money to support their campaigns. In the most important gauge of a candidate, votes, women candidates do as well as men. As was the case with the state legislatures, if more women run, more will be elected. Once a woman becomes a congressional candidate, she faces the same barriers faced by men running in similar races. Why so few women run remains a problem, however. This is something we will return to in Part Three.

Notes

1. See Gary Jacobson and Samuel Kernell, *Strategy and Choice in Congressional Elections* (New Haven, Conn.: Yale University Press, 1981); Kirsten Monroe, ed., *The Political Process and Economic Change* (New York: Agathon Press, 1983).
2. See Angus Campbell, Philip Converse, Warren Miller, and Donald Stokes, *Elections and the Political Order* (New York: Wiley, 1966).
3. Barbara Hinckley, *Congressional Elections* (Washington, D.C.: Congressional Quarterly Press, 1981), 81–91.
4. Walter Kohn, *Women in National Legislatures* (New York: Praeger, 1980); Elina Haavio-Mannila et al., *Det Uferdige Demokratiet: Kvinner i Nordisk Politikk* (Oslo: Nordisk Ministerrad, 1983); Joni Lovenduski and Jill Hills, eds., *The Politics of the*

Second Electorate: Women and Public Participation (London: Routledge & Kegan Paul, 1981).

5. For this view see Robert Lane, *Political Life: Why People Get Involved in Politics* (Glencoe, Ill.: Free Press, 1959); Angus Campbell, Philip Converse, Warren Miller, and Donald Stokes, *The American Voter* (New York: Wiley, 1960).

6. See Jean Lipman-Blumen, "Role De-differentiation as a System Response to Crisis: Occupational and Political Roles of Women," *Sociological Inquiry* 43 (1973): 105–129.

7. Jonathan Kelley and Ian McAllister, "Ballot Paper Cues and the Vote in Australia and Britain: Alphabetic Voting, Sex, and Title," *Public Opinion Quarterly* 48 (Summer 1984): 452–466.

8. Marian Sawyer, "Women and Women's Issues in the 1980 Federal Election," *Politics* 16 (1981): 243–249; Malcolm Mackerras, "Do Women Candidates Lose Votes? Further Evidence," *Australian Quarterly* 52 (1980): 450–455; Jorgen Rasmussen, "The Electoral Costs of Being a Woman in the 1979 British General Election," *Comparative Politics* 15 (July 1983): 461–475.

9. R. Darcy and Sarah Slavin Schramm, "When Women Run against Men," *Public Opinion Quarterly* 41 (Spring 1977): 1–12.

10. Jacobson and Kernell, *Strategy and Choice.*

11. See Lee Sigelman and Susan Welch, "Race, Gender, and Opinion toward Black and Female Presidential Candidates," *Public Opinion Quarterly* 48 (Summer 1984): 472.

12. Quoted in the *Washington Post*, July 15, 1975, 8:5; see also Virginia Currey, "Campaign Theory and Practice: The Gender Variable," in Marianne Githens and Jewell Prestage, eds., *A Portrait of Marginality: The Political Behavior of American Women* (New York: McKay, 1977), 157.

13. John Peters and Susan Welch, "The Effects of Charges of Corruption on Voting Behavior in Congressional Elections," *American Political Science Review* 74 (September 1980): 697–708. Interestingly, up to the time of their study no female member of Congress had even been the target of a corruption charge.

14. See Thomas Mann, *Unsafe at Any Margin: Interpreting Congressional Elections* (Washington, D.C.: American Enterprise Institute, 1978); Hinckley, *Congressional Elections;* Barbara Hinckley, "Interpreting House Midterm Elections," *American Political Science Review* 70 (September 1976): 694–700; Barbara Hinckley, Richard Hofstetter, and John Kessel, "Issues, Information Costs, and Congressional Elections," *American Politics Quarterly* 2 (April 1974): 131–152.

15. Jacobson and Kernell, *Strategy and Choice;* Hinckley, *Congressional Elections.*

16. Roderick Kiewiet, "The Rationality of Candidates Who Challenge Incumbents in Congressional Elections," Social Science Working Paper 436 (Pasadena: Division of Humanities and Social Sciences, California Institute of Technology, 1982); Hinckley, *Congressional Elections.*

17. Robert Huckshorn and Robert Spencer, *The Politics of Defeat: Campaigning for Congress* (Boston: University of Massachusetts Press, 1971); Jeff Fishel, *Party and Opposition: Congressional Challengers in American Politics* (New York: McKay, 1973).

18. See Hinckley, *Congressional Elections;* Edie Goldenberg and Michael Traugott, "Congressional Campaign Effects on Candidate Recognition and Evaluation," *Political Behavior* 2 (Spring 1980): 61–90; Paul Dawson and James Zinser, "Broadcast

Expenditures and Electoral Outcomes in the 1970 Congressional Elections," *Public Opinion Quarterly* 35 (Fall 1971): 398–402; Gary Jacobson, "The Impact of Broadcast Campaigning on Electoral Outcomes," *Journal of Politics* 37 (August 1975): 769–793; Lyn Ragsdale, "Incumbent Popularity, Challenger Invisibility, and Congressional Voters," *Legislative Studies Quarterly* 6 (May 1981): 201–218.

19. See also James Payne, "The Personal Electoral Advantage of House Incumbents," *American Politics Quarterly* 8 (October 1980): 465–482; James Payne, "Career Intentions and Electoral Performance of Members of the U.S. House," *Legislative Studies Quarterly* 7 (February 1982): 93–99.

20. Donald Stokes and Warren Miller, "Party Government and the Salience of Congress," *Public Opinion Quarterly* 26 (Winter 1966): 531–546; Susan Tolchin and Martin Tolchin, *Clout: Womanpower and Politics* (New York: Coward, McCann & Geoghegan, 1973): Jeane Kirkpatrick, *Political Woman* (New York: Basic Books, 1974), 101.

21. Robert Bernstein, "Why Are There So Few Women in the House?" *Western Political Quarterly* 39 (March 1986): 155–164.

22. See Emmy Werner, "Women in Congress, 1917–1964," *Western Political Quarterly* 19 (March 1966): 16–30; Kirkpatrick, *Political Woman;* Diane Margolis, "The Invisible Hands: Sex Roles and the Division of Labor in Two Local Political Parties," in Debra Stewart, ed., *Women in Local Politics* (Metuchen, N.J.: Scarecrow, 1980), 22–41; Marilyn Johnson and Susan Carroll, "Statistical Report: Profile of Women Holding Public Office, 1977," in Kathy Stanwick and Marilyn Johnson, eds., *Women in Public Office: A Bibliographic Directory and Statistical Analysis* (Metuchen, N.J.: Scarecrow, 1978); Irene Diamond, *Sex Roles in the State House* (New Haven, Conn.: Yale University Press, 1977); Susan Gluck Mezey, "The Effect of Sex on Recruitment: Connecticut Local Offices," in Stewart, *Women in Local Politics,* 61–85; Maureen Fiedler, "Congressional Ambitions of Female Political Elites," paper presented at the meeting of the Capital Area Political Science Association, Washington, D.C., April 1975; Diane Fowlkes, Jerry Perkins, and Sue Tolleson Rinehart, "Gender Roles and Party Roles," *American Political Science Review* 73 (September 1979): 772–780.

23. See Currey's autobiographical account, "Campaign Theory and Practice"; M. Kent Jennings and Norman Thomas, "Men and Women in Party Elites: Social Roles and Political Resources," *Midwest Journal of Political Science* 12 (November 1966): 462–492; Peggy Lamson, *Few Are Chosen* (Boston: Houghton Mifflin, 1968); Naomi Lynn, "Women and American Politics: An Overview," in Jo Freeman, ed., *Women: A Feminist Perspective* (Palo Alto, Calif.: Mayfield, 1975), 264–285; Susan Carroll, "Women Candidates and State Legislative Elections, 1976: Limitations on the Political Opportunity Structure and Their Effects on Electoral Participation and Success," paper presented at the meeting of the American Political Science Association, Washington, D.C., September 1977.

24. Johnson and Carroll, "Statistical Report"; Lawrence Miller, "Political Recruitment and Electoral Success: A Look at Sex Differences in Municipal Elections," paper presented at the meeting of the Southwest Political Science Association, Fort Worth, April 1984; Marcia Manning Lee, "Why So Few Women Hold Public Office: Democracy and Sex Roles," *Political Science Quarterly* 91 (Summer 1976): 297–314; Kirkpatrick, *Political Woman;* Sarah Slavin Schramm, "Women and Representation: Self-government and Role Change," *Western Political Quarterly* 34 (March

1981): 46–59; R. Darcy, Margaret Brewer, and Judy Clay, "Women in the Oklahoma Political System: State Legislative Elections," *Social Science Journal* 21 (January 1984): 67–78; Kathleen Carroll, "The Age Difference between Men and
Women Politicians," *Social Science Quarterly* 63 (June 1982): 332–339.

25. See Johnson and Carroll, "Statistical Report."
26. See Ruth Mandel, *In the Running: The New Woman Candidate* (New York: Tich-
    nor & Fields, 1981); Tolchin and Tolchin, *Clout;* Currey, "Campaign Theory and
    Practice."
27. See Hinckley, *Congressional Elections,* 17–35.
28. See Stokes and Miller, "Party Government."
29. See Darcy and Schramm, "When Women Run against Men"; Mann, *Unsafe at
    Any Margin;* Hinckley, *Congressional Elections.*
30. See Jacobson and Kernell, *Strategy and Choice;* Alan Abramowitz, "Name Fa-
    miliarity, Reputation, and the Incumbency Effect in Congressional Elections,"
    Western Political Quarterly 28 (December 1975): 668–684; Gary Jacobson, *Money
    in Congressional Elections* (New Haven, Conn.: Yale University Press, 1980); Mann,
    Unsafe at Any Margin.
31. The MCA technique was used to adjust the means. This adjusts categories of one
    independent variable such that other independent variables are equally distributed
    among the categories of that independent variable.
32. See Mann, *Unsafe at Any Margin,* 44–47; Hinckley, *Congressional Elections,* 95–
    111.
33. See Philip Converse, "The Structure of Belief Systems in Mass Publics," in David
    Apter, ed., *Ideology and Discontent* (New York: Free Press, 1964), 206–261.
34. The binomial formula ($n = 12$; $k = 9, 10, 11, 12$; $p = .5$) indicates that this is
    not likely to have happened by chance ($p = .072$).
35. Darcy and Schramm, "When Women Run against Men."
36. For discussions of the congressional widow as a candidate, see Diane Kincaid, "Over
    His Dead Body: A Positive Perspective on Widows in the U.S. Congress," *Western
    Political Quarterly* 31 (March 1978): 96–104; Charles Bullock and Patricia Heys,
    "Recruitment of Women for Congress: A Research Note," *Western Political Quar-
    terly* 25 (September 1972): 416–423; Irwin Gertzog, "Changing Patterns of Female
    Recruitment to the U.S. House of Representatives," *Legislative Studies Quarterly*
    4 (August 1979): 429–445; Irwin Gertzog, *Congressional Women: Their Recruit-
    ment, Treatment, and Behavior* (New York: Praeger, 1984).
37. See Jacobson and Kernell, *Strategy and Choice.*
38. See David Mayhew, *Congress: The Electoral Connection* (New Haven, Conn.: Yale
    University Press, 1974).
39. See Louis Maisel, *From Obscurity to Oblivion: Running in the Congressional Pri-
    mary* (Knoxville: University of Tennessee Press, 1982).
40. Raisa Deber, " 'The Fault, Dear Brutus': Women as Congressional Candidates in
    Pennsylvania," *Journal of Politics* 44 (May 1982): 474.
41. Irwin Gertzog and M. Michele Simard, "Women and 'Hopeless' Congressional
    Candidacies: Nomination Frequency, 1916–1978," *American Politics Quarterly* 9
    (October 1981): 449–466; Jody Newman, Carrie Costantin, Julie Goetz, and Amy
    Glosser, *Perception and Reality: A Study of Women Candidates and Fundraising*
    (Washington, D.C.: Women's Campaign Research Fund, 1984).

42. Janine Brody, *Point of Entry: The Election of Women in Canada* (Montreal: McGill–Queen's University Press, 1984).

43. Jorgen Rasmussen, "The Role of Women in British Parliamentary Elections," *Journal of Politics* 39 (November 1977): 1044–1054; Vicky Randall, *Women and Politics* (London: Macmillan, 1982); Kelley and McAllister, "Ballot Paper Cues."

44. Kelley and McAllister, "Ballot Paper Cues."

45. Thomas Kazee and Mary Thornberry, "Can We Throw the Rascals Out? Recruiting Challengers in Competitive Districts," paper presented at the meeting of the American Political Science Association, Chicago, September 1983.

46. Bernstein, "So Few Women."

47. Deber, "'The Fault, Dear Brutus'"; Gertzog and Simard, "Women and 'Hopeless' Congressional Candidacies."

48. See Robert Erikson, "Malapportionment, Gerrymandering, and Party Fortunes in Congressional Elections," *American Political Science Review* 66 (December 1972): 1234–1245; Albert Cover, "One Good Term Deserves Another: The Advantage of Incumbency in Congressional Elections," *American Journal of Political Science* 21 (August 1977): 523–542.

49. See Sandra Baxter and Marjorie Lansing, *Women and Politics: The Invisible Majority* (Ann Arbor: University of Michigan Press, 1980); Mandel, *In the Running.*

50. Eugene Declercq, James Benze, and Elisa Ritchie, "Macha Women and Macho Men: The Role of Gender in Campaigns involving Women," paper presented at the meeting of the American Political Science Association, Chicago, September 1983; see also James Benze and Eugene Declercq, "The Importance of Gender in Congressional and Statewide Elections," *Social Science Quarterly* 66 (December 1985): 954–963.

51. Barbara Burrell, "Women's and Men's Campaigns for the U.S. House of Representatives, 1972–1982: A Finance Gap?" *American Politics Quarterly* 13 (July 1985): 251–272.

52. Carole Uhlaner and Kay Schlozman, "Candidate Gender and Congressional Campaign Receipts," *Journal of Politics* 48 (February 1986): 30–50.

53. See Jacobson, *Money in Congressional Elections.*

54. Uhlaner and Schlozman, "Candidate Gender," 44.

55. Ibid.

56. Newman et al., *Women Candidates and Fundraising.*

57. Ibid., 17.

PART III

Structural Barriers
to the Representation of Women

Careful scrutiny of U.S. elections indicates that when women run, they are treated like similar male candidates by voters and political elites. The reason there are few women in public office, at least today, has nothing to do with prejudice against women candidates or elected officials. So what does account for the fact that there are so few women in public office?

One answer (to which we do not subscribe) is to blame the victim, to find inadequacies in women themselves. For example, perhaps women are not ambitious or lack the aggression necessary for political life. Or perhaps women are too naive and really do not understand what goes on in politics. Perhaps women are too concerned with issues relating to their traditional roles, such as child care and education, and not enough concerned with issues more central to the political agenda, such as inflation, the military, the budget, and taxes. The blame-the-victim approach shifts responsibility for a lack of representation onto women themselves. Perhaps the ultimate in the blame-the-victim view is to tell women who are thinking of entering political life that they have to be prepared to work twice as hard as a man. Lack of success, from this point of view, is due to women just not working hard enough.

From the scientific point of view, blaming the victim has weaknesses. It can never be shown that men and women have no politically relevant differences because we can never be confident that we have isolated all politically relevant traits. Further, it cannot be demonstrated that a particular characteristic is necessary to political life because political life takes many forms, and we can never be sure that new forms will not emerge. Yet the characteristics we all might agree are desirable in public officials seem to be the joint property of both sexes. Certainly character, honesty, ability to make decisions, ability to work with others, ability to empathize, capacity for hard work, and intelligence are all desirable characteristics in public officials. We are unaware of any argument that any of these characteristics are found exclusively or predominantly in men.

There is another difficulty with the blame-the-victim approach. In Chapter 1 we argued that our democratic system needs the full participation of women. If we accept this argument, women are needed not just to the extent to which they can approximate certain male characteristics.

A third argument against the blame-the-victim approach is related to the first two. Blaming the victim requires that women must adapt *themselves* to the political system. But it is more plausible to turn the argument on its head. If our political system needs women—and we have argued that this is the case— and if our system has demonstrably failed to include these women, as it clearly has, it is the political system that needs to be blamed, not the women.

What we mean by the "system" is our complex set of institutions and formal and informal procedures designed to elect our officials democratically. Although there are many ways to do this, political scientists and politicians have long been aware of possible political advantages or disadvantages associated with different practices. Every year we change or alter the rules and procedures we use to conduct elections. We redistrict, change ballot formats and registration rules, reform nomination procedures, alter campaign regulations and the laws controlling campaign donations, and many other things. These changes are made with a careful eye on how they will influence the electoral chances of particular groups or individuals.

Seldom do even women themselves consider how changes might affect them; indeed, this question is rarely raised. Yet there are, perhaps, aspects of the political system not specifically directed against women that do affect them differently than men in ways that reduce their chances of obtaining office. In Part Three we will examine how our system works, with special attention given to effects on the election of women. If two election rules are both democratic and fair but women are more likely to be elected under one than under the other, we will argue that people who wish to further the election of women should support the more favorable rule. This approach may bring women into conflict with other groups; nevertheless, in a pluralist system such as ours, no group can expect its interests to be looked after if it does not articulate and fight on its own behalf. People who feel that women need to be better represented must be alert to the consequences for women of different electoral arrangements and be prepared to compete for their interests in the same way other groups do.

Of course, women are not the only underrepresented group in our system, and it would be unfortunate if conflicts were to develop *among* underrepresented groups. We do not think that such an outcome is inevitable. As we shall discuss, election arrangements exist whereby the quite different situations of many underrepresented groups can be advanced.

5

The Eligibility Pool

We will begin our examination of the impact of the political system itself on women and electoral office by focusing on the social eligibility requirements for public office. The political system does not exist in isolation. Instead, it is only a part of our broader social and economic system. Although the formal rules by which we choose our leaders may provide no barriers to women serving in public office, the norms and informal rules may present severe impediments, given the position of women in our society. For example, if most political officeholders are recruited from occupations where there are few women, the selection rules, no matter how informal, will prevent women from holding office. Some people have argued that it is futile to discuss a political role for women until fundamental changes in the broader social system give women an equal role there. Only then, they argue, will it be possible for women to exercise political influence commensurate with their numbers.[1]

One connection between the broader social system and the selection of political leaders is through eligibility requirements for public office. How does one become part of the ''eligible pool'' from which political leaders are chosen? Our focus on eligibility requirements is not on the formal, legal requirements. Indeed, those are usually rather minimal, frequently requiring a candidate to be a certain age (25 for the House, for example), hold U.S. citizenship, reside in the state for a length of time, and pay a filing fee, usually fairly small. These legal requirements do not seem to work to the disadvantage of women relative to men.

The informal requirements of candidacy, however, are much more extensive. Holders of elective office in the United States are not a random group of citizens. As a group, they are distinguished by their very high levels of income; their more prestigious occupational status, especially employment as professionals; and their high levels of education, often at the graduate level. In other words, officeholders are part of the socioeconomic elite.

In the U.S. Congress of 1985 and 1986, for example, there were no blue-collar workers, and one-third of all senators and one-sixth of representatives are millionaires. Over 45 percent are lawyers. This is a typical pattern for recent Congresses.

Women, through achievement, birth, or marriage, are found at all social levels, including the social elite. As members of a social elite they will share the personal and political contacts of male elites. Yet there are reasons for thinking that women may not be as able as men to turn elite status into political eligibility. The criteria for membership in the intangible pool of potential candidates place heavy emphasis on educational and occupational status, as well as personal and political ties. Here women may be disadvantaged.

To a considerable extent, women have traditionally been barred from prestige education and occupations. Where they have been admitted, it has been in reduced numbers compared to males. This has occurred for two reasons. One is deliberate and systematic discrimination, as when women were not admitted to graduate or professional schools and were barred from employment in prestigious law firms or as executives in large corporations. Sandra Day O'Connor, the first woman justice of the U.S. Supreme Court, reports being denied employment by private law firms after her graduation from law school. Though some were willing to hire her as a legal secretary, none were willing to hire her as a lawyer. This sort of discrimination may still exist, especially at the highest levels, but it has diminished.

Women's access to prestige occupations and education has also been limited by the socialization process, which taught both men and women that certain kinds of jobs were "men's jobs" and others were for women. Through this socialization process, women themselves came to believe that important jobs in business and the professions were for men, not for them.

Let us examine some of the socioeconomic criteria that are important in running for office. We will test the assumption that an important reason for the exclusion of women from public office has been their severe underrepresentation in the "eligible pool" of the population from which candidates for public office are drawn.

Prior Research

Women's Role as Wife and Mother

The traditional role assigned to women makes it difficult for her to enter public office. The role of homemaker and mother as traditionally defined is isolated from, and perhaps mutually exclusive of, many societal roles, including intensive political activity.[2] Men can be breadwinners and political leaders as well as fathers, but mothering has traditionally been seen as a full-time job. Some roles, such as being a lawyer and a political activist, seem to converge, but the role of mother does not "naturally" seem to converge with being a politician.[3]

Once a woman has been socialized into a full-time wife and mother role, the role often leaves little time for activities outside the home. This is especially true when the family has small children. The demands of many political offices are extensive and may require relocation for lengthy periods of time in a state capital or Washington. For a traditional wife and mother of small children, this poses difficult choices.

Not all observers agree on the extent to which these time demands inhibit women from running for office. Most evidence is indirect. For example, most studies have found that women legislators delay their entrance into politics until their forties, when their children are in school or out of the home.[4] A study of men and women state legislators and local officeholders in 1981 found that newly elected women are less likely to have small children than newly elected men.[5] This was true at both the state legislative and the council level. Among state legislators, women newcomers were more likely to be over 40 years old (only one-third of the women were under 40, compared to two-thirds of the men). These differences suggest that having small children is a reason for women to delay their entrance into elective politics.

Certainly, however, having small children does not extinguish all political activism. Women have long comprised the core of workers in local political party organizations and voluntary associations of all kinds. Homemakers, at least in the second half of the twentieth century, have not been tied to hearth and home to the exclusion of other activities. Further, the kind of male-female age differences found in entering the state legislature have not been found in studies of candidates for local councils nationwide or in selected areas.[6]

Others have also argued that the strains faced by women officeholders may not arise from conflicts between the politician and wife and mother roles but rather from striving for acceptance by their male political peers.[7] Another researcher takes a different tack by arguing that although role strains do affect women who want to be legislators, they also affect men.[8] There is some evidence that both men and women are deterred from running for office when small children are at home.[9] We have recently seen a few male-members of Congress announce decisions not to run again because they have to spend too much time away from their growing children. In one sample of (mostly men) legislators who decided not to run again, half cited interference with family life as an important reason.[10] Whether or not this is the real or only reason, it is an interesting commentary on changing sex-role norms.

Still, it is difficult to dismiss the argument that women are more inhibited than men by child-care responsibilities. Interviews with women political elites in a wide variety of circumstances consistently document a concern with care for their children not found among men political elites.[11] One suggestion is that the presence of young children does not decrease women's political activity but rather influences the mode it takes. Women with young children may feel uneasy about committing large scheduled blocks of time but may participate in more spontaneous and less structured political activities. Then, too, local office, not requiring travel or absences from home, may be more compatible with the role of mother of small children than state or national offices.

Education and Occupations

Traditionally, women have been socialized to become housewives to the near exclusion of other occupations. Thus they were socialized not to pursue "male" occupations such as business, science, law, medicine, and other professions.[12] Even if they did try to pursue such occupations, outright discrimination barred all but the most persistent and single-minded. The implications of this for political officeholding are clear, though indirect. Public officials are disproportionately drawn from just that group of individuals who hold such positions. As two observers declared, though American politics is open to participation by a wide range of citizens, "it is also a rather highly selective system in which recruitment to public office emphasizes certain well-defined strata of the population."[13] Thus legislators tend to come from different social and political strata than the public, characterized by rural or small-town origins, middle- or upper-class backgrounds, certain prestigious occupations, high educational levels, and political families. There are few working-class individuals in any legislature, nor are there members from among the unemployed or from those receiving welfare designed for the poor.

Membership in the legal profession is particularly important in establishing the appropriate credentials for political office. Although the proportions of lawyers in legislatures has declined somewhat since the 1960s, in 1980 fully 20 percent of the members of state legislatures were lawyers.[14] In some legislatures this can be as high as 60 percent (New York), while in others it is much lower.[15] In most legislative bodies, law is the background of the most members. The higher the legislative body, the more likely lawyers are to dominate it (in the U.S. Congress, lawyers make up 41 percent of the House and 61 percent of the Senate).

Obviously, not all who meet the criteria are recruited into the political arena. Nor are all public officeholders from these strata. But it is largely from this pool that the recruitment is done. One scholar of the 1960s admitted this, while at the same time unconsciously revealing the exclusion of women from the pattern, by noting that "the ambitions of any politician flow from the expectations which are reasonable for a *man* in his position."[16] The certification process of political recruitment means that candidates from the appropriate social and economic strata and having the appropriate political credentials must be found.[17]

We are arguing that a substantial part of the underrepresentation of women in public office is due to their underrepresentation in this eligible pool: the business and professional occupations from which most officials are recruited. This effect will be strongest at the state and national levels of government, but it is likely to be present to a lesser degree in local government, too. This is a structural explanation that posits that changing the occupational distribution of women would influence their recruitment to public office.

Demographic Evidence for the "Eligible Pool" Explanation

Is there evidence that this "eligible pool" explanation has any merit? These demographic arguments are strong, on their face. While women are not at a disadvantage vis-à-vis men in terms of class, ethnic status, or small-town origins, as a group they are at a definite disadvantage in terms of education and occupation. Though women and men have similar mean years of education (see Table 5.1), and though women now outnumber men on college campuses, fewer women than men complete college or obtain graduate or professional training. The 1980 census reported that over 20 percent of all men, but only 13 percent of all women, complete college. Since college seems to be nearly a prerequisite for the modern legislator, at least at the state or national level, women are somewhat disadvantaged.

Among the women members of Congress serving in 1986, fully 18 of 22 had college degrees, and only one lists no college in her background. Six have masters or law degrees.[18] Like their male counterparts, then, they exceed the public in their educational achievements.

Women are even more handicapped when occupation is considered. Male and female occupations still tend to be highly segregated in our society. A study in the late 1970s indicated that at least 66 percent of white women would have to change their occupations to have an occupational distribution matching that of white males.[19] Among black and Mexican-American women, even more change was necessary, 69 and 75 percent, respectively. Women tend to be congregated into what is called the "pink ghetto" of clerical employment, nursing, teaching at the elementary level, and many low-paying service jobs. Though these jobs might be compatible with part-time, local officeholding, none offers the kind of independence and economic security necessary to embark upon a political career.

Occupational choices among women are clearly changing, however, and changing in a direction that holds some promise for public officeholding. In 1970 only 3 percent of all lawyers were women. Beginning in the mid-1970s women began to enter the profession in vastly greater numbers. By 1984 women made up 13 percent of the legal profession, and in the mid-1980s, 35 to 40 percent of entering law school freshmen were women. It will take many years for the growing wave of women law students to reflect itself in the profession at large. But to the extent that law is the prerequisite to a political career, women are more and more part of the eligible pool.

Women are also a growing proportion of managers and administrators. While only about one-sixth of such individuals were women in 1970, by 1980 the census reported that about one-third were. Women now constitute nearly half of all professionals, representing a very large increase from 1970. However, over

Table 5.1   Selected Comparative Occupational and Educational Data for Men and Women, 1970 and 1980

Occupations	Men	Women	Ratio
1970			
Number of lawyers	315,715	9,103	34.7:1
Number of managers and administrators	5,386,000	1,007,000	5.0:1
Number of insurance and real estate brokers	584,000	143,000	4.1:1
Number of professional, technical, and kindred occupations	6,917,000	4,644,000	1.5:1
Less nurses, elementary and secondary school teachers	6,137,000	1,944,000	3.2:1
Farmers and farm managers	1,357,000	72,000	18.8:1
Mean school years	11.9	11.9	1.0:1
Percent completing four or more years of college	13.8	8.1	1.7:1
Percent completing one to three years of college	10.7	9.7	1.1:1
1980			
Number of lawyers	456,000	74,000	6.1:1
Number of executive, administrative, and managerial	7,210,000	3,169,000	2.2:1
Number in properties and real estate	118,000	82,000	1.4:1
Number of professionals	6,248,000	6,027,000	1.0:1
Less nurses, elementary and secondary school teachers	5,158,000	2,159,000	2.3:1
Farmers and farm managers	1,185,000	130,000	9.1:1
Median school years	12.5	12.3	1.0:1
Percent completing four or more years of college	20.2	13.0	1.5:1
Percent completing one to three years of college	15.4	13.95	1.1:1

Source: U.S. Bureau of the Census, *Statistical Abstract of the United States* (Washington, D.C., 1975); U.S. Bureau of the Census, *1980 Census of Population Supplementary Reports* (PC80 St 8).

half the women professionals are employed as nurses and elementary and secondary school teachers, whereas only a small minority of male professionals hold these positions.

Previous Research and the Eligible Pool Explanation

Research done in the early 1970s supported the eligible pool argument. In her analysis of women's recruitment for and behavior in state legislatures, Jeane

Kirkpatrick discovered that women who succeed in getting elected very much resemble men officeholders in both personality and social background.[20] She concluded that women legislators differ from their male counterparts mainly with regard to economic role, occupational experience, and age of entry into the legislature. A larger and somewhat more systematic study also found men and women state legislators to be similar in their personality traits.[21] Even more directly, data collected in the 1950s from four states (New Jersey, California, Ohio, and Tennessee) indicated that occupation was an important factor limiting women's access to state legislative bodies.[22]

Studies of candidates for local government have shown that they also have higher-than-average socioeconomic status.[23] In the early 1980s, among such candidates, income was a good predictor of whether a candidate would win or lose. This was true of both men and women. Levels of education and occupation, however, distinguished between winners and losers among men candidates in the predicted way (winners were more likely to have more education and higher occupational status), but not among women: Education did not predict winning or losing, and having a professional occupation was associated with losing, not winning.[24] This might suggest that having a high socioeconomic status is more important in screening potential candidates than in affecting their chances of winning.

Clearly, too, the nature of the eligible pool varies. Eligibility requirements are less stringent for local than state offices and less demanding for state than national ones. Within the same level of government, eligibility pools also differ. Interstate differences can be illustrated by contrasting New York and Oklahoma. In Oklahoma, legislators are drawn as much from traditional "women's occupations," such as teaching and social work, as from law, whose practitioners compose 14 percent of the legislature.[25] A very high proportion of that legislature (36 percent) did not hold a college degree. Thus the eligible pool is much broader than for the New York senate, where over half the members are lawyers, or the assembly (New York's lower house), where one-third are. And the eligible pool has increased considerably in New York, where less than two decades ago fully 75 percent of the members of the senate and over half the assembly were lawyers.[26]

It would be an error to leave the impression that only women who have somehow managed to enter "male-dominated" fields are ever elected. Many women legislators list their occupation as "housewife" or "homemaker," and others come from the female-dominated professions such as elementary school teaching. Further, activity in volunteer groups is strongly associated with the political success of women candidates. As we saw in Chapter 2, activity in religious, civic, charity, or political groups can be functionally equivalent for women to male prestige occupations. Like prestige occupations, voluntary groups can form the base for developing leadership skills and experience, community visibility, and widespread contacts.

Women members of the U.S. Congress have backgrounds not typical of the men members, beyond the fact that most are highly educated. Among members elected in 1984, only Patricia Schroeder (D, Colorado) and Marjorie Holt (R, Maryland) were lawyers; five were teachers (Nancy Johnson, R, Connecticut; Lynn Martin, R, Illinois; Lindy Boggs, D, Louisiana; Margaret Roukema, R, New Jersey; Mary Rose Oakar, D, Ohio). One, Barbara Mikulski (D, Ohio), was a social worker; another (Marcy Kaptur, D, Ohio), an urban planner.

A sizable number entered politics with no significant other occupational experience, though they gained political experience before being elected to Congress. Jan Meyers (R, Kansas) was a member of the city council, then of the Kansas senate; Olympia Snowe (R, Maine) served in the Maine house and senate before being elected to Congress. Claudine Schneider (R, Rhode Island) was a housewife active on energy and environment issues, and Virginia Smith (R, Nebraska), in agricultural organizations, while Bobby Fiedler (R, California) was a school board member. Sala Burton (D, California) was active in California Democratic party politics and married to Phillip Burton, her predecessor in her House seat; Beverly Bryon (D, Maryland), another congressional widow, had worked in her husband's campaigns. Paula Hawkins (R, Florida), one of only two women in the Senate, was a housewife before being elected and reelected as Florida's public service commissioner. Barbara Kennelly (D, Connecticut), daughter of John Bailey, longtime Democratic state chairman in Connecticut and later national Democratic chairman, was also a housewife before entering a full-time political career, including local and then statewide office as secretary of state.

Other women members of Congress worked in business and other professions such as journalism. Barbara Boxer (D, California) was a stockbroker and a journalist. Marilyn Lloyd (D, Tennessee) co-owned and managed a radio station, while Nancy Kassebaum (R, Kansas) was an executive in a radio station and worked briefly on the staff of a Kansas senator. Helen Bentley (R, Maryland) was a reporter and businesswoman and a former chair of the Federal Maritime Commission. Barbara Vucanovich (R, Nevada) owned small businesses before going to work for Senator Laxalt of Nevada. Only Cardiss Collins (D, Illinois) might be thought of as coming from a typical low-status "women's job." She started as a stenographer, though later moved into positions as an accountant and an auditor for the Illinois Department of Labor.

These examples from the U.S. Congress illustrate the diversity of backgrounds of women who serve there. Some parallel those of the typical male representative, such as law and small businesses. Though others come from predominantly women's occupations, such as teaching, social service, and volunteer work, given the lack of women in elected office, it is safe to say that women's occupations and activities have not provided the same sort of gateway to political office as prestigious male occupations.

Testing the Relationship between Women's Occupations and Election to Office

The extent to which women's occupational background is a deterrent to political office can be illustrated systematically. A simple test of the relationship between women's occupational status and their entrance into politics can be made by charting the relationship between the proportion of various offices held by women and their changing occupational status. If we look, for example, at the relationship between women entering the law profession and women entering the state legislature, we find a very strong relationship. In 1970, when women made up 3 percent of the law profession, 4 percent of all state legislators were women. In 1984, when women constituted 13 percent of the law profession, 14 percent of all state legislators were women (see Figure 5.1). The parallelism in the growing presence of women in these two occupations is quite striking.

Obviously our simple chart may not accurately reflect the impact of occupation on women's entrance into political office. The relationship of law to legislative membership is not nearly as strong at the national level, for example, as at the state level, even though being a lawyer is more common in Congress than in state legislatures. Further, the trend in Figure 5.1 may tell us more about changing societal attitudes toward women in nontraditional roles than it does about the impact of occupation on legislative membership. So a more sophisticated test is needed. Such a test was done using the membership of the legislatures of 12 central states: Illinois, Indiana, Iowa, Kansas, Michigan, Minnesota, Missouri, Nebraska, North Dakota, Ohio, South Dakota, and Wisconsin. This analysis, first reported in 1978,[27] was performed using data from

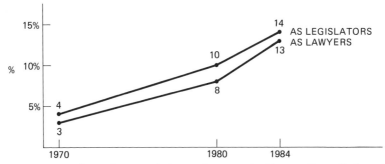

Figure 5.1 Comparison of women in law and as state legislators. (From Barbara Curran, *Lawyers' Statistical Report,* Chicago: American Bar Foundation, 1985, and National Women's Political Caucus, *National Directory of Women Elected Officials, 1985,* Washington, D.C., 1985).

the early 1970s and thus in some ways is a historical snapshot. But the underlying patterns found in that analysis are still relevant today, as we shall see.

Data and Study Methods

The data used for this analysis are from a 20 percent sample of the state legislators in these states plus data from a random sample of the public in these states. The public sample is the University of Michigan's Survey Research Center (SRC) 1972 election survey, which drew a national sample in such a way that each of the four regional subsamples was an accurate random sample from that region. These states comprise the SRC's central region. Data on the legislatures were drawn from the Blue Books of each state for 1972 or 1974, except in the case of Kansas, Missouri, and North Dakota. For these states only data on state senators could be used, and those data were obtained by means of a mail questionnaire in 1975. Nebraska, you will remember, has a unicameral legislature with no lower house.

If women were represented in the legislative bodies of the United States in proportion to their membership in the population as a whole, which we will call the proportional or random model, they would comprise about 53 percent of the membership. In 1972, the year that our data were collected, they comprised only 2.5 percent of the membership of state upper houses and 4.9 percent of state lower houses.[28] In the central states examined here they were better represented than in the nation as a whole; 4.3 percent of the upper and 7.7 percent of the lower house were women. Recalling from Table 5.1 that in 1970 only 3 percent of all lawyers were women, one could say that if all legislators were lawyers, it would be logical to argue that women were overrepresented in these central states in proportion to their being in the legal profession, the eligible pool (4.3 percent versus 3 percent in the upper houses, 7.7 percent versus 3 percent in the lower houses). Thus if being a lawyer were a prerequisite to state legislative membership, it would follow that if we wanted more women as legislators, we would need more women as lawyers. The question to be explained, then, would be "Why don't women become lawyers?" rather than "Why don't women become legislators?"

In reality, of course, we cannot make these deductions so easily. Not all legislators are lawyers; a complex mix of occupations and educational backgrounds is found in the statehouse. But we do have a way of examining the mixture of occupations in the statehouse and comparing it with the public to determine the extent to which women are disadvantaged by their particular occupational mix. It is a method of analyzing data called discriminant analysis.

In discriminant analysis, a set of discriminant (or predictor) variables is used to predict membership of each case in one of two or more groups.[29] Here our predictor variables are years of education, number of voluntary associations to which an individual belongs, and a set of variables measuring whether the individual is a lawyer, another professional, a white-collar or self-employed worker, or a farmer. Based on these, we can calculate an equation allowing each case to be classified as a member of one or another of the target groups. Our groups are first, members of the state legislature, and second, a random sample of adult citizens from the same states. Discriminant analysis will tell how well the factors of occupation, education, and voluntary association membership can predict whether or not the individual is a legislator.[30]

Using our sample of the public and legislators, we computed classification functions for the males. This allowed us to see how the mix of male occupations translated into legislative membership. We then applied these functions to the data on women. Assuming no discrimination or other impediments to women's membership (and assuming that sex is an irrelevant factor in legislative membership), how many women legislators would be predicted using the same formula that is used to predict male membership? This procedure allows us to see how many legislative memberships women "should" have on the basis of their occupational, educational, and voluntary group characteristics.[31] Obviously, we would expect a prediction that is lower than 53 percent because occupational and group membership are being assessed as the crucial factors in legislative membership. The difference between the percent predicted on that basis and the actual proportion in the legislatures we can attribute to factors that have an impact on women's recruitment only. These other factors may include discrimination as well as political socialization.

In Table 5.2 we see the characteristics of our public and legislative sample. As we predicted, legislators are more highly educated than members of the public, who average a little more than high school graduate status. The proportion of lawyers in the legislature is around 24 percent for men but only 4.5 percent for women, conforming to what we know about the lack of legal training for women during this time. Legislators are more active than the public in group activities. On other characteristics legislators resemble male members of the public, with females lagging behind in proportion professional and proportion white-collar or self-employed.

Table 5.2   Characteristics of Legislator and Public Samples by Sex

	Legislators		Public	
	Men	Women	Men	Women
Mean years of education	16.0	15.4	12.8	12.3
Mean number of group memberships	3.4	4.2	1.9	1.6
Percent lawyers	23.8	4.5	0.8	0.0
Percent white-collar or self-employed	28.2	27.3	34.7	17.1
Percent farmers	2.9	0.0	8.8	0.1
Percent professionals other than lawyers	14.6	13.6	15.6	8.7

Using the male members of the sample, these characteristics do reasonably well in predicting male membership in the legislature, with about four-fifths correctly classified. That is, on the basis of these group, education, and occupational criteria alone, we can predict whether or not the vast majority of the men are legislators or members of the public.

Being a lawyer is important in predicting legislative status in both upper and lower houses, while white-collar status is of little importance in either. Group membership is the most powerful predictor of lower house membership but has much less importance as a predictor of membership in state senates. Education, however, is more important in predicting upper house than lower house status. The combined predictive power of the variables is about the same (between 50 and 55 percent) for lower and upper house membership.

Table 5.3 shows the results when the classification functions are applied to women. If female structural characteristics predicted membership in legislatures exactly the same as for males, there would be three times as many women in these lower houses and 3.7 times as many in the upper houses as there are in reality. Instead of women making up less than 10 percent of the membership of these central state legislatures, they would constitute 23 and 28 percent in the upper and lower houses, respectively. These figures represent less than half of direct proportionality based on the percent of women in the total adult population but considerably more than are actually elected. Thus we can conclude that factors of occupation and education play a very important role in limiting women's membership in state legislatures.

We also examined selection to the more or less "professional" legislatures. Using salary as the criterion, the legislatures of Illinois, Indiana, Iowa, Michigan, Minnesota, Ohio, and Wisconsin were categorized as professional; the others, less professional. We examined only membership in upper houses since the data on lower houses were incomplete.

Women are less represented in the more professional legislatures.[32] The figures in Table 5.3 indicate that on the basis of structural characteristics, one

Table 5.3 Actual and Predicted Proportions of Women in Central State Legislatures

	All States		Upper House Professional	
	Upper House	Lower House	More	Less
Prediction proportional to population	53.0%	53.0%	53.0%	53.0%
Predicted by structural statistics	23.4	28.5	11.6	23.8
Sample percent women	6.3	9.5	2.9	11.9
Actual percent women	4.3	7.8	4.2	4.4

would predict fewer women in the more professional legislatures. This is due to the greater weight given in more professional legislatures to education and to being a lawyer or a white-collar employee and the lesser weight given to membership in groups. Women in our sample are less disadvantaged in terms of voluntary association participation than they are in terms of education and occupation. Thus it would appear that recruitment to the more professional legislatures is more selective in terms of education and occupation rather than simply being more discriminatory on the basis of sex.

Implications

In these 1970s data we found that women's occupation and educational status accounted for a large part of their absence in the state legislatures. With the same occupational and educational status as men, women would make up about 25 percent of the legislatures in these states rather than less than 5 percent of the upper houses and 8 percent of the lower houses. This assumes that the process would be blind to sex but sensitive to education and occupation. However, even 25 percent of the membership would not come close to purely proportional representation of women. Thus while education and occupation are very important factors in determining women's representation, they are far from the only factors.

Keep in mind that our model of representation is only suggestive. Perhaps some relevant characteristics, such as age and marital status, are missing from the model. Nevertheless, we believe that this model illuminates the traditional barriers of education and occupation to adequate representation for women.

Today, of course, women are moving from their 4 percent representation in 1970 closer to the 25 percent predicted, though in most statehouses they still have far to go. Nonetheless, this analysis gives us some reason for optimism that given the dramatic change in the proportion of women in just those occupations that seem to lead to the statehouse, a new generation of legislators will include far more women than the past generations.

We cannot be sure that women are moving at a rate faster than one would predict on the basis of their increasing educational and occupational status. For as they come to resemble the educational and occupational pattern of men, their predicted membership in the legislature increases. Clearly there are still other explanations for limited women's representation.

Notes

1. Jean Bethke Elshtain, *Public Man, Private Woman* (Princeton, N.J.: Princeton University Press, 1981); Zillah R. Eisenstein, *The Radical Future of Liberal Feminism* (White Plains, N.Y.: Longman, 1981).
2. Jeane Kirkpatrick, *Political Women* (New York: Basic Books, 1974), 17.

3. Heinz Eulau and John Sprague, *Lawyers in Politics: A Study of Professional Convergence* (Indianapolis: Bobbs-Merrill, 1961).
4. Susan Carroll and Wendy Strimling, *Women's Routes to Elective Office* (New Brunswick, N.J.: Rutgers University, CAWP, 1983); Kirkpatrick, *Political Women*, 55.
5. Carroll and Strimling.
6. Sharyne Merritt, "Winners and Losers: Sex Differences in Municipal Elections," *American Journal of Political Science* 21 (November 1977): 731–744; Lawrence Miller, "Winners and Losers: Another Look at Sex Differences in Municipal Elections," paper presented at the meeting of the Southern Political Science Association, Memphis, November 1981; Lawrence Miller, "Political Recruitment and Electoral success: A Look at Sex Differences in Municipal Elections," paper presented at the meeting of the Southwestern Political Science Association, Fort Worth, April 1984; Lawrence Miller and Lillian Noyes, "Winners and Losers: Women Candidates for Municipal Elections Revisited," paper presented at the annual meeting of the Midwest Political Science Association, Chicago, April 1980; Carroll and Strimling.
7. Marianne Githens and Jewell Prestage, "Women State Legislators: A Reconsideration of Characteristic Values and Attitudes" (1981) and "Education and Marginality: Some Observations on the Behavior of Women State Legislators" (1980), unpublished manuscripts reported in Marianne Githens, "The Elusive Paradigm: Gender, Politicals and Political Behavior," in Ada Finifter, ed., *Political Science: The State of the Discipline* (Washington, D.C.: American Political Science Association, 1983), 485.
8. Emily Stoper, "Wife and Politician: Role Strain among Women in Public Office," in Marianne Githens and Jewell Prestage, eds., *A Portrait of Marginality* (New York: McKay, 1977), 471–502.
9. Kathleen Carroll, "The Age Difference between Men and Women Politicians," *Social Science Quarterly* 63 (June 1982): 332–339.
10. Lee Bernick, "Legislative Reform and Legislative Turnover," paper presented at the annual meeting of the American Political Science Association, Washington, D.C., August 1977.
11. Vicky Randall, *Women and Politics* (New York: St. Martin's Press, 1982); R. Darcy and Sunhee Song, "Men and Women in the Korean National Assembly," *Asian Survey* 26 (June 1986): 670–687; M. Phillips, *The Divided House* (London: Sidgewick & Jackson, 1980); Sharon Wolchick, "Eastern Europe," in J. Lovenduski and J. Hills, eds., *The Politics of the Second Electorate* (London: Routledge & Kegan Paul, 1981), 252–277.
12. Cynthia Fuchs Epstein, *Woman's Place* (Berkeley: University of California Press, 1970).
13. Malcolm Jewell and Samuel Patterson, *The Legislative Process in the United States* (New York: Random House, 1973), 69.
14. Alan Rosenthal, *Legislative Life* (New York: Harper & Row, 1981), 44.
15. R. Darcy, Margaret Brewer, and Judy Clay, "Women in the Oklahoma Political System: State Legislative Elections," *Social Science Journal* 21 (January 1984): 68.
16. Joseph Schlesinger, *Ambition and Politics* (Chicago: Rand McNally, 1966), 9; emphasis added.
17. Lester Seligman, Chong Lim Kim, and Roland Smith, *Patterns of Recruitment* (Chicago: Rand McNally, 1974), 14.

18. Backgrounds of members of Congress can be found in Michael Barone and Grant Ujifusa, *The Almanac of American Politics, 1986* (Washington, D.C.: National Journal, 1985).
19. U.S. Commission on Civil Rights, *Social Indicators of Equality for Minorities and Women* (Washington, D.C.: Government Printing Office, 1978).
20. Kirkpatrick, *Political Women*, 221.
21. Emily Werner and Louise Bachtold, "Personality Characteristics of Women in American Politics," in Jane Jacquette, ed., *Women in Politics* (New York: Wiley, 1974), 75–84.
22. Mary McPherson, "Sex, Race, and Political Participation," unpublished paper, University of Nebraska, Department of Sociology, 1975.
23. Merritt, "Winners and Losers"; Miller, "Winners and Losers"; Miller, "Political Recruitment and Electoral Success."
24. Miller, "Winners and Losers"; Miller, "Political Recruitment and Electoral Success"; see also Merritt, "Winners and Losers."
25. Darcy et al., "Women in Oklahoma."
26. Madeline Adler and Jewell Bellush, "Lawyers and the Legislature: Something New in New York," *National Civic Review* 68 (May 1979): 245.
27. A lengthier report of this is found in Susan Welch, "Recruitment of Women to Public Office," *Western Political Quarterly* 31 (September 1978): 372–380.
28. Irene Diamond, *Sex Roles in the State House* (New Haven, Conn.: Yale University Press, 1977).
29. These equations consist of a weighted coefficient for each predictor variable plus a constant. A separate equation is computed for each group. For each case, each classification coefficient is multiplied by the raw value of the relevant variable, the products are summed, and the coefficient is added. As many scores are computed as there are groups. A case is classified into the group with the highest score. Discriminant functions are similar in interpretation to beta weights in regression in that they represent the relative importance of each predictor variable in allowing the case to be classified into one group or another.

Here is a simple example: the classification of membership in the legislature on the basis of education alone. Two classification equations would be computed, one for membership in the legislature, one for nonmembership.

$$S_m = C_m \text{(education)} + K_m$$
$$S_n = C_n \text{(education)} + K_n$$

where S_m = classification score for membership in the legislature
S_n = classification score for nonmembership in the legislature
C_m = classification function for membership in the legislature
C_n = classification function for nonmembership in the legislature
K_m = constant for the membership equation
K_n = constant for the nonmembership equation

Assume that $C_m = 2.0$, $C_n = 1.5$, $K_m = -15$, $K_n = -8$, and the individual to be classified has an educational level of 12 years. Thus $S_m = 9$ and $S_n = 10$. The individual would be classed in the nonmember group because the score on that function is higher. If a second individual was a college graduate and had an educational level of 16, then $S_m = 17$ and $S_n = 16$; this individual would be predicted to be a member of the legislature. In the analysis done here, more than one variable is used to predict membership; thus each of the two classification functions takes the following form:

$$S_1 = C_1(X_1) + C_2(X_2) + \ldots + C_n(X_n) + K_1$$

where S_1 = the classification score for the ith group
$C_1, C_2, \ldots C_n$ = the classification coefficients for the first through nth variables
$X_1, X_2 \ldots X_n$ = a case's scores on the first through nth variables
K_1 = the constant for the ith classification equation

30. The technique used here is an adaptation of a regression procedure introduced by Otis D. Duncan in "Inheritance of Poverty or Inheritance of Race?" in Daniel P. Moynihan, ed., *On Understanding Poverty* (New York: Basic Books, 1969), and widely used subsequently. Duncan was interested in explaining the extent to which black-white differences in income could be accounted for by educational, occupational, and other structural differences. Using a sample of whites, he regressed income on these structural factors in order to obtain regression coefficients. White income could then be predicted on the basis of these factors. He used the white regression coefficients to predict black income by substituting in his equation black education, occupation, and other structural characteristics. In other words, he argued that if the same processes of converting education and occupation into income are at work for blacks as for whites, an accurate prediction of black income can be made knowing black educational and occupational characteristics. The difference between the actual mean black income and that predicted can thus be attributed to some form of bias against blacks. The difference is the degree to which black educational and occupational status cannot be converted to income in the same manner as it is possible for whites. Duncan did find that on the basis of these black characteristics, one would expect a higher mean income than actually existed.

In our sample we are predicting not income but status as a member of the legislature. Because our sample is stratified on the dependent variable (that is, we have collected data for two separate samples—the legislators and the adult population), we cannot use regression. We would have to weigh the nonlegislators so that they approximate their weight in the population. But every different weight assigned results in a different set of regression coefficients. As long as one uses regression, there is no real solution to these problems. Hence we use discriminant analysis.

31. Diamond, *Sex Roles*.
32. Ibid., 4.

6

Women Candidates and the Electoral System

For decades blacks and other minorities have challenged some of the ways in which the American electoral system works. First they fought blatantly discriminatory procedures such as the white primary, poll taxes, and literacy tests. More recently they have pointed to the negative effects of at-large election systems on black political representation and worked to change these systems in many cities.

Although most observers now recognize that at-large election procedures hurt black chances to gain political power, a similar awareness of the potential effect of electoral systems on women's representation has not occurred. Yet today women are much further from being represented in proportion to their numbers than are still underrepresented blacks. Are women also hindered in their quest for political office by the nature of the election systems used in this country? It is this question that we will address in this chapter.

Despite the decades-long debates over fair representation for blacks and other minorities, most Americans give little thought to their election system. Ours seems a simple and fair way to select public officials. Yet, as the black experience reveals, the election systems we use are far from neutral in their effects on groups competing for political power. Rarely are their effects as transparent as they have been on blacks; nevertheless, more subtle effects are still far from inconsequential.

Unlike the general public, politicians are aware of at least some of the ways in which election systems are not neutral. They have strong beliefs about the importance of shaping election laws to help parties and causes they favor. For example, party leaders prefer their candidates to be listed first on the ballot because they believe that some small portion of the electorate automatically votes for the first listed candidate. Anticipating close elections, each party naturally wants that advantage. Similarly, parties struggle fiercely to create or preserve advantages when drawing electoral districts.[1] In Europe, many nations use proportional representation to select representatives to the national legislature. Very early, party leaders learned that this system could be manipulated to provide advantage to larger or smaller parties or to national or regional parties.[2]

Political parties are not the only groups to discover ways they can gain ad-

vantages or be disadvantaged through electoral arrangements. Blacks and Hispanics in the United States have challenged a number of election systems that
diminish their voting strength and elected representation.[3] Most whites cast
their votes for white candidates, and most blacks and Hispanics cast theirs for
black or Hispanic candidates. In a city with a white majority, whites intent on
subordinating blacks favor at-large elections in which the entire city votes for
each of the council members. This would likely produce a nearly all-white
council. Black or Hispanic citizens, therefore, have frequently worked for district systems where each neighborhood selects its own representative. This usually leads to more proportionate minority city council representation.

In district systems, drawing district lines is also a contentious issue. Some
plans might be more favorable to the white majority, others to the black or
Hispanic minority. Such struggles have taken place throughout the country
since the mid-1960s, and they show every indication of continuing to occupy
the attention of legislatures and courts. Many groups—political parties; urban,
suburban, and rural interests; ethnic groups; and others aside from racial
groups—have come into conflict over districting plans.

From the point of view of politicians, then, electoral arrangements are by
no means taken for granted. Instead, they are evaluated for possible advantages
or disadvantages to one's own causes. Those in power usually want to design
a system to help them maintain that power. For those not in power, the courts,
the mass media, or even public protest are used to call attention to arrangements seen as unfair.

Since suffrage was achieved, women seem to be an exception to this process.
Instead of examining the impact of different electoral systems and challenging
arrangements that disadvantage them, women candidates and women's organizations have tried to work within systems designed to the advantage of others. Political arrangements are not neutral, and we suspect that there are situations under which women are more likely to gain public office than others.
Let us explore some of these.

Election Systems and Procedures: An Overview

Quotas

The most obvious method of increasing the number of women in public office
is to establish quotas. The Constitution of the Republic of China (Taiwan), for
example, has a requirement that female membership of legislative bodies cannot fall below 10 percent.[4] In India the ruling Congress party mandates that
15 percent of its candidates in state elections be female.[5] The French government in 1979 required that no more than 80 percent of the candidates for local
office could be of one sex.[6] In Norway, the nation with the largest proportion
of women in its national legislature, the Liberals and the Socialist Left party
require in their party rules that equal numbers of men and women be nomi-

nated, and the Labor party mandates that neither sex shall have less than 40 percent of the candidates. Of the parties represented in the Norwegian Storting after the September 1985 election, only one had fewer than 40 percent women among its candidates.[7] Elsewhere in Scandinavia parties are also moving toward establishing quotas for women candidates.[8] In Great Britain the two major parties (Conservatives and Labour) nominate candidates for Parliament through the local constituency party organizations. These local parties, however, use lists of approved candidates prepared by the national party organization. Some effort has been made to increase the proportions of women on these approved lists, although it is not clear exactly what effect this will ultimately have on female nominations.[9]

Appointment

One method of selection that seems to favor women is appointment. As we noted in Chapter 2, women are more likely to be selected as mayors of cities when the mayor is chosen by the city council itself (appointed) than when the mayor is elected directly by the people. Likewise, upper legislative chambers in Canada, Ireland, and Great Britain, where members are appointed, have larger proportions of women members than the lower, elected chambers. This was the situation in Denmark also before the upper chamber was abolished in 1953.[10] In South Korea's Fourth Republic there were two routes to the National Assembly. Some members were elected to the National Assembly in districts, and others were appointed by the president. Women were more likely to be found among the appointed than the elected members.[11]

Evidence from a number of places, then, shows that when there are a number of positions to fill by appointment, women will do better than when the system calls for direct election of individuals. There are several reasons for this. First, appointment implies accountability. Those doing the appointing, whether a party congress, a city council, or a single individual such as a sovereign or a president, will be expected to answer for their appointments. A pattern of appointments excluding women has become difficult to explain in the fourth quarter of the twentieth century. The mass electorate, in contrast, is not held to account for its actions.

Next, the authorities making appointments have, over the years, found it useful to "balance" their appointments among the relevant social groupings. It is usually not in their interest to give the impression that some groups are favored to the exclusion of others. Once such patterns of appointment have developed with religious, ethnic, and racial groups, it is but a short step to include women in the process as well—especially if the women can be drawn from a minority group and thus do double duty in creating a balance in appointments.

Finally, elites can typically eliminate a lot of wrangling by establishing and following rules for appointments. City councils, boards of education, and similar bodies often rotate the chair by seniority, each member becoming chair for a certain period, in turn. At least through the 1970s, in American cities, such procedures resulted in more female mayors than direct election did.[12] Likewise, in Switzerland the president is selected annually on a rotating basis from the members of the Federal Council.[13] By tradition, one of the seven councillors serves as president for a year. Thus Elisabeth Kopp, elected to the Federal Council in 1984, stands a good chance of being elected to a turn as Swiss president.

Appointed positions are usually less politically important than elected positions. This could be another reason for the willingness of political elites to appoint women. The positions are more honorary and symbolic, and less is at stake.

Runoff Elections

Runoff elections have attracted attention from people concerned with increasing the number of elected women. If there are a number of candidates for only one office, such as a legislative seat, plurality election (where the candidate with the most votes wins) can result in a winner who has the support of only a small minority.[14] One solution to this is to require a runoff between the two top vote-getters. While not without its own problems, such a method does allow a majority candidate to be chosen. But do runoffs lessen the chances of women candidates compared with a simple plurality system?

In the 1984 presidential election campaign, Democratic candidate Jesse Jackson charged that runoff elections lessened the chances of black candidates being elected. Runoff election systems are largely a phenomenon of the South. Jackson reasoned that black voters would be likely to unite behind one candidate while white voters would divide their votes among several white candidates. In a heavily, but not majority, black district, the result would be a plurality for the black candidate. If there were a runoff, however, the black candidate would be defeated since the white voters would unite behind the remaining white candidate.

Jackson argued that a similar process would also work against women candidates in runoff elections, a charge echoed by feminist Eleanor Smeal.[15] However, the reasoning, even if valid for blacks, does not necessarily apply to women as well. Most people vote for candidates of their own race, but few, if any, cast votes on the basis of sex. Still, some believe that the French runoff election, in place between 1958 and 1985, was the cause of a decrease in the number of women elected to the French National Assembly.[16] We will look more closely at France shortly; here let us examine the American evidence.

Between 1970 and 1983, in several states, there were 79 runoff elections involving women candidates, mostly in elections for the lower house of the state legislature. In some of these elections the women candidates led in the first round (and would have won under a plurality system); others lost. Some women who would have won the plurality vote were defeated in the runoff; other women won only because there was a runoff (they had come in second in the first round). The net result was that in the 79 elections, one more woman was elected than would have been the case with simple plurality voting.[17] Thus there is no evidence of women candidates being harmed by runoff primaries.

Proportional Representation

Nations using proportional-representation legislative election systems elect more women than nations using single-member districts.[18] Further, nations using both proportional representation and district systems for their national legislatures elect a greater proportion of women by proportional vote than by district vote.[19] Finally, we have already seen that when France switched from proportional representation to single-member district elections in 1958, the proportion of women elected to the national assembly dropped.[20]

So it is clear that in proportional-representation systems more women are elected to national legislatures than in single-member district systems; why this is so, however, remains obscure.

The question of why proportional representation returns more women than single-member district systems is complicated in a number of ways. First, there is a great variety of proportional election systems—in fact, no two countries use precisely the same system.[21] Further, single-member district systems are used almost exclusively by English-speaking nations: Great Britain, the United States, Australia, Canada, and New Zealand. The political heritage of these nations, largely British, differs in many ways from that of the continental European democracies where proportional representation is the rule.

Given these differences, it is difficult to isolate the particular barriers single-member district systems pose for the election of women. Clearly if the important barriers are rooted in political cultures, increasing female representation must rely on education and socialization. Such traditions change slowly. If the problem lies with the party systems found in the English-speaking nations, the problem is perhaps even more difficult. The party system in the United States, for example, has shown great resilience with respect to fundamental change, in large part because it is compatible with the decentralization in other aspects of American politics. However, if the barriers are in the election system itself, we might be more sanguine, since Americans have proved willing to experiment in this area. Let us examine some of these differences between European and American systems as they relate to electing women to office.

One important difference between proportional representation and single-member district systems concerns political parties. Proportional representation tends to favor multiparty competition, whereas district systems tend to favor two major parties.[22] The nature of the party organization also tends to differ. Continental Europe and Scandinavia have developed mass parties with strong central control, while the party systems in the English-speaking nations have tended toward decentralized national parties with local control over candidate selection.[23] In addition, continental European nations all have strong Marxist socialist or communist parties or both. The Marxist socialist tradition is much less strong in English-speaking nations.

In some nations the Socialist and Communist parties take the lead in nominating and electing women.[24] The decline in female representation in France after 1956 may be only indirectly related to change from proportional representation to single-member constituencies.[25] This change was designed to reduce the strength of the French Communist Party,[26] and in this it succeeded. The decline in women elected to the national assembly may have resulted from the decline of the Communists who elected them and not to the election system itself.

However, there is quite a bit of evidence that the parties of the left are no more likely to run or elect women than the parties of the center or the right. Reports from Scandinavia and Germany indicate that conservative parties are just as likely to nominate women as the parties of the left.[27] In West Germany the Socialists (SPD) did not run or elect more women in the 1976 Bundestag elections than the more conservative Christian Democrats (CDU) and Free Democratic Party (FDP).[28] Likewise, about half the women elected to the Austrian Nationalrat in 1983 were Socialists and half Conservatives. In Britain the Labour party was slow in sending women to Parliament, although it managed to make up for this in time.[29] It was the Liberals who took the lead in nominating women, though their minority party status meant that relatively few were elected. The Conservatives currently send fewer women to Parliament than either of the two leftist parties, though the differences are fairly small. However, in local elections, at least in Scotland, the Conservatives nominate and elect many more women than Labour. The absence of strong Socialist and Communist parties in the English-speaking democracies, then, is probably not the cause of the low representation of women there.

The organization of political parties is another possible explanation for the greater number of women elected to the national legislatures in continental Europe compared with English-speaking nations. Continental parties generally have mass dues-paying memberships with centralized leadership. Candidates run as representatives of a party with the intention of following the party leadership in the legislature. They are less independent than party candidates in the English-speaking nations. Campaigns, too, are different. Candidates, especially those on a list in proportional-representation systems, play a relatively small role. Voters choose the party and its leadership rather than the individual candidates. Under these circumstances women candidates may do better than when forced to campaign on their own in single-member constituencies.[30] This assumes that either the women candidates are less effective campaigners or that voters are biased against women but ignore this bias in list systems.

In the American and British settings, at least, these assumptions seem invalid. Women are not weaker candidates, nor do voters in single-member districts discriminate against women. Evidence from a number of proportional-representation systems also demonstrates women candidates to be equal or stronger vote-getters than men. For example, in Belgium the political parties offer a list of candidates from which the elected representatives will be chosen, based on the party's vote percentage. Voters, however, are free to change the order of the names on the list. Hence, a personal vote is possible in addition to the party vote. Likewise, in Ireland, voters are given a list of candidates nominated by the various parties and asked to provide their *own* rankings. In both systems women candidates are advantaged by these personal votes, as voters move the women candidates higher on the list.[31] Similar evidence has been reported from Finland and Denmark.[32]

Thus the evidence from Belgium, Ireland, Finland, and Denmark is that women candidates are as effective as men in reaching and persuading voters in proportional-representation systems. The argument that women have a greater need for a party to campaign for them is not borne out.

One key characteristic of proportional-representation systems is that each party nominates a list of candidates and votes are counted for the list as a whole. Some nations—Israel and the Netherlands, for example—vote on the party list in a nationwide constituency. In other nations, as in Scandinavia, the country is divided into several districts. Each district elects a number of representatives, and each party contesting in the district presents a list of candidates in that district. Voting is quite stable in European elections, and parties are able to predict their vote accurately. When the party prepares its list for a district, candidates are nominated for three types of positions: *Mandate* places are ones the candidate is almost certain to win, *fighting* places are ones that will give the party an additional seat if things go particularly well, and *ornamental* positions are ones there is no chance of winning.[33]

Parties are most likely to nominate women to mandate positions only when they expect to win more than two seats.[34] Thus in elections to the Norwegian Storting in 1981 women were nominated for 16 percent of the mandate positions by parties expecting to win one or two seats, but for 35 percent of the mandate positions in places where parties expected to win more than two seats.[35] Enid Lakeman offers the following explanation:

> A party which is reluctant to select a woman as its *only* candidate may be much more willing to include her as one of a list with several men. Refusal to select a woman as a sole candidate may be due to real prejudice or to a belief that the electors are prejudiced—that a woman candidate is likely to win fewer votes for the party than a man would. But if several candidates have to be selected the pressure is in the opposite direction—not to offend either sex by excluding it but to widen the party's appeal by including both.[36]

By this reasoning, then, the fact that the election system is proportional is not the relevant factor. Nor is the number of candidates elected in each district in proportional-representation systems relevant. The key to the nomination and election of women is the expected number of seats to be won in the district by the party.

The general statement of this argument is that the political risk to a party is less in a multimember district than in a single-member, all-or-nothing district, where a party risks losing everything. Women may be nominated in inverse proportion to the political risks involved.[37]

The example of Israel is instructive. Israel uses proportional representation to elect all 120 members of the Knesset in one national constituency but returns few women—6.6 percent in 1981.[38] However, Israeli politics is very factionalized, with many very small groupings, each offering candidates. The number elected by any one faction will be relatively small, even though the constituency itself is quite large.[39]

These findings from European electoral systems indicate that proportional representation, strong centralized parties, and the presence of competitive Socialist and Communist parties are less important in increasing the numbers of women elected than the electoral system itself. In particular, the presence of multimember districts in which parties can expect to elect three or more of their candidates seems to stimulate female representation. But does the influence of electoral arrangements on the nomination and election of women in Europe apply to the very different political world of the United States?

Single-Member and Multimember District Systems in the United States

Elections in the United States differ from those in continental Europe and Scandinavia in a number of ways. We do not have disciplined mass parties, nor do we have proportional representation, or party lists from which candidates are elected. Candidates in the United States run for office as individuals, using the party only as a label.

One aspect of American and continental European elections, however, is similar. A large number of elections here are conducted in multimember districts similar to those in European nations using proportional representation. The districts vary widely in size from the two-member districts used in Georgia and other states to the bizarre 177-member "district" used in the 1964 Illinois election (because of a failure to apportion the state into legislative districts, each voter was forced to select 177 individuals from among the 236 candidates).[40] These multimember districts are used to elect representatives to state legislatures and to local bodies such as school boards and city councils.

Given the differences between Europe and the United States in political culture and the nature of the party systems, do the European findings hold for the United States? Do multimember district systems encourage the election of women in the United States as they appear to have done in Europe?

Local Elections

With regard to British local elections there is some belief (though as far as we know unsubstantiated) that multimember district local councils elect more women candidates than in single-member district elections.[41] In the United States there is evidence of a similar pattern, although the associations between the proportion of women serving and the type of election are weak.[42]

Table 6.1 presents data gathered from 256 U.S. cities that have a population of 25,000 or more and a black population of at least 10 percent. The few cities using the commission form of government are excluded, as are those applying district residency requirements to at-large elections. In cities using district residency requirements, candidates for a particular seat must live in a certain district, but voters from all districts select the representative for that seat.

Three kinds of cities are presented in the table. Some cities elect all their city councils in at-large elections; voters from the entire city vote on each member. Other cities elect their city councils in single-member districts. The proportion of women elected in each of these two types of cities is compared in the first part of the table. A third type of city is one in which some of the city council is elected at large and some by districts. In these cities the proportion of women elected by each electoral system within the city is compared.

Women were slightly more likely to be elected to city councils in cities using at-large procedures than in cities using district procedures. Further, in cities employing both methods, women were slightly more likely to be elected to the at-large seats than the district seats. While consistent with previous research, the differences are small and statistically insignificant. The evidence for the proposition that at-large elections will increase the proportion of women elected, though in the right direction, remains inconclusive at the local level.

There is also some contrary evidence from cities using both district and at-large systems. In these cities there are more cities with no women members at

Table 6.1   Female Representation on City Councils

Type of Election	Women Elected		Councils with No Women (%)
	Percentage (Mean)	Number	
Cities with Only District or Only At-Large Seats			
At-large	14	138	40
District	10	62	45
Cities with Some Members Elected At Large, Some from Districts			
At-large seats	12	56	62
District seats	9	56	51

Source: Data from Susan Welch and Albert Karnig, "Sex and Ethnic Differences in Municipal Representation," *Social Science Quarterly* 60 (December 1979): 487.

all elected at large than there are with no women elected from districts. Again, however, we should not make too much of these insignificant differences.

One reason for the weak support for the theory of multimember districts favoring women candidates might be the greater permeability of local politics to women, something we discussed in Chapter 2. For a number of reasons local politics do not present the same barriers to the election of women as politics at other levels.

State Legislative Elections

There is no uniform method of electing state legislatures in the United States. Each state is more or less free to adopt a method best suited to its particular circumstances and political realities. This results in a great variety of procedures. Further, states change their procedures regularly so that over time a particular state will likely have used a variety of methods. Though confusing, this great variability can prove useful to political scientists. In our case the variety of election procedures can be examined with regard to how they affect the nomination and election of women candidates.

Our particular interest will concern the effect of multimember and single-member district systems on the nomination and election of women candidates. European research indicates that the nomination and election of women candidates in proportional-representation systems is a function of the number of candidates the parties expect to elect in districts. When that number is one or two, few women will be elected; when that number is greater than two, more women will be elected.

Whereas in proportional-representation systems the number of seats being contested is less relevant than the number of seats a party expects to win, in American multimember districts the situation is different. Each voter in the United States has as many votes as there are seats to fill and may distribute them among any combination of candidates. Parties have little control over which candidates get which votes. In American multimember districts, parties can reasonably seek to win *each* seat they contest. The key to the nomination and election of women in these elections is the number of seats being contested. The more seats available, the more likely parties will nominate at least some women.

We expect to find more women candidates running and more elected from multimember districts than from single-member districts. First, although party slate making plays a smaller role in American elections than in nations using proportional representation, it still does occur here.[43] Since women are a legitimate grouping with political relevance, slate makers will be under greater pressure to include them as candidates as the number to be nominated increases. So there is more pressure in a multimember district of three than in a single-member district.

Next, voters, too, may exercise a sort of affirmative action in favor of women candidates when there are many votes to cast for an office in which women are underrepresented.

Third, running as a woman among a number of candidates may give the candidate novelty value and distinctiveness. This in turn should help with voter recognition and ultimately with getting votes.

Finally, women may be more willing to step forward as candidates in multimember districts than in single-member districts. Many women candidates prefer to campaign *for* themselves, running on their qualifications and programs, rather than *against* their opponents.[44] Such a campaign is very appropriate to multimember district elections where there is no specific opponent.[45]

Let us examine three sorts of evidence concerning multimember and single-member districts in American state legislative elections. First we will look at states using both multimember and single-member systems. We expect that a greater proportion of women candidates and winners will be from the multi-member districts. Next we will look at states that have changed their method of electing the state legislature. States changing toward greater use of multi-member districts are expected to have greater increases in the proportion of women candidates running and being elected than states changing toward single-member district systems. Finally, we will contrast the proportions of women running and being elected to the upper house and the lower house of the legislature in the same state where one body uses one election method and the other body uses the other method.

We turn first to states using both single and multimember districts to elect members to the lower house of the state legislature. In each of these states candidates ran at large within a district and were not paired off against one another for particular seats. For some states data for several years were available, and that is presented in Table 6.2.

As can be seen, with only two exceptions, women ran in a greater proportion of multimember districts than single-member districts. The proportion of women running in the multimember districts was almost double that running in the single-member districts.[46] This is quite unlikely to have occurred by chance. The record of the multimember districts is also good when the election of women is considered. In 16 of the 20 instances the proportion of the elected candidates in multimember districts exceeded that in the single-member districts.[47] The proportion of those elected who were women in the multimember districts was more than half again as large as that in the single-member districts.

We were able to locate election data from nine states that changed their district systems between elections. There were eight instances of change from multimember or a combination of multimember and single-member districts to single-member districts only. In seven of the eight instances the change was associated with either a drop in the proportion of women elected that was greater than the national drop that year, or an increase in the proportion of women elected that was less than the national proportion of women elected[48] (see Table 6.3). In the case of Hawaii, Idaho, and Montana, the second election,

*Table 6.2   The Female Proportion of All Major Party Candidates
in the General Election and All Elected Legislators to the Lower House
by State, Year, and District Type*

State	Year	Type of District	Female Percent of All Candidates	Female Percent of All Elected
Connecticut	1962	Single	11	9
		Multiple	18	16
Hawaii	1980	Single	14	20
		Multiple	18	19
Idaho	1970	Single	3	7
		Multiple	8	3
	1966	Single	7	7
		Multiple	4	5
	1964	Single	3	7
		Multiple	5	4
Indiana	1980	Single	2	3
		Multiple	15	14
Iowa	1966	Single	5	3
		Multiple	9	6
	1964	Single	2	0
		Multiple	6	8
Louisiana	1968	Single	0	0
		Multiple	2	3
Maine	1976	Single	16	15
		Multiple	26	30
	1974	Single	10	10
		'Multiple	18	20
Maryland	1978	Single	0	0
		Multiple	16	18
Montana	1970	Single	0	0
		Multiple	5	1
New Hampshire	1978	Single	22	21
		Multiple	32	29
Pennsylvania	1964	Single	6	4
		Multiple	7	7
	1962	Single	4	3
		Multiple	7	6
South Dakota	1968	Single	0	0
		Multiple	6	5
West Virginia	1980	Single	0	0
		Multiple	13	16
Wyoming	1982	Single	36	12
		Multiple	25	30
	1980	Single	6	10
		Multiple	24	20

Source: Election data supplied by the states.

Table 6.3   Effect of Changes in the Electoral System on Female Candidacy and Election to the Lower House of State Legislatures in the General Election[a]

State	Year	Type of District[b]	Female Percent of All Candidates	Female Percent of All Elected	Change in Percent Elected	
					State	National
Changed in 1960s						
Conn.	1962	M & S	17	15		
	1966	S	11	11	−4	−0
Iowa	1966	M & S	7	4		
	1968	S	6	4	−0	0
Pa.	1964	M & S	6	5		
	1966	S	3	3	−1	−0
Changed in 1970s and 1980s						
Hawaii	1980	M & S	18	19		
	1982	S	24	23	+3	+1
	1984	S	17	13	−9	+1
Idaho	1970	M & S	7	4		
	1972	M	12	7	+3	+0
	1974	M	11	11	+3	+2
	1976	S	12	11	0	+1
	1978	S	9	8	−2	+1
Ill.	1980	M	14	15		
	1982	S	14	16	+0	+1
Me.	1976	M & S	18	19		
	1978	S	19	19	−0	+1
	1980	S	22	23	+4	+1
Mont.	1970	M & S	5	1		
	1972	M	10	7	+6	+0
	1976	S	12	10	+3	+3
	1978	S	14	10	0	+1
S. Dak.	1968	M & S	4	3		
	1972	M	7	7	+3	+1

Sources: Election data supplied by the states.

[a]Major party candidates only.

[b]M = multiple, S = single.

[c]Data for 1962–1968 from Emmy Werner, "Women in The State Legislature," *Western Political Quarterly* 21 (March 1968): 40–50, and *The Book of the States* (Lexington, Kentucky: The Council of State Governments, 1975), various editions. Data for 1970–1982 from National Women's Political Caucus, *National Directory of Women Elected Officials, 1983* and *1985* (Washington, D.C., 1983, 1985). National estimates combine the two legislative houses.

after changing to all single-member districts produced either no change or drops in the female proportion of elected legislatures at times when the national trend was in the opposite direction. Maine, however, was an exception.

We were able to locate only three instances where a state moved toward more multimember districts. Each of these instances was accompanied by an increase in the proportion of women elected that was greater than what occurred nationally in the same year.

These findings may underrepresent the effects on women. Given the inertia of incumbency, it might be that the effects of changing the election system will not be fully felt until several elections have passed.

Each state except Nebraska has a two-house legislature. The upper house is typically smaller and its members have longer terms than is the case for the lower house. Because of the longer term, members of the upper house have more job security than lower house members. In addition, because the chamber is smaller, a member of the upper house has more individual influence and power. This makes service in the upper house more attractive than service in the lower house. It is not uncommon for a member of the lower house to give up a seat in the lower house for a try at a seat in the upper house; the reverse is uncommon. Irene Diamond has argued that these conditions work against women gaining access to the upper legislative house because "all of this spells status and no women." "Women are less likely to be elected to the upper houses: the average proportion in the senates is 2.5 percent, whereas the average proportion in the lower houses is 4.9 percent." "The sheer fact of the senate's being 'upper' partially explains the sparse representation of women. . . . Recruitment for the upper house is more selective."[49]

From this we would expect that fewer women would be elected to the upper house than to the lower house, even though the evidence presented earlier indicated that women candidates are at least as able as similar male candidates, in which case there should not be much difference between the two houses with regard to the proportion of women running or elected, all things being equal. But the election system might make a difference.

We were able to find four states in which the upper chamber of the state legislature was elected using a combination of multimember and single-member districts. These are presented in Table 6.4. In each instance, as expected, women were more likely to be candidates and to win in the multimember districts than in the single-member districts.

In three of these cases the lower houses also have a combination of single-member and multimember districts. Very little difference between the success of women in the house and senate is seen. In fact, in two of the three cases, the proportion of candidates who are women is greater for the upper than the lower chamber multimember districts. In each instance women are more likely to be elected in upper house multimember districts than in single-member lower house ones.

Even from this limited sample it is apparent that in elections to the state legislature women do better in multimember districts than in single-member districts regardless of the house. In determining female success, the type of election is much more important than whether it is for the upper or lower house.

Table 6.4   Women Candidates in State Legislative General Elections, Upper and Lower House[a]

State	Year	House	Type of District[b]	Female Percent of All Candidates	Female Percent of All Elected
Hawaii	1980	Senate	S	0	0
			M	17	25
		House	S	14	20
			M	18	19
Mont.	1970	Senate	S	0	0
			M	9	8
		House	S	0	0
			M	5	1
Nev.	1980	Senate	S	N.A.[c]	0
			M	N.A.	20
		House	S (all)	N.A.	12
S. Dak.	1968	Senate	S	2	0
			M	7	11
		House	S	0	0
			M	6	5

Source: Election data supplied by the states.
[a]Major parties only.
[b]M = multiple, S = single.
[c]Not available.

Voters and Women Candidates in Primaries

Primary election data are also of importance in comparing single-member and multimember districts. Today, political parties tend to play a smaller role in recruiting and backing candidates in primaries than they do in the general elections, although there are states where parties still endorse candidates in primaries. Thus candidates, both women and men, are more on their own when contesting the primary election than when contesting the general election. The extent to which women contest primaries, then, is more an indicator of the candidate's self-recruitment than the general election itself. Further, the vote in a primary is a clearer indicator of the voters' reaction to a candidate than the general election, where party has a major impact on the vote.

For the years 1968–1980, we have data on women candidates in primary elections in Wyoming, a state which has elected the lower house of the legislature using both single-member and multimember districts for some time. Table 6.5 shows that as the number of seats increases, the proportion of women candidates contesting primary elections increases. Districts having four or more seats witness over twice the proportion of women candidates as the single-member districts.

Table 6.5   *District Size and Proportion of Men and Women Candidates in Wyoming Primaries, 1968–1980*

	District Size					
					4 or More	
Candidate Gender	1 Member		2–3 Members		Members	
Men (%)	93		89		85	
Women (%)	6		10		15	
Total (%) (Number)	100	(139)	100	(276)	100	(587)

Source: Election data supplied by the state of Wyoming.

Table 6.6 indicates that women candidates run much stronger races in the multimember district primaries than in the single-member district primaries. When the percent of vote gained by the average woman candidate is adjusted for party, incumbency, number of candidates, and time period, the advantage of multimember districts for women candidates becomes very apparent. The female proportion of the vote in the larger multimember districts is more than twice that of the single-member districts. These Wyoming primary election data suggest that the advantage of multimember districts for women candidates in the United States is due to both the greater willingness of women to run in the larger districts and the advantage they have as candidates in that situation.

The Electoral College

We have one last piece of evidence concerning the relationship between the election system and the representation of women. The one American political body that comes closest in terms of the nomination and election process to that typically found in continental European democracies is the electoral college. Certainly this body plays only a minor part in our political system today. Nevertheless, nominations are sought after, and there is competition for the limited number of positions a party has available. Like the situation in European pol-

Table 6.6   *MCA Breakdowns of Votes Received by Wyoming Women Candidates in Primaries*

	Vote (%)		Number of Women
District Size	Unadjusted	Adjusted	Candidates
1 member	32	27	139
2–3 members	58	47	276
4 or more members	54	57	587

Source: Election data supplied by the state of Wyoming.

itics, the list of nominations is made by party organizations at the state level, and the election turns on the party, not on the campaigns of the nominees. They are elected or not elected depending on how the party has done in the state. Under these circumstances it would be expected that there will be pressure to include women on the list. Political parties, whether out of a desire to bring women into the system or simply to deflect pressure with symbolic acts or tokens, will include women among their nominees.

In the 1984 presidential election, 538 electors were chosen. Given the fact that parties were required to nominate lists of candidates and that the candidates would be voted for at large in highly partisan elections, it would be expected that a large proportion of women would be nominated and elected. That was, indeed, the case. Of the 538 electors chosen, over 31 percent were female. This is a far greater percentage than elected in the other federal elections and a higher percentage than elected to all but one of the state legislatures. The credit for this is very likely the nomination and election system. If the electors were nominated and elected in a manner similar to our legislative bodies, as some people have in fact proposed, we could anticipate far fewer female electors.

Conclusions

There is a great variety of election procedures that satisfy the abstract ideas of democracy. At any given time the adoption of one system of election over another can provide an advantage to particular groups. Even in the Athens of 501 B.C., disputes over the election of generals resulted in a change from electing by districts (actually tribes) to at-large elections with residency requirements—each general had to come from a different tribe.[50] Twenty-five centuries later the relative merits of at-large and district systems are still being debated, in the context of American municipal elections. While the origins of the Athenian dispute have been lost, today the concern is over the representation of racial and ethnic minorities.

It is curious that women, one of the most underrepresented groups in American politics and perhaps the most underrepresented, have subjected election systems to very little challenge. Other groups do not hesitate to cry foul when they perceive a disadvantage for themselves in the methods adopted for conducting elections. Yet there are electoral circumstances under which women candidates are more likely than others to run and be elected. Two selection methods, quotas for women and indirect methods of choosing public officials (basically appointment), appear to work in favor of bringing women into office. Runoff elections, thought by some to work against the election of women, do not appear to have that effect.

Strong evidence from Europe that multimember election systems are more conducive to the election of women than single-member district systems is confirmed in the United States. In legislative elections in states using both single-member and multimember districts, a greater proportion of women run and are elected in multimember districts than in single-member districts. The consequence of a change to more multimember districts is a jump in the proportion of women among the candidates and among those elected. This jump is greater than the national trend of increasing numbers of women elected. When states change toward less use of multimember districts there is the opposite effect. Compared to the national trend, these states suffer decreases in the proportion of women running and being elected to the legislature.

Other groups have successfully argued that *they* are disadvantaged by multimember districts, which advantage women. At-large systems disadvantage the most minority groups that are clustered together in a particular part of a city or district; when minorities are dispersed, single-member districts are of no particular advantage to them. Thus it is clear that at-large elections pose a severe impediment to black male representation. Hispanic males are also sometimes disadvantaged by at-large elections, though the effect is not so clear or consistent as the effects on blacks because Hispanics are often not as spatially segregated as blacks.

Minority women, however, do not gain from single-member districts. Black women do almost the same in multimember as in single-member districts.[51] Female blacks and Hispanics are exceptions to the generally favorable effect of multimember districts on the election of women and to the generally favorable effect of single-member districts on the election of minorities. Must we trade electoral equality for male minorities to achieve it for women? It would be disastrous if that were to happen.

Perhaps a reasonable strategy is to look for other kinds of electoral arrangements that might be fair to all groups. There are, in fact, versions of the multimember district system that could be adopted that would be fair to both women and minority men. The single transferable vote, for example, virtually guarantees minority representation, especially in *large* multimember districts.[52] Voters rank all the candidates running from first choice to last. First choices for a candidate are counted only until the candidate has enough votes to be elected. After that, first choices for the candidate are transferred to the next preference. The practical consequence is that in a contest to fill three seats, for example, a candidate with a third of the first preferences will be elected to represent those voters.[53] This method is currently used in national elections in Ireland, Australia, and Malta, and in council elections in Cambridge, Massachusetts, and school board elections in New York City. Between 1915 and 1956 it was used by two dozen American cities, including Cincinnati and Cleveland.[54] In fact, Cleveland is now studying returning to that system.

Notes

1. Regarding ballot effects, see R. Darcy, "Position Effects with Party Column Ballots," *Western Political Quarterly* 39 (December 1986); regarding districting, see

Bruce E. Cain, "Assessing the Partisan Effects of Redistricting," *American Political Science Review* 79 (June 1985): 320–333.

2. See Arend Lijphart and Bernard Grofman, eds., *Choosing an Electoral System: Issues and Alternatives* (New York: Praeger, 1984).

3. See Albert Karnig and Susan Welch, *Black Representation and Urban Policy* (Chicago: University of Chicago Press, 1980); Richard Engstrom and Michael McDonald, "The Election of Blacks to City Councils: Clarifying the Impact of Electoral Arrangements on the Seats/Population Relationship," *American Political Science Review* 75 (June 1981): 244–354; Chandler Davidson, ed., *Minority Vote Dilution* (Washington, D.C.: Howard University Press, 1984); Rufus Browning, Dale R. Marshall, and David Tabb, *Protest Is Not Enough: The Struggle of Blacks and Hispanics for Equality in Urban Politics* (Berkeley: University of California Press, 1984).

4. Bir-Er Chou and Janet Clark, "Women Legislators in Taiwan: Barriers to Women's Participation in a Modernizing State," *Working Papers on Women in Development* (East Lansing: Michigan State University, 1986); Alice Ai-Fen Wang and Helen Hsieh-chin Yeh, "Women's Contributions to National Development of the Republic of China," in *Proceedings of Asian Woman Parliamentarian's Seminar* (Seoul, 1982), 37–50.

5. Vicky Randall, *Women and Politics* (New York: Saint Martin's Press, 1982), 100.

6. Ibid.

7. See Henry Valen, "The Storting Election of September 1985: The Welfare State under Pressure," *Scandinavian Political Studies* (forthcoming); "Norway's New Parliament: One Third Women," *News of Norway* (published by the Embassy of Norway, Washington, D.C.), October 15, 1985, 58.

8. Elina Haavio-Mannila et al., *Det Uferdige Demokratiet: Kvinner i Nordisk Politikk* (Oslo: Nordisk Ministerrad, 1983), 56.

9. See Randall, *Women and Politics,* 96; Susan Welch and Donley T. Studlar, "British Public Opinion toward Women in Politics: A Comparative Perspective," *Western Political Quarterly* 39 (March 1986): 138–154.

10. Haavio-Mannila et al., *Det Uferdige Demokratiet,* 81–82; Welch and Studlar, "British Public Opinion."

11. R. Darcy and Sunhee Song, "Men and Women in the Korean National Assembly: Social Barriers to Representational Roles," *Asian Survey* 26 (June 1986): 670–687.

12. Susan Welch and Albert Karnig, "Correlates of Female Office Holding in City Politics," *Journal of Politics* 41 (May 1979): 478–491.

13. Arend Lijphart, *Democracies: Patterns of Majoritarian and Consensus Government in Twenty-one Countries* (New Haven, Conn.: Yale University Press, 1984).

14. See Philip Straffin, *Topics in the Theory of Voting* (Boston: Birkhauser, 1980); Hannu Nurmi, "Voting Procedures: A Summary Analysis," *British Journal of Political Science* 13 (April 1983): 181–208.

15. Charles S. Bullock and Loch Johnson, "Sex and the Second Primary," *Social Science Quarterly* 66 (December 1985): 933–944.

16. See Karen Beckwith, "Structural Barriers to Women's Access to Office: The Case of France, Italy, and the United States," paper presented at the meeting of the American Political Science Association, Washington, D.C., September 1984; Wilma Rule, "Twenty-three Democracies and Women's Parliamentary Representation," paper presented at the meeting of the International Political Science Association, Paris, July 1985.

17. Bullock and Johnson, "Sex and the Second Primary."

18. See Maurice Duverger, *The Political Role of Women* (Paris: UNESCO, 1955); Ingunn Means, *Kvinner i Norsk Politikk* (Oslo: Cappelen, 1972); Maud Eduards, "Sweden," in Joni Lovenduski and Jill Hills, eds., *The Politics of the Second Electorate: Women and Public Participation* (London: Routledge & Kegan Paul, 1981), 208–227; Torild Skard, *Utvalgt til Stortinget* (Oslo: Gyldendal, 1980); Walter Kohn, *Women in National Legislatures* (New York: Praeger, 1980); Wilma Rule, "Why Women Don't Run: The Critical Contextual Factors in Women's Legislative Recruitment," *Western Political Quarterly* 34 (March 1981): 60–77; Rule, "Twenty-three Democracies"; Maud Eduards, *Kvinnor och Politik: Fakta och Forklaringar* (Stockholm: Liber Forlag, 1977); Ingunn Means, "Political Recruitment of Women in Norway," *Western Political Quarterly* 25 (September 1972): 491–521; Elizabeth Vallance, *Women in the House: A Study of Women Members of Parliament* (London: Athlone, 1979); Vernon Bogdanor, "Conclusion: Electoral Systems and Party Systems," in Vernon Bogdanor and David Butler, eds., *Democracy and Elections* (Cambridge: Cambridge University Press, 1983); L. Culley, "Women in Politics," in L. Robins, ed., *Updating British Politics* (London: Politics Association, 1984); Joni Lovenduski and Jill Hills, "Conclusions," in Joni Lovenduski and Jill Hills, eds., *The Politics of the Second Electorate: Women and Public Participation* (London: Routledge & Kegan Paul, 1981), 320–328; Francis Castles, "Female Legislative Representation and the Electoral System," *Politics* 1 (April 1981): 21–26; Elizabeth Vallance, "Where the Power Is, Women Are Not," *Parliamentary Affairs* 35 (Spring 1982): 218–219; Torild Skard and Elina Haavio-Mannila, "Equality between the Sexes: Myth or Reality in Norden?" *Daedalus* 113 (Winter 1984): 141–167; Janneke van der Ros, "Women and Politics in the Nordic Countries: A Complex Picture," in Howard Penniman, ed., *Women at the Polls* (Washington, D.C.: American Enterprise Institute, unpublished manuscript).

19. Duverger, *Political Role of Women;* Darcy and Song, "Korean National Assembly."

20. Enid Lakeman, "Electoral Systems and Women in Parliament," *Parliamentarian* 56 (July 1976): 159–162; Rule, "Twenty-three Democracies."

21. See Lijphart and Grofman, *Choosing an Electoral System.*

22. See Lijphart, *Democracies;* but see also Richard Rose, "Electoral Systems: A Question of Degree or of Principle?" in Lijphart and Grofman, *Choosing an Electoral System,* 73–81.

23. See Maurice Duverger, *Political Parties* (London: Methuen, 1954); Leon Epstein, *Political Parties in Western Democracies,* rev. ed. (New Brunswick, N.J.: Transaction Books, 1980).

24. See Beckwith, "Structural Barriers"; Rule, "Twenty-three Democracies," 2.

25. Jaine Mossuz-Lavau and Mariette Sineau, "France," in Lovenduski and Hills, *Politics of the Second Electorate,* 112–133.

26. See Domenico Fisichella, "The Double-Ballot System as a Weapon against Antisystem Parties," in Lijphart and Grofman, *Choosing an Electoral System,* 181–190.

27. See Haavio-Mannila et al., *Det Uferdige Demokratiet;* Eduards, "Sweden."

28. Jane Hall, "West Germany," in Lovenduski and Hills, *Politics of the Second Electorate,* 153–181.

29. Kohn, *Women in National Legislatures,* 238.

30. Duverger, *Political Role of Women,* 79; Rule, "Why Women Don't Run," 77.

31. Lakeman, "Electoral Systems and Women in Parliament."
32. Haavio-Mannila et al., *Det Uferdige Demokratiet.*
33. Ibid., 85.
34. Ibid.; Means, *Kvinner i Norsk Politikk;* Skard, *Utvalgt til Stortinget.*
35. Haavio-Mannila et al., *Det Uferdige Demokratiet,* 86.
36. Lakeman, "Electoral Systems and Women in Parliament," 161.
37. Beckwith, "Structural Barriers"; Monica Charlot, "Women in Politics in France," in Howard R. Penniman, ed., *The French National Assembly Elections of 1978* (Washington, D.C.: American Enterprise Institute, 1980), 189–190.
38. See S. Weis and Yael Yishai, "Women's Representation in Israeli Political Elites," *Jewish Social Studies* 42 (Spring 1980): 165–176.
39. See Alan Arian, "Stability and Change in Israeli Public Opinion and Politics," *Public Opinion Quarterly* 35 (Spring 1971): 19–35.
40. John E. Mueller, "Choosing among 133 Candidates," *Public Opinion Quarterly* 34 (Fall 1970): 395–402.
41. Enid Lakeman, *How Democracies Vote* (London: Faber & Faber, 1970); David Butler and M. Pinto-Duschinsky, "The Conservative Elite, 1918–1978: Does Underrepresentativeness Matter?" in Z. Layton-Henry, ed., *Conservative Party Politics* (Atlantic Highlands, N.J.: Humanities Press, 1980).
42. Welch and Karnig, "Correlates"; Albert Karnig and Oliver Walter, "Election of Women to City Councils," *Social Science Quarterly* 56 (March 1976); 605–613; Susan MacManus, "Determinants of the Equitability of Female Representation on 243 City Councils," paper presented at the meeting of the American Political Science Association, Chicago, August 1976.
43. Sid Groeneman, "Candidate Sex and Delegate Voting in a Pre-primary Party Endorsement Election," *Women and Politics* 3 (Spring 1983): 39–56.
44. Jeane Kirkpatrick, *Political Woman* (New York: Basic Books, 1974), 94–95.
45. Despite these plausible explanations, there are some reasons why multimember districts may not facilitate women's election as much as we expect. Women candidates have sometimes been found to do less well in urban areas than in rural areas. The reason for this, these authors suggest, is that political campaigns are more difficult, expensive, and competitive in the urban areas compared to the rural areas. Since multimember districts in the United States are more likely to exist in urban than rural areas (though not always so), women candidates will also be disadvantaged in the multimember districts.

A related argument is that the size of a district affects a woman's chance of being elected. The larger the population of the district, the more effort is needed to reach voters and the stiffer the male competition likely to be encountered. Like the argument relating to urban and rural districts, this argument, too, is premised on the notion that women are less able campaigners than men.

The evidence developed in Part Two, however, indicates that this premise is not correct. Women candidates for local, state, and congressional offices are as competitive as or more competitive than similar male candidates. See Emmy Werner, "Women in the State Legislatures," *Western Political Quarterly* 21 (March 1968): 40–50; Irene Diamond, *Sex Roles in the State House* (New Haven, Conn.: Yale University Press, 1977); David B. Hill, "Political Culture and Female Political Representation," *Journal of Politics* 43 (February 1981): 159–168; Rule, "Why Women Don't Run"; but for the opposite argument see Elina Haavio-Mannila, "Changes in Sex Roles in Politics as an Indicator of Structural Change in Society," *International Journal of Sociology* 8 (Spring 1978): 56–85.

46. The binomial formula (k = 18, 19, 20; n = 20; p = .5) gives a probability of p < .001.

47. The binomial formula (k = 16, 17, 18, 19, 20; n = 20; p = .5) gives a probability of p < .01.

48. The binomial formula (k = 7, 8; n = 8; p = .5) indicates that this cannot be attributed to chance (p < .03).

49. Diamond, *Sex Roles,* 9, 10, 11.

50. E. S. Staveley, *Greek and Roman Voting and Elections* (Ithaca, N.Y.: Cornell University Press, 1972), 41–47.

51. Albert Karnig and Susan Welch, "Sex and Ethnicity in Municipal Representation," *Social Science Quarterly* 56 (March 1979): 605–613.

52. George Hallett, "Proportional Representation with the Single Transferable Vote: A Basic Requirement for Legislative Elections," in Lijphart and Grofman, *Choosing an Electoral System,* 113–125.

53. At-large voting systems typically found in the United States today give each voter as many votes as there are seats to be filled and require winning candidates to have a majority or a plurality of the votes cast. The consequence is that the majority elects each representative and the minority none. Consider a hypothetical at-large district with 300,000 voters selecting three representatives. In this district 100,000 voters are black and 200,000 are white. Voters are racially polarized, so blacks vote only for blacks and whites vote only for whites. If three white candidates and one black candidate run, each white candidate gets 200,000 votes and the black candidate gets 100,000 votes. All the whites are elected.

Now let us see how the single transferable vote works. Each voter gets just one vote. Further, each voter ranks the candidates from first choice to last. The whites all rank the three whites among their first three choices and the blacks all rank the black candidate as their first choice.

As there are 300,000 voters and three seats to be filled, a candidate requires 100,000 votes to be elected. Two whites and one black will be elected. To see how, we will look at the white voters. One white candidate gets 90,000 first-choice votes, another gets 80,000, and the last white candidate gets 30,000 first-choice votes. Thus for first choices, the black candidate has 100,000 votes (and is elected) and the white candidates have 90,000, 80,000, and 30,000 votes. None of the white candidates has enough votes to be elected. The candidate with the fewest votes is eliminated, and that candidate's votes are transferred to the other candidates by taking the voters who choose that candidate first and looking at those voters' second choice. These second choices are then added to the totals of the remaining candidate. If these 30,000 voters consisted of 20,000 preferring the first white candidate next, and 10,000 preferring the second white candidate next, the first white candidate would now have 110,000 (and be elected), and the remaining white candidate would have 90,000 votes, still not enough to be elected. With the single transferrable vote, once a candidate has enough votes to win (here, 100,000), no more votes are counted for that candidate. The first white candidate, then, would have been elected before the 10,000 remaining votes were counted. For these voters, their *third* choice would get their votes, in this case the second white candidate, who would now have 100,000 votes and be elected: 80,000 first-choice votes, 10,000 second-choice votes transferred from the third white candidate, and 10,000 third-choice votes transferred from the first and third white candidates.

54. Hallett, "Proportional Representation"; Leon Weaver, "Semi-proportional Representation Systems in the United States," in Lijphart and Grofman, *Choosing an Electoral System,* 191–206.

7

Women Candidates and Legislative Turnover

To unravel the puzzle of the vast underrepresentation of women in American political life, we have carefully examined a number of propositions concerning the election of women to public office. We have reviewed previous research and gathered and examined our own data as well. Rather than solving the puzzle, in many ways this has made it seem even further from solution. For example, we have found that voters, party leaders, and financers of political campaigns either are not biased against women candidates or actually favor women. Similarly, we have found that while the eligible pool of available candidates for state legislative races did not include nearly the proportion of women we find in the adult population, the female proportion of the eligible pool was considerably larger than the proportion of women actually elected to state legislatures. Clearly some pieces of the puzzle are missing.

So far we have tried to gather data and test hypotheses and explanations concerning actual elections and candidates. Here our purpose will be different. Instead of examining individual pieces, we will develop models of elections that will tie these pieces together. We will then be able to see how the system works over a period of time. This will also help us to understand the role played by various elements in slowing women's entrance into electoral office.

In Chapter 5 we suggested that, in general, the gender composition of the eligible pool of candidates will eventually determine the gender composition of elected bodies. Now it will be useful to be more precise in describing both the changing gender composition of eligible pools and the relationship between this and the gender composition of elected public officials. The purpose of doing so will be to determine what can be expected or anticipated from projected changes in eligible pools.

Our focus is on women's representation in state legislatures and the U.S. House of Representatives. First, we will examine the eligible pool itself and the process by which the female proportion in it is changing. Then we will relate that changing eligible pool of candidates to the changing male and female proportions in state legislatures. Finally, we shall take the state legislatures themselves as an eligible pool of new candidates for the House of Representatives in Washington. The model will relate changes in society, through changes in the state legislatures, to changes in the male and female composition of the House of Representatives. Figure 7.1 expresses the model in a simple way.

Notice that in developing a model we have simplified a complex situation. For example, people who have not previously been elected to a state legislature certainly do get elected to Congress. The state legislature is simply the most used route to Congress. By making things more simple than they really are, we make the model manageable. We gain something else as well. It is much easier to examine the processes we are concerned with in a simple model. But despite our model's simplicity, it does capture key aspects of the movement of women into American political life.

Eligible Pools

In Chapter 5 we suggested that we can expect the proportion of female candidates for an office such as state legislator to be determined by the female proportion of the eligible pool of candidates for that position. We also have shown that there are changes taking place in society and that more and more women are moving into these eligible pools. Now we will try to model the process by which female proportions of eligible pools are growing.

Let us look at the case of lawyers. While lawyers are not the majority of the eligible pool for state legislators, they are perhaps the single most important element. Today over 40 percent of the people entering law school are women, and between 1980 and 1984 about 34 percent of the new lawyers were female.[1] In 1980, by contrast, there were about a half million practicing lawyers, only 8 percent of which were female. The new lawyers over the period 1980–1984 represented an average increase of about 26,000 per year, or a little less than 5 percent of the total number of lawyers. If this additional 5 percent is 34 percent female (which it was), the net change in the female proportion of lawyers will increase the female proportion of all practicing lawyers by only about 1.5 percent per year. Thus between 1980 and 1984 the female proportion of practicing lawyers rose only from 8.1 to 12.8 percent. The slow growth occurred despite great changes in the process of admitting women into the profession and the consequently large proportions of women among new lawyers.

The reason for this, of course, is that the vast bulk of existing lawyers were trained in a time when very few women entered that profession. And each year's pool of new lawyers is very small in comparison with the total number of lawyers. Even if the proportion of women among the new lawyers increased to 50 percent, it would be some time before the female proportion among all

Figure 7.1 General Model of Legislative Recruitment.

lawyers would approach this level. Despite great changes, the legal profession will remain largely male for some time.

Eventually, of course, things will change. That change, when it comes, will be relatively rapid as males of the older generations retire at much higher rates than the female proportion of the profession, most of whom will be considerably younger. But for the next two decades there will be slow growth in the female proportion of practicing attorneys; nevertheless, even at this rate, women will constitute nearly 30 percent of the profession in another decade.

This reasoning assumes that the numbers of new lawyers remains constant each year and that the female proportion of new lawyers is also constant. If the number of new lawyers diminishes, the male domination of the profession will continue somewhat longer, unless the proportion of new lawyers who are female increases. If the number of new lawyers begins to increase while the percent of women among them stays constant, female proportions among all attorneys will increase at a greater rate.

The process we have outlined for lawyers is taking place throughout our society for many other groups. Women are entering new fields in greater numbers and are taking their places in what had been previously almost exclusively male enclaves. For young women, that means that their chances of entering some desired profession is almost or entirely equal to those of similarly situated males. However, it also means that the gender composition of the whole profession or group will be changing only slowly because of the large numbers of males already established.

State Legislatures

State legislatures are typically the point at which a partisan political career begins. Here we will focus on the lower house, except in the case of Nebraska, which has only one house. In some ways it is very difficult to specify exactly what constitutes the eligible pool of candidates for state legislatures. In fact, we can be pretty confident that the eligible pool of candidates varies quite a bit from state to state and even from year to year. Nevertheless, we can go some way toward estimating what proportion of the candidates in any particular year are women.

Using data collected by the National Women's Political Caucus and the Council of State Governments,[2] we can estimate that in the years 1980–1984 there were over 10,000 candidates running for about 5,500 legislative seats. Of these 10,000 candidates we can further estimate that about 4,700 were incumbents and the remaining 5,300 were new candidates. This last group can be considered the eligible pool of new candidates for the lower house of the state legislature. This eligible pool was 16.14 percent female in 1980, 17.84 percent female in 1982, and 18.67 percent female in 1984. The increase in the proportion of women in this pool is about 1.3 percent for each election, or about .5 percent per year. This is about half that expected from our examination of the growth in the proportion of women among lawyers. No doubt there is a lag of several years between achieving a particular occupational status and establishing oneself sufficiently to consider running for office.

How will this increasing eligible pool of women translate into women elected to state legislatures? To examine this process, we need to examine what happens in the many state legislative races.

In 1982 state legislative elections for the lower house took place in 46 states— all but New Jersey, Mississippi, Louisiana, and Kentucky. There were 5,187 individuals serving in these lower houses before the election, 4,437 men and 750 women. After the election 68.06 percent of the men and 67.20 percent of the women had been reelected. Only 32 percent retired, died, or were defeated in the election; the rest were back. Most legislators decide to run for reelection. When they do, most are reelected. Any model of legislative turnover, therefore, must account for this incumbency factor.

We can use incumbent return rates to estimate the incumbent replacement probability. The probability of a male incumbent being replaced is slightly less than the probability of a female incumbent being replaced, but both have a very high probability of returning, .6806 for men and .6720 for women. What if they do not return? Who will replace them? In 1984 we have already estimated that 18.67 percent of the nonincumbent candidates (the eligible pool) were female and 81.33 percent were male. Based on the findings of previous chapters, we can reasonably assume that an individual woman candidate has the same chances of being elected as a similar male individual. Thus we will assume that the sex of the candidate has no effect on the election outcome. It implies that 18.67 percent of officeholders replacing incumbents in 1984 would be female and 81.33 percent male. Expressed as a probability, in 1984 the likelihood of a male replacing an incumbent would be .8133 and a woman replacing an incumbent would be .1867. What about 1986? We can assume that the proportion of women in the eligible pool will have increased, thus changing the probabilities of a woman succeeding an incumbent. If we are somewhat liberal and assume that the proportion of women in the eligible pool is increasing 1.5 percent per year, or 3 percent in the two years between elections, for 1986 we can expect that the female proportion of the candidates will be .1867 + .03, or .2167. Likewise, there will be a decrease in the male proportion of the new candidates, .8133 − .03, to .7833. If we assume changes in the eligible pool to be constant over the next few decades, then for any particular election the proportion of women among the new candidates will be .1867 + (.03 × e), where e is the number of elections since 1984, and the proportion of men among the new candidates will be .8133 − (.03 × e). We have provided the proportions to four decimal places for readers who wish to examine the calculations themselves and perhaps explore the effects of changed assumptions. An appendix to this chapter provides a BASIC computer program enabling this to be done.

Figure 7.2 diagrams the model just specified. There are two starting places,

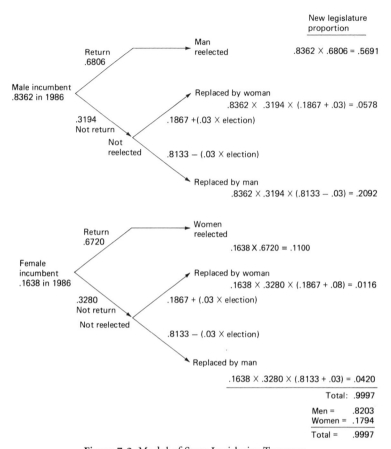

Figure 7.2 Model of State Legislative Turnover.

a male incumbent or a female incumbent. In each case there are three things that can happen. The incumbent can return, the incumbent can be replaced by a male, or the incumbent can be replaced by a female. The probabilities associated with each segment are specified. The probability associated with each particular outcome is the product of each of the segment probabilities on that path. Thus if we start with a male incumbent, the probability that he will return after the election is .8362 × .6806 = .5691. This means that 56.91 percent of the new legislature will consist of men from the old legislature. The probability that a male incumbent will be replaced by a female is .8362 × .3194 × (.1867 + .03 × 1), or .0578. Thus in the new legislature 5.78 percent of the members will be women who have replaced male incumbents. The total proportion of women will be the *sum* of the probabilities of a woman being elected, .0578 + .1100 + .0116 = .1794. Thus we expect that after the 1986 state legislative elections the proportion of women in the lower houses of the nation's state legislatures will be .1794, or 17.94 percent, an increase of about 1.5 percent over 1984. These new proportions can be used to base projections for 1988. The model can be continued indefinitely by recycling the new male and female proportions as the starting point for the next electoral cycle. Table 7.1 presents the results of the model carried well into the next millennium, assuming two-year election cycles for the state legislatures.

First notice the slow but steady growth of the female proportion of the eligible pool. By 2006 women are projected to make up the majority of nonincumbent candidates. This growth, however, is quite slow, especially as women will likely have been the majority of new people entering various relevant professions for some time before that. Notice also that we have used a rather optimistic increase of 1.5 percent per year, or 3 percent for each two-year election cycle; the actual 1980–1984 increase was only half that.

Turning to the women elected to state legislatures, we can also notice a projected increase over the years, the proportion of 1984 being doubled by 1998. However, even well into the next century, women still are not projected to hold a majority of the legislative seats even though they will have made great gains elsewhere in the economy. The reason is the drag of incumbency. By 2006 women will constitute the majority of the new candidates. However, if incumbents keep returning at the rates they have been, much less than half the legislature will be replaced, and most of those eventually elected will still be male. Eventually the proportion of women in the legislature will equal their proportion in the eligible pool of new candidates,[3] but that may take some time to achieve, as the results of this model have shown.

One more observation deserves some comment. Notice the slight difference

Table 7.1 *Projected Female Proportions among State Legislative Candidates and Lower House Members of State Legislatures*

Year	Female Proportion of Eligible Pool	Female Proportion of Lower House	
		State Legislature Actual Estimates	Female Incumbent 5% Advantage
1984	.1867	.1638	.1638
1986	.2167	.1794	.1897
1988	.2467	.1998	.2179
1990	.2767	.2231	.2475
1992	.3067	.2485	.2779
1994	.3367	.2752	.3088
1996	.3667	.3029	.3400
1998	.3967	.3313	.3712
2000	.4267	.3601	.4023
2002	.4567	.3893	.4333
2004	.4867	.4186	.4641

in the probability of a woman returning to the legislature compared to a man. *Women are less likely to return than men.* The difference is small, but it is in an unexpected direction, for the following reason. Women have recently increased their numbers in state legislatures greatly, at the expense of men. In 1971 only 4.7 percent of the legislators (upper and lower house) were women; by 1986 the figure had become 14.8 percent. Most of that increase came between 1977 and 1986. It suggests that women constitute the newer legislators, while men are typically more senior and older. We would expect, then, that retirements among men would exceed those among women for some time into the next century. Women should be more likely to return, not less likely.

The last column in Table 7.1 shows the female proportion of state legislators (lower house) that would exist if female incumbents had a 5 percent greater chance of returning than male incumbents. Notice that this increased retention rate speeds the process by which the female proportion of the legislators increases. Basically it makes the female proportion roughly what it would have been one election in the future.

There are several possible explanations for the low rate of return of female incumbents. One is that it was a simple artifact of the year examined. If we had looked at other years, perhaps something different would have been found. Another possibility is that women enter the legislature at an older age than men. That might imply that they leave earlier as well. A third possibility is that women are a small minority in what is still a male environment. Women may get fewer of the intangible benefits legislative membership brings, causing them to leave. A final explanation is that women may be seen as attractive candidates for higher office and are actively recruited and encouraged to leave the legislature to seek statewide or federal office. Parties need women candidates, and governors and presidents need able women to serve in a variety of appointed positions. One place to seek these women is in the state legislature.

U.S. House of Representatives

Two recent papers tried to develop models of the growth of women in the U.S. House of Representatives. The first developed a computer program that simulated the growth of women representatives.[4] The second developed a completely mathematical model from a set of axioms concerning the election system and some assumptions concerning incumbents and women candidates.[5]

The mathematical model assumes that a legislature is selected from single-member districts. It also assumes that the proportion of women among new candidates remains constant and that the return rate of incumbents also remains constant. If these assumptions are valid, the eventual proportion of women in the legislature will equal the proportion of women among the new candidates. The rate at which this maximum is approached depends only on the proportion of incumbents who return. The higher the proportion of incumbents returning, the longer it will take for the proportion of women in a legislature to stabilize at the proportion of women among the new candidates. There are also some interesting findings concerning bias. Bias *against* women candidates will have a small effect both on the ultimate level of women in a legislature and on the rate at which that level is reached. Bias *in favor* of women candidates will have even larger effects.

The mathematical model can be used to generate predictions as to the growth of the female membership of the House of Representatives. Figure 7.3 presents the model. It has the same form as the model already used for state legislatures (Figure 7.2). Using several congressional elections up to 1984, it was found

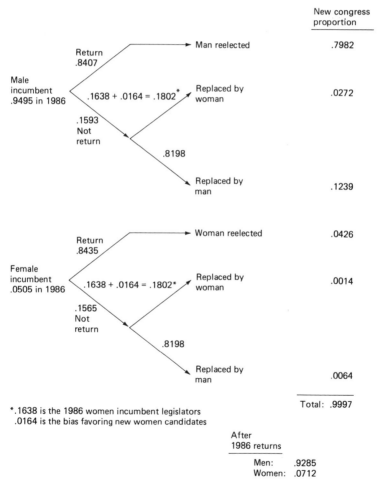

Figure 7.3 Model of Turnover in the U.S. House of Representatives.

that the proportion of male incumbents returning after the election was .8407, while the proportion for women was .8435, showing a slight bias in favor of women incumbents. Turning to new candidates, it was found that women consisted of .0813 of the total. However, the proportion of women among the *elected* new candidates was .0977. Thus among the new candidates there was also a bias in favor of women. They had a larger chance of being elected than a man.

Table 7.2 presents the results of the mathematical model projected for 20 years. Eventually, the proportion of women in the House reaches .0992, somewhat larger than the proportion of women among the new candidates (.0813). This is due to the bias in favor of both women incumbents and new women candidates. The results are not very encouraging, however, for those looking forward to greater representation of women. Women are still expected to constitute less than 10 percent of the representatives well past the millennium.

Our model assumes that the proportion of women among the new candidates will remain at the present level and that the return rate of incumbents will also remain constant. It is possible that the number of members who voluntarily retire will increase, as it did in the 1970s, but we cannot be sure. Overall, the number of incumbents who do not run again has stayed relatively stable during the 1980s.[6] But we have very good reasons for thinking that the proportion of women among the new candidates will increase.

We have already discussed the increase in the number of women in the state

Table 7.2 Projected Female Proportions among Members of the U.S. House of Representatives, 1984-2004

	Female Proportion of U.S. House of Representatives		
		Dynamic Model	Woman Incumbent 5% Advantage
Year	Mathematical Model[a]	Actual Estimates[b]	
1984	.0505	.0505	.0505
1986	.0582	.0712	.0797
1988	.0646	.0913	.1093
1990	.0700	.1114	.1396
1992	.0746	.1320	.1708
1994	.0785	.1534	.2027
1996	.0817	.1758	.2352
1998	.0845	.1990	.2681
2000	.0868	.2230	.3013
2002	.0887	.2479	.3346
2004	.0904	.2734	.3679

[a]The percent of women candidates remains fixed at 1984 levels.

[b]The percent of women candidates equals the levels of predicted membership in state legislatures (Table 7.1, col. 3).

legislatures. We also know that state legislators serve as a major part of the eligible pool of new candidates for the U.S. Congress,[7] although women are somewhat less likely than men to come from the state legislatures.[8] From the analysis of state legislators it would be reasonable to project that the eligible pool of women candidates for the House will increase. We then can develop an alternative model for the House that has the proportion of women among state legislators (lower house) as an estimate of the proportion of women among new congressional candidates. The other aspects of the model presented in Figure 7.3 will remain the same. The only change will be the increasing proportion of women among the new candidates for each election to equal the proportion of women serving in the lower house of the state legislatures. This will be the proportion previously presented in the third column of Table 7.1. The results of this model for the House of Representatives are presented in Table 7.2. As can be seen, under these assumptions, the proportion of women will be expected to rise more rapidly, and to a higher level. By the year 2004, for example, the female proportion of the House of Representatives is expected to be .2734 rather than the .0904 projected for the mathematical model. But still, this is a very small proportion, especially given that the female proportion among state legislators will have reached .41 by this time and that women will be close to a majority of the eligibility pool for the legislature.

The obvious reason for the very slow response of the House of Representatives to changes in the eligible pool of candidates is the very large incumbency factor. The House of Representatives turns itself over very slowly. Most incumbents run again, and most of them win. This means that significant changes in membership will be long delayed.

We have used a model of the electoral system to project a number of trends 20 years into the future. The model cycles the parameters supplied (see the appendix to this chapter for the BASIC computer program used) and calculates predicted proportions of women in the House of Representatives for various years. The parameters were calculated from various recent elections. One parameter is the proportion of male incumbents returning, calculated to be .8407 for the House. Another is the difference between the return rate for women and men, calculated to be +.0028.

The same model can be used to examine the consequences of various changes in the situation of male and female candidates. For example, if the male incumbent return rate were reduced by .05 to .7907, and women incumbents were .05 more likely to remain in the House, their return rate would become .8407. To this we might add a similar advantage for women incumbents in the state legislatures. Such changes might result from a combination of policies designed to make legislative life more attractive for women and, further, might reflect the aging nature of the male incumbents compared to younger and newer women incumbents.

The last column in Table 7.2 presents the new projections based on these changed assumptions. The predicted results indicate a dramatic increase in the proportion of women elected to the House of Representatives over what can be expected from the return rates estimated from recent elections. Nevertheless, even these changes, optimistic as they are, demonstrate the enormous advantage of incumbency. Even greatly advantaged women will still constitute only a little over a third of the representatives 20 years from now. There will be change, and if present trends continue, women will eventually form the majority in the House of Representatives. But that time is still a very long way off.

Curiously, because of limitations on terms and other factors reducing the incumbency factor, women may make faster gains as governors and senators than in the legislatures or Congress.

This model of the electoral process shows that the number of women in office, now and in the future, is related to the operation of the system itself. Although more women are now entering the occupations that form the eligible pools, the increase in the number of women holding office will be slowed by the drag of incumbency.

Notes

1. Barbara Curran, *Lawyer Statistical Report* (Chicago: American Bar Foundation, 1985).
2. National Women's Political Caucus, *National Directory of Women Elected Officials, 1981, 1983,* and *1985* (Washington, D.C., 1981, 1983, 1985); Council of State Governments, *State Elective Officials and the Legislatures, 1981–1982* and *1983–1984* Lexington, Ky., 1981, 1983).
3. R. Darcy and James Choike, "A Formal Analysis of Legislative Turnover: Women Candidates and Legislative Representation," *American Journal of Political Science* 30 (February 1986): 237–255.
4. Kristi Andersen and Stuart Thorson, "Some Structural Barriers to the Election of Women to Congress: A Simulation," *Western Political Quarterly* 37 (March 1984): 143–156.
5. Darcy and Choike, "Legislative Turnover."
6. John R. Hibbing, *Choosing to Leave: Voluntary Retirement from the U.S. House of Representatives* (Washington, D.C.: University Press of America, 1982).
7. Gary G. Jacobson and Samuel Kernell, *Strategy and Choice in Congressional Elections* (New Haven, Conn.: Yale University Press, 1981).
8. Diane Sainsbury, "Women's Routes to National Legislatures: A Comparison of Eligibility and Nomination in the United States, Britain, and Sweden," paper presented at the ECPR Workshop on Candidate Selection in Comparative Perspective, Barcelona, March 1985.

APPENDIX

BASIC Computer Program to Project Female Legislative and Congressional Representation

The following program is written in the BASIC language. This language can be used by nearly all home computers and many university and college computers. Several steps in the program may seem a bit obscure, but if the program is entered into a computer as written, it should work.

This is the program we used for the model discussed in this chapter. The model could be used to explore a great many situations; we managed to discuss only a few. You may wish to use it to test the consequences of other assumptions or conditions—for example, changes in the bias affecting female candidates, or parameters from a particular state legislature.

```
10 REM THIS PROGRAM MODELS THE RELATIONSHIP OVER TIME BETWEEN CHANGING
20 REM PROPORTIONS OF WOMEN IN THE SOCIETY'S ELIGIBLE POOL, THE ELECTION
30 REM OF WOMEN TO STATE LEGISLATURES AND THE ELECTION OF WOMEN TO THE
40 REM U.S. HOUSE OF REPRESENTATIVES. THE PROGRAM PROMPTS THE USER FOR
50 REM A SERIES OF PARAMETERS WHICH ARE DEFINED AS FOLLOWS:
60 REM    A: THE GROWTH IN THE FEMALE PROPORTION OF THE ELIGIBLE POOL;
70 REM       HERE THIS IS THE INCREASE IN THE FEMALE PROPORTION AMONG
80 REM       LAWYERS OVER A TWO YEAR ELECTION CYCLE, .03.
90 REM    S: THE INITIAL PROPORTION OF MEN IN THE STATE LEGISLATURES;
100 REM      HERE THIS IS THE 1984 FIGURE, .8362.
110 REM   R: THE RETURN RATE OF MALE LEGISLATIVE INCUMBENTS. HERE THIS
120 REM      HAS BEEN ESTIMATED TO BE .6806.
130 REM   X: THE BIAS FAVORING FEMALE LEGISLATIVE INCUMBENTS COMPARED
140 REM      WITH MALE LEGISLATIVE INCUMBENTS, THIS IS ESTIMATED
150 REM      THE FEMALE INCUMBENT RETURN RATE LESS THE MALE INCUMBENT
160 REM      RETURN RATE: .6720 − .6806 = − .0086.
170 REM   W: THE INITIAL PROPORTIONS OF WOMEN AMONG NEW LEGISLATIVE
180 REM      CANDIDATES. HERE THIS IS ESTIMATED FOR 1984 TO BE .1867.
190 REM   Y: THE BIAS FAVORING NEW WOMEN LEGISLATIVE CANDIDATES COMPARED
200 REM      WITH NEW MEN CANDIDATES. THIS IS ESTIMATED TO BE THE
210 REM      DIFFERENCE BETWEEN THE PROPORTION OF WOMEN AMONG LEGISLATIVE
220 REM      CANDIDATES AND THE PROPORTION OF WOMEN AMONG THE NEW
230 REM      CANDIDATES ACTUALLY ELECTED. HERE THIS IS ASSUMED TO BE
240 REM      ZERO.
250 REM   T: THE INITIAL PROPORTION OF MEN IN THE U.S. HOUSE OF
260 REM      REPRESENTATIVES, FOR 1984 THIS IS .9495.
270 REM   I: THE CHANCES OF A MALE INCUMBENT RETURNING TO THE HOUSE OF
```

```
280 REM      REPRESENTATIVES. HERE THIS IS ESTIMATED TO BE .8407.
290 REM   J: THE BIAS IN FAVOR OF A FEMALE INCUMBENT RETURNING TO THE
300 REM      U.S. HOUSE OF REPRESENTATIVES COMPARED WITH MEN INCUMBENTS.
310 REM      HERE THIS IS .8435 − .8407 = +.0028.
320 REM   K: THE BIAS IN FAVOR OF NEW WOMEN HOUSE CANDIDATES COMPARED
330 REM      TO NEW MEN CANDIDATES. HERE THIS IS THE PROPORTION OF NEW
340 REM      CANDIDATES ELECTED WHO ARE WOMEN LESS THE PROPORTION OF
350 REM      NEW CANDIDATES THAT ARE WOMEN. HERE THIS IS
360 REM      .0977 − .0813 = +.0164.
370 PRINT 'INPUT THE TWO YEAR GROWTH OF WOMEN IN THE ELIGIBLE POOL'
380 INPUT A
390 PRINT 'INPUT THE EXISTING PROPORTION OF MEN IN THE LEGISLATURE'
400 INPUT S(1,1)
410 PRINT 'INPUT THE CHANCES OF A MAN LEGISLATOR BEING ELECTED'
420 INPUT R
430 PRINT 'INPUT THE BIAS IN REELECTION FOR WOMEN INCUMBENTS'
440 INPUT X
450 PRINT 'INPUT THE PROPORTION OF NEW WOMEN LEGISLATIVE CANDIDATES'
460 INPUT W
470 PRINT 'INPUT THE ELECTION BIAS FOR NEW WOMEN LEGISLATIVE CANDIDATES'
480 INPUT Y
490 PRINT 'INPUT THE INITIAL PROPORTION OF MEN IN THE U.S. CONGRESS'
500 INPUT T(1,1)
510 PRINT 'INPUT THE REELECTION CHANCES OF A MAN IN THE U.S. CONGRESS'
520 INPUT I
530 PRINT 'INPUT THE BIAS IN THE ELECTION OF A WOMAN IN CONGRESS'
540 INPUT J
550 PRINT 'INPUT THE BIAS IN THE ELECTION OF A NEW WOMAN TO CONGRESS'
560 INPUT K
570 S(1,2)=1−S(1,1)
580 T(1,2)=1−T(1,1)
590 FOR E=1 TO 11 STEP 1
600 REM BEGIN PRINTING RESULTS
605 PRINT 'FEMALE PROPORTION'
608 PRINT 'ELECTION', 'POOL', 'LEGISLATURE', 'CONGRESS'
610 PRINT E,W,S(1,2),T(1,2)
620 REM RESULTS OF CONGRESSIONAL ELECTION
630 REM TRANSITION MATRIX
640 Q(1,1)=I+(1−I)*(S(1,1)−K)
650 Q(2,1)=(1−I−J)*(S(1,1)−K)
660 Q(1,2)=1−Q(1,1)
670 Q(2,2)=1−Q(2,1)
680 REM NEW MALE AND FEMALE PROPORTIONS
690 T(1,1)=T(1,1)*Q(1,1)+(T(1,2)*Q(2,1))
700 T(1,2)=1−T(1,1)
710 REM GROWTH OF ELIGIBLE POOL TO A MAXIMUM OF 50% WOMEN
720 IF W<.53 THEN W=W+A
730 REM STATE LEGISLATIVE RESULTS
740 TRANSITION MATRIX
750 P(1,1)=R+((1−R)*(1−W−Y))
760 P(2,1)=(1−R−X)*(1−W−Y)
```

```
770 REM NEW MALE AND FEMALE LEGISLATIVE PROPORTIONS
780 S(1,1)=(S(1,1)*P(1,1))+(S(1,2)*P(2,1))
790 S(1,2)=1-S(1,1)
800 NEXT E
810 END
```

PART IV

Conclusions: The Tasks Ahead

We began this book with a puzzle and a problem. The puzzle is an intellectual one. Its solution is the understanding of why there is a paucity of women elected to public office. The problem is practical. It concerns the need of our political system for the fairer representation of women and the additional talent that will bring. The solution here will be in the political arena. The puzzle and the problem are related in that once we come to understand how our political system has managed to bypass women, we can use that knowledge as the basis for a political agenda directed at change.

In the conclusions we will draw on the research presented in Chapters 1 through 7 to review the answers to our questions and to make some recommendations both for future research and for ways to bring more women into political life.

8

Opening Up Political Life to Women

By noting that "where power is, women are not," Elizabeth Vallance has aptly summed up the traditional fate of women in American politics.[1] Yet, as we have seen throughout this book, the role of women in American politics is changing; as barriers drop, women are running for office in record numbers. Some of them are winning, assuming a prominent role in the political life of their city, state, and nation.

But progress has been slow. The increase of women has not been constant at all levels; at the national level it has been minute. The increase in the number of winning women candidates has not really kept pace with the increased number of candidates. We have documented both the progress women have made and some of the impediments that remain for them. In this chapter we will briefly summarize some of the major findings of the book and then turn to a consideration of what this bodes for American politics. Finally, we offer some recommendations for a political agenda directed at bringing more women into political life.

In seeking to explain why there are so few women in politics, analysts have turned to two kinds of explanations. One is that women cannot win when they run; the other is that not enough women run. Let us examine each of these two reasons in turn.

Can Women Win When They Run?

Voters

There is a popular belief that women are discriminated against by many voters, that a woman candidate automatically loses a lot of votes merely because of her sex. In fact, public opinion polls indicate that less than 20 percent of the public says they will not vote for a woman for president; this is a substantial number, but fewer than admitted they would not vote for a Catholic in 1960. The proportion agreeing they would not vote for a woman for lesser office, including the House of Representatives, is much lower: only around 10 to 11 percent.

Despite this admission of prejudice, as we have shown in Chapters 3 and 4, it is difficult to detect any penalty levied against women candidates. Once party and incumbency are taken into account, women candidates do as well as men in both primary and general elections. Whereas in the 1950s and 1960s women were discriminated against at the polls, at least in some places, this has become largely a historical, rather than a contemporary, problem.

Of course, some voters vote against women because of prejudice against them. Older, conservative voters who hold traditional religious beliefs are somewhat more likely to be against women taking a role in politics. Given the overall success of women who run, it appears that these antiwomen voters are equaled by those who go out of their way to cast a vote for a woman. It is also likely that some prejudice expressed to a pollster may not be carried out in actual voting when faced with the choice of a woman of one's own party or a man of the opposition party.

Party Leaders

Another popular explanation for the lack of women's success is that party leaders discriminate against them. Traditionally, party leaders who had some influence on party slating could deny women a place on the slate. In situations where party leaders did not have this power (as where party nominations were decided by primaries), party leaders could have refused to encourage women candidates to run or actively discouraged them. There is no question that there were such actions in the past. There is little question that there will be such actions in the future as well. But our systematic evidence from before the 1970s is scanty, and there are many stories of party leaders working against the aspirations of male candidates as well. Our more recent systematic evidence does not find that party leaders discriminate against women candidates. Women do not appear to be running disproportionately for unwinnable seats. And women are just as likely as men, and in some cases more likely, to say that party leaders encouraged their candidacy.[2]

Incumbency

A major reason for the slow entrance of women into political office, particularly at the national level, is the power of incumbency. As we saw in Chapter 7, incumbents have a tremendous advantage in House elections. About 90 percent of all House members who run are reelected, and almost the same is true in state legislatures. This advantage, combined with the fact that only a small minority of members voluntarily give up their seats in any one election, means that newcomers in legislative bodies are rare. This is particularly true for the House of Representatives, where the number of open seats for any election is only about 10 percent of the total.

The power of incumbency and turnover is an excellent explanation for two puzzling phenomena. First, it helps explain why women are entering state legislatures faster than the House of Representatives. While both bodies have extremely high rates of incumbency election success, in the state legislatures voluntary turnover is much higher. State legislators are much more likely than members of the House to decide to return to private business or run for higher office. Thus women can run for more open state legislative seats and win a fair share of them. The power of incumbency also explains why, at the national level, so many fewer women are winning elections than are running. Most women candidates for the House of Representatives (like most nonincumbent male candidates) are running against incumbents, not for open seats. Thus their chances of electoral victory are very low.

Overall, then, it appears that while voter discrimination now plays at best a small part in keeping women out of office, the impact of incumbency and low turnover for many offices is a major explanation. This incumbency factor is in turn a consequence of changes in the structure of American politics begun early in this century.[3] As more women run, more will benefit from incumbency. Women incumbents have just about the same advantage as male incumbents.

Why Don't More Women Run?

If every woman who ran won, we would still not have proportional representation for women. Women still represent only a small proportion of the new political candidates. Thus we must turn to a consideration of why more women do not run for office.

Trying to figure out who constitutes a pool of potential candidates and then learning the members' reasons for running or not are nearly impossible tasks. So our conclusions about why women do not run must be based more on inference and less on direct evidence than our conclusions about what happens to women when they do run.

Fear of Losing

One explanation for the small number of women candidates is that women who are potential candidates believe that voters and party elites will not support them because they are women. This fear may have had some basis as recently as 20 years ago, but it is certainly no longer the case. Nonetheless, if it is believed, some women candidates will be discouraged.

Women candidates may also believe that should they become candidates, they will encounter opposition from party leaders, political activists, and fundraisers simply because they are women. Again, this fear may be rooted in historical fact. As we have indicated, it has not been too many years since party leaders were quite blatant about admitting that they did not want a woman on their tickets. Further, many women candidates, even now, report difficulty with fund-raising.

Yet again, these beliefs have been disproved in systematic investigations of recent campaigns. As we have shown at both the congressional and state legislative levels, women candidates do just as well as men candidates in raising funds. Investigations of patterns of candidacies for men and women have illustrated that women are not more likely to be found running for hopeless seats. These findings indicate a relative equity between male and female candidates. Our research shows that women candidates will not have to carry an extra burden because they are women. We hope these findings will make it easier for more women to decide to become political candidates.

Patterns of Women's Socialization

Some people have suggested that rather than blaming the voters or party leaders for the reluctance of women to become political candidates, it is the victims themselves who are to blame. This very global explanation has at least three components. One is that women were socialized to believe that politics is a man's game and hence to stay away from it. In recent U.S. history, this explanation falls short. Women have participated at the grass-roots level as much as men, have been the backbone of many political campaigns, and have taken part in all sorts of political activities at the same rates as men. However, women, as well as men, have only recently come to believe that women can and should play a leadership role in political life. In some surveys, for example, the proportion of people saying that men are better suited for politics than women fell from 47 percent to 36 percent between 1974 and 1983.

Occupational Segregation

Women have traditionally been directed into only limited occupational channels. As we discussed in Chapter 5, the very occupations that lead to politics— law and business—are the ones that traditionally contained few women. The absence of women from these stepping-stones to political office does explain a good portion of women's underrepresentation in public office.

Very much related to this is that women in our society are traditionally given primary child-care responsibility. The impact of that role on political office-holding is probably great, and we have a good deal of indirect evidence for that. We know that women are much more likely to be elected to local offices, where time away from home is more limited than at the state and national levels. We know that women tend to defer political careers until children are in school. We know that the distance from the statehouse is related to the proportion of women elected as state representatives. But what we do not know is how many women have completely dropped aspirations for a political career in favor of a homemaker role.

However, we must not assume that the stepping-stones into politics are set in concrete, as it were. There is no necessity that the stepping-stones used by men must also be used by women. Research is beginning to show that women who are elected to state legislatures and to the House of Representatives, for example, do have somewhat different backgrounds from those of their male colleagues. Though many women in these bodies are lawyers and business executives, many others come to the legislature from more traditional women's roles, including homemaking. More research is needed on how women can enter political life using their existing backgrounds and experiences.

Impact of the Electoral System on Women

The electoral system is a factor related to both the absence of women running for office and their electoral fate when they do run. We have seen in Chapter 6 that women are more likely to be elected in multimember districts than in single-member systems. The difference is fairly great when one compares nations with multimember proportional election systems with nations such as the United States with a predominantly single-member district system. Even in the United States, however, where multimember plurality systems are used, women do somewhat better than in the single-member plurality systems. Though the strength of the relationship varies, this pattern obtains at both the state and local levels. It appears that our system of single-member districts leads to a focus on finding the ''best man for the job'' rather than forcing us to seek ways to represent community diversity.

This pattern is particularly interesting and somewhat disturbing because it is counter to the pattern for geographically segregated racial and ethnic minorities. In areas where they form a significant minority, minority males benefit from single-member districts, especially at the local level. Finding an electoral system that is politically acceptable while being fair both to women generally and to minority men may prove to be a challenge, but it is a challenge our political system will have to meet.

Does Having a Woman in Office Make a Difference?

In Chapter 1 we discussed some reasons for needing women in office. Having a more proportional representation of important societal groups such as women accords government greater legitimacy, allows us to fulfill more closely the requirements of the democratic form of government we claim to prize, provides a previously excluded group with an indication that its interests are now likely to be more thoroughly considered, and makes better use of the talents available in society. These assessments were made abstractly. We might now address whether increased representation of women has actually changed the nature and outcomes of policymaking in government.

To answer that question, several analysts have compared the attitudes and behavior of women and men policymakers at various levels of government. Their findings have been reasonably, though not completely, consistent.

Women and men do behave slightly differently in office. In the U.S. House of Representatives, for example, women vote in a more liberal direction, even after party affiliation has been taken into account.[4] This gap is particularly apparent among southern Democrats and Republicans and is hardly visible among northern Democrats. Women members of the House were also more likely to support feminist concerns than were their male counterparts.[5] In state legislatures, women supported the Equal Rights Amendment more than did male legislators.[6] Furthermore, in these same legislatures, women provided important cues in determining how male legislators would vote on the ERA issue.[7]

At the local level, in surveys among city councillors, women have been shown to be the most egalitarian in their attitude toward male and female roles,[8] more likely to declare themselves "liberal,"[9] and more likely to support city planning measures.[10] Election of women mayors encourages egalitarianism in city employment as well.[11] However, in terms of placing issues in priority order, male and female council members were found not to differ very much.[12]

Women judges have been found to be similar to male judges in their overall decision making[13] but to behave in a more egalitarian way toward women defendants[14] and to have more egalitarian sex-role attitudes.[15]

Overall, then, it appears that women in public office are more liberal. They are also more sensitive to women's rights issues. The differences are not very large in most instances, but they are consistent over time and from place to place.

There is, however, no assurance that these differences will persist as more women enter the political elite. For example, the voting gap between men and women in the U.S. House of Representatives decreased steadily between 1972 and 1982.[16] This decrease came primarily because women members became less liberal, relative to men, over time. Even though they were still more liberal in their voting than men, the difference diminished. It could be projected that this difference will disappear entirely in a few more years. It is possible that as women begin routinely entering public office, they will behave in less divergent ways. As more opportunities arise for women to move up in the political world, pressures for conformity on women may also increase. But a decrease in male-female differences can also be produced by women exercising stronger influence on the political agenda and the thinking of male colleagues. Thus we might see women moving in a more conservative direction and men moving in a more liberal one.

Strategies for Change

Where does this leave us in terms of strategies for bringing about increased equality for women? Radical and Marxist feminists have argued that extreme changes in society must occur before women can achieve equality with men. They argue that our society is based on the subjugation of women. Only a radical restructuring of society itself will lead to political possibilities for women.[17] Modest reform will not be successful because it does not challenge the basic male dominance built into the social system. Thus if we are to have real change, we must complete a revolutionary reorganization in our economic, social, and political structures. The underlying premise is that little can be accomplished by gradual change within the existing social system.

Curiously, this argument also played a role in the suffrage movement almost a century ago. In Europe, socialists who were expected to support female suffrage argued that the real problem was capitalism. In their view the struggle for women's rights, futile as long as the capitalist system provided the basis for social organization, would misdirect political energy away from the struggle against the real oppressor, the capitalist system.[18] Ending capitalism, so the argument ran, was the only way to achieve equality for women.

Our analysis finds the radical and Marxist feminist argument inadequate as it pertains to women's representation. We found no evidence of a "male conspiracy," overt or covert. While the problems women face in getting elected reflect to some extent their position in the larger social world, most of the problems women encounter are within the political and electoral system. Further, these problems are not specific to women. The problem of incumbency, for example, slows all change, not just change relating to female representation. Further, though these factors only delay the accession of women to political roles, they have not stopped it. An examination of election systems, both here and in Europe, indicates that the democratic arrangements of the present social system are flexible enough to accommodate change favorable to women.

One further argument against the radical or Marxist feminist argument is that the political roles of women have not been enhanced in societies that have attempted radical social reordering. China and the Soviet Union, for example, remain overwhelmingly male in their most visible and real positions of political power.

Liberal feminists believe that equality for women can come about through incremental change, working within the broad framework of our political and social institutions. They believe that by making relatively modest changes in these political and social institutions, women can gain greater political power within the existing structure.

The situation at this point indicates both the strength and weakness of the liberal feminists' position. They are right in that changes are occurring in the direction of greater equality for women. Many despair at the slow rate of change. But to step back and compare the situation of women as recently as 1970 with that of women today is to see that in most areas of society women are closer to equal; they are more likely to be found in statehouses, local councils, and on judges' benches; they are entering former male bastions such as the legal and medical professions and corporate headquarters in ever greater numbers; they have achieved equality in areas as diverse as obtaining financial credit and college admissions; and they have far greater equality than before in activities such as athletics and business.

Yet incremental change is by definition slow, and the hopes of liberal feminists have yet to be realized. Despite the dramatic gains of women since the 1960s, much remains to be done. We can observe existing inequality in many places in society. In politics we observe it most acutely in the absence of women from the highest offices and their near absence from both houses of Congress. In economic life we observe it clearly in the continuing occupational segregation of women to the pink ghettos of clerical work, retail clerking, and other low-paying jobs with little opportunity for advancement. We also find it in the wage patterns that reward workers in traditional male occupations much more highly than those in traditional female ones and hence consign 30 percent of all female-headed households to poverty. In the social arena we observe it in emerging patterns of divorce settlements that condemn ever higher proportions of newly divorced women and their children to poverty.

The entrance of more women into public office promises to change these conditions but also promises that change will be slow. The alternative, however, offered by the more radical feminists, promises a quicker solution but one that has little chance of being delivered. Neither women nor men have shown much interest in a radical overhaul of our institutions. Support for greater women's equality exists among the public, but support does not exist for erasing the basic institutions of our society, whether it be the family or our system of indirect democracy. Indeed, the difficulty of making relatively minor changes in laws and procedures involving a shift in sex roles is much greater than attempts to change laws that try to achieve equality within existing roles. Such was the conclusion of a recent study of federal women's rights legislation.[19]

We can expect that the numbers of women officeholders will continue to increase. This expectation is based on the changing economic and social roles of women. Public opinion has undergone a significant change in the direction of supporting women's ambitions outside the home. Party leaders and fundraisers have become more egalitarian, as we have seen. Women comprise significant proportions of the law and other professions and are graduating from college at increasing rates, thus becoming a larger part of the eligible pool of candidates. More and more women are being elected to office at lower levels, thus providing a base for attempts at higher office. All of this certainly leads us to expect more women candidates, and more women elected, at all levels of government.

But there are other things that can be done to achieve greater representation for women. Based on our findings, we can suggest several things that might speed the pace of incremental change. We can also suggest that this is an area in which fruitful research has only just begun.

Political Parties and Women Candidates

The Republican and Democratic parties, at both the national and state levels, are aware of the need to bring more women candidates forward. We certainly can credit party leadership with some enlightened desire for change, but it is also true that both parties recognize potential advantages from increases in their pools of candidates, and the disadvantages of being perceived as the party *not* concerned with bringing women into the political mainstream.

The two parties have for some time opened up their organizations to women, and women are represented in leadership positions from the national level to the county and precinct levels. In some nations, such as Sweden,[20] where the parties draw candidates from their own organizations, such a program would result in more women candidates. But in the United States the movement from the party organization to electoral office is less regular, and enhanced party roles have not translated directly into increased candidacies for women.

Recently, prompted perhaps by the activities of groups such as the National Women's Political Caucus, the parties have adopted two additional strategies for bringing forward more women candidates. Even though these two strategies are based on outmoded premises as to why so few women have been elected, they may still have some positive payoffs.

First, the two parties have developed specific fund-raising efforts designed to aid women candidates, based on the assumption that women candidates are discouraged by lack of financing or by unique problems in raising funds. The Republicans have the GOP Women's Political Action League (GOPAL), the Democrats, the Eleanor Roosevelt Fund. Each is designed to raise money for women candidates at all levels. These complement a number of nonparty PACs also focusing on raising money for women candidates.[21] Certainly additional funding will make any candidate stronger. But women are not disadvantaged in this area, either at the level of the state legislatures or the House of Representatives.

Party fund-raising specifically for women candidates is relatively new. Whether or not it makes a difference still needs to be researched. We can speculate, however, that unless fund-raising for women generates the massive amounts necessary to make challengers competitive with incumbents, the results, in terms of electing more women, will be marginal. What evidence there is indicates that these PACs are only raising a minuscule portion of the total political money.[22] Nevertheless, some PACs, such as the Women's Political Committee in Los Angeles, have given up to $16,000 to a single woman candidate.[23]

The female PAC with the most funds is controlled by the National Organization of Women (NOW). Like many feminist organizations, NOW pursues several related goals that can sometimes conflict. One goal is to build the organization and its membership.[24] Another goal is to elect women to public office. A third is to advance the feminist agenda. Organization building requires militancy; electing women requires moderation.[25] Further, the goal of electing women, even women who are strong feminists, can conflict with advancing the feminist agenda itself. NOW has had that problem in New Jersey:

For many groups, particularly for the national organizations, a special problem is created by races between men who are seen as friends of progressive causes and acceptable women who oppose them. Recent examples include Assemblywoman Marie Muhler's 1980 and 1982 races against Congressman James Howard in New Jersey. The recent race for New Jersey's open Senate seat provided a slightly different case, with Congresswoman Millicent Fenwick facing political newcomer Frank Lautenberg, who adopted pro-feminist positions and rhetoric, although he had no political track record. In these cases, the question arises of whether the goal of electing more women overrides the goal of electing the candidate seen as most supportive of feminist policies.

The Women's Campaign Fund, after long and difficult deliberation, concluded that its limited resources could be used most effectively by staying out of such races in *general* elections. However, they will support a woman in a primary where she is vying for the opportunity to face a "good" man, on the theory that the general election will then feature two strong candidates and a positive outcome will be ensured. Thus, WCF contributed to Marie Muhler in her 1982 primary race, but did not support her in the general election.

NOW has taken a very different position, choosing to support the candidate they perceive as *most* feminist. In 1982, they also took note of party affiliation, preferring in general a worthy Democrat over a comparable Republican because of the importance of committee chairmanships distributed to the members of the majority party in each house. Thus, NOW supported both Howard and Lautenberg over their Republican female opponents.[26]

The unwillingness of women's campaign fund managers to support women candidates who do not publicly support the more controversial women's issues such as gay rights, abortion, and ERA is also a problem. In some states such positions could consign an otherwise staunch woman supporter of women's issues to defeat. Making such positions a prerequisite for funding can be self-defeating. As Jane Hickie, a Texas fund-raiser, put it: "What kind of friend is it who wants to *print* in Dallas County, Texas, 'Yes, indeed I will hire a qualified gay or lesbian on my staff'? They're supposed to be on *our* side."[27]

A second strategy is premised on the idea that women, as political outsiders, do not really know what campaigning involves, or need special encouragement to come forward as candidates. To address this, parties sponsor special programs or workshops on political campaigning targeted specifically at women with the potential to run for office. Scholarships and other inducements are available to encourage women to attend. Again, this is a relatively new device and has received little scholarly assessment of its usefulness in increasing the number of women candidates. Although we have found that women have no special impediments as campaigners, these workshops may serve to develop enthusiasm and increase women's awareness that their candidacies will be welcomed and successful. They certainly can be useful in dispelling lingering myths concerning barriers women face in electoral politics.

The current activities of the two political parties are certainly a good beginning, but a lot more remains for them to do. For one thing, fund-raising and seminars do not address the *causes* of low female representation, which lie in the functioning of the electoral system itself. The political parties need to take steps to deal with problems caused by electoral arrangements.

Recommendations for Change

1. People who are interested in increasing the number of women in office should be as inclusive as possible in the kind of women candidates they encourage to run and support. There should be no litmus tests beyond, perhaps, a general acceptance of equality for women. The efforts of the two parties, which provide only a partisan test, may be more useful in increasing the numbers of women officeholders than some issue-oriented women's groups, which require endorsed candidates to adhere to certain, often divisive, issue positions.[28]

2. Whether they be party leaders, fund-raisers, activists, or members of women's groups, people who play a role in encouraging women candidates should direct their attention particularly to encouraging women to run for open seats. Of course, in Congress there are generally few open seats; there, in order to increase their rate of entry, women must defeat some incumbents. Nevertheless, the potential for winning should be a factor considered in allocating scarce time and resources to political campaigns. Incumbency is a large part of that factor.

3. Changes from multimember to single-member districts at the state level, or any other electoral changes, need to be carefully considered for their impact on women as well as on minority males. At the local level, changes to single-member districts can greatly enhance the proportionality of black male representation, and are often made for precisely that reason. Modest differences between women's representation in at-large and single-member districts at the local level do not outweigh the necessity for implementing systems that bring about dramatic increases in equity of minority representation. But at the state legislative level, changes to single-member districts are usually done for other reasons than equity of minority representation, and to our knowledge they have not brought about greater equality in that respect. The reason for the difference is the much smaller proportion of the black population statewide compared to the large urban areas.

Thus the evidence needs to be carefully considered when proposals for changes in election arrangements are made. To what extent is the change likely to enhance equitability of different groups in the state? People interested in increasing the representation of women should be prepared to add their evidence to that of other groups on this matter.

4. Political party leaders and activists need to be continually mindful of recruiting women for political office. A political affirmative action program is in order. Strengthening the role of party organizations might help in this regard; conventions, for example, can balance tickets in a way that primaries cannot.

In Scandinavia, India, Taiwan, France, and England political parties have made commitments to nominating more women candidates. That can be done here as well. In some states political parties endorse candidates before primaries. These endorsed candidates receive favored ballot positions or other advantages should they be challenged in a party primary. Political parties in these states can set specific goals for the nomination of women. It is not unreasonable, for example, to set the goal that not more than 60 percent of endorsed candidates come from one sex. That is already being done in European political parties. The exact form these goals take would have to vary with the particular circumstances of the party. If the representation of women is to increase substantially in the near future, the political parties are going to have to shoulder more responsibility.

Where political parties do not endorse candidates prior to primaries, people seeking to increase women's representation should work to bring the party back into the nomination process as a preliminary step in having the party play a more active role in recruiting and nominating women candidates.

5. Any strategies that reduce the power of incumbents to gain reelection will benefit women, who make up a larger portion of challengers than of incumbents. People interested in increasing the numbers of women, then, should be particularly aware of proposed changes in campaign financing and disclosure laws as well as the electoral advantages that incumbents vote themselves. Placing limits on PACs and campaign financing generally needs to be examined in light of incumbency effects.

Incumbents are aided in other ways as well. Typically, legislative districts are gerrymandered to protect incumbents, often incumbents of both parties. To the extent that gerrymandering protects incumbents, any more neutral districting, such as by court order, will probably give women, as predominantly nonincumbents, a better break.

6. Increasing the likelihood of women incumbents returning will also help. In Chapter 7 we showed that women state legislators were slightly less likely to return than men. In Congress the difference was reversed but also small. Yet women generally have less seniority than men (as a group) and should be more likely to return. Why women do not stay in office needs to be examined, and, if necessary, strategies must be devised to keep them in once elected.

7. Strategies are needed to identify, recruit, and elect women with more traditional backgrounds. Though things are changing, the present eligible pools are predominantly male and will remain so for some time to come. Women with backgrounds different from those of males in public office can get elected. Political parties and others interested in recruiting substantially more women candidates need to learn more ways to use the many able women presently not considered part of candidate eligible pools.

Of course, there are other changes that could be made that would likely increase the proportion of women officeholders: In particular, increasing the size of the legislature and limiting the number of terms served in order to increase turnover, would clearly be to the advantage of women in the short and medium run. Increasing the size of the legislature would, on a one-shot basis, dramatically reduce the proportion of the candidates who are incumbents, increase the number of open seats, and result in more women being elected. Limitations on legislative terms, similar to those imposed on the president and many state governors, would also increase legislative turnover and the probability that women would be elected. Likewise, abandonment of a system of single-member districts in favor of some form of proportional representation, such as a single transferable vote, should improve women's representation.

We have argued that the representation of women is an important challenge to our political system and to the scholars who seek to understand our political life. Further, we have argued that the problem of the representation of women lies not in women themselves nor in hostility toward women on the part of society and its leaders. Instead we argue that the problem and the solution lie in the working of the political system. There is the challenge. For scholars the task is to learn much more about how our political system can be made more accessible. For those involved in politics, the task is to work to bring about the changes that will open and enrich our political life.

Notes

1. Elizabeth Vallance, "Where the Power Is, Women Are Not," *Parliamentary Affairs* 35 (Spring 1982): 218–219.
2. Sophonisba P. Breckenridge cites examples of both party support for women candidates and party opposition to women candidates from the early 1920s in *Women in the Twentieth Century* (New York: McGraw-Hill, 1933), 327–332.
3. See David R. Mayhew, *Congress: The Electoral Connection* (New Haven, Conn.: Yale University Press, 1974); Morris P. Fiorina, *Congress: The Keystone of the Washington Establishment* (New Haven, Conn.: Yale University Press, 1977).
4. Shelah Gilbert Leader, "The Policy Impact of Elected Women Officials," in Louis Maisel and Joseph Cooper, eds., *The Impact of the Electoral Process* (Beverly Hills, Calif.: Sage, 1977); Susan Welch, "Are Women More Liberal than Men in the U.S. Congress?" *Legislative Studies Quarterly* 10 (February 1985): 125–134.
5. Leader, "Policy Impact."
6. David B. Hill, "Women State Legislators and Party Voting on the ERA," *Social Science Quarterly* 63 (June 1982): 318–326.
7. Ibid.
8. Sharyne Merritt, "Sex Differences in Role Behavior and Policy Orientations of Suburban Officeholders: The Effect of Women's Employment," in Debra W. Stewart, ed., *Women in Local Politics* (Metuchen, N.J.: Scarecrow, 1980), 115–129; Susan Gluck Mezey, "Support for Women's Rights Policy: An Analysis of Local Politicians," *American Politics Quarterly* 6 (October 1978): 485–497.
9. Susan Welch and Timothy Bledsoe, "Differences in Campaign Support for Male and Female Candidates," in Glenna Spitze and Gwen Moore, eds., *Research in Politics and Society* (Greenwich, Conn.: JAI Press, 1985).
10. Ibid.
11. Grace Saltzstein, "Female Mayors and Women in Municipal Jobs," *American Journal of Political Science* 30 (February 1986): 140–164.
12. Mezey, "Support for Women's Rights Policy."

13. Herbert M. Kritzer and Thomas Uhlman, "Sisterhood in the Courtroom: Sex of Judge and Defendant in Criminal Case Disposition," *Social Science Journal* 14 (April 1977): 77–88; John Gruhl, Cassia Spohn, and Susan Welch, "Women as Policymakers: The Case of Trial Judges," *American Journal of Political Science* 25 (May 1981): 308–322.

14. Gruhl et al., "Women as Policymakers."

15. Beverly Blair Cook, "Will Women Judges Make a Difference in Women's Legal Rights?" in Margherita Rendel, ed., *Women, Power and Political Systems* (London: Croon Helm, 1981), 216–239; but see also Thomas G. Walker and Deborah J. Barrow, "The Diversification of the Federal Bench: Policy and Process Ramifications," *Journal of Politics* 47 (May 1985): 596–617.

16. Welch, "Are Women More Liberal?"

17. See Jean Bethke Elshtain, *Public Man, Private Woman* (Princeton, N.J.: Princeton University Press, 1981); Zillah R. Eisenstein, *The Radical Future of Liberal Feminism* (White Plains, N.Y.: Longman, 1981).

18. See Nancy McGlen and Karen O'Connor, *Women's Rights: The Struggle for Equality in the 19th and 20th Centuries* (New York: Praeger, 1983).

19. Joyce Gelb and Marian Lief Palley, *Women and Public Policies* (Princeton, N.J.: Princeton University Press, 1982).

20. See Diane Sainsbury, "Women's Routes to National Legislatures: A Comparison of Eligibility and Nomination in the United States, Britain, and Sweden," paper presented at the ECPR Workshop on Candidate Selection in Comparative Perspective, Barcelona, March 1985.

21. Katherine Kleeman, *Women's PACs* (New Brunswick, N.J.: Eagleton Institute, 1983).

22. Ibid.

23. Ibid.

24. See Janet Boles, "Building Support for the ERA: A Case of Too Much, Too Late," *PS* 15 (Fall 1982): 572–577.

25. See Jerry Perkins and Diane Fowlkes, "Opinion Representation versus Social Representation: Or Why Women Can't Run as Women and Win," *American Political Science Review* 74 (March 1980): 92–103.

26. Kleeman, *Women's PACs*, 15.

27. Ibid., 11.

28. For a contrary view, see Thomas J. Volgy, John E. Schwarz, and Hildy Gottlieb, "Female Representation and the Quest for Resources: Feminist Activism and Electoral Success," *Social Science Quarterly* 67 (March 1986): 156–168.

References

Abramowitz, Alan. "Name Familiarity, Reputation, and the Incumbency Effect in a Congressional Election." *Western Political Quarterly* 28 (December 1975): 668–684.

Abzug, Bella. *Bella!* New York: Saturday Review Press, 1972.

———, with Mim Kelber. *Gender Gap*. Boston: Houghton Mifflin, 1984.

Adams, William C. "Local Television News Coverage and the Central City." *Journal of Broadcasting* 24 (Spring 1980): 253–265.

Addams, Jane. "The Larger Aspects of the Woman's Suffrage Movement." *Annals of the American Academy of Political and Social Science* 56 (November 1914): 1–8.

Adler, Madeline, and Jewell Bellush. "Lawyers and the Legislature: Something New in New York." *National Civic Review* 68 (May 1979): 245.

Ambrosius, Margery, and Susan Welch. "Women and Politics at the Grassroots: Women Candidates for State Office in Three States, 1950–1978." *Social Science Journal* 21 (January 1984): 29–42.

Andersen, Kristi, and Stuart Thorson. "Some Structural Barriers to the Election of Women to Congress: A Simulation." *Western Political Quarterly* 37 (March 1984): 143–156.

Antolini, Denise. "Women in Local Government: An Overview." In Flammang, *Political Women*, 23–40.

Arian, Alan. "Stability and Change in Israeli Public Opinion and Politics." *Public Opinion Quarterly* 35 (Spring 1971): 19–35.

Barker, Ernest. *Greek Political Theory*. London: Methuen, 1918.

———. *The Political Thought of Plato and Aristotle*. New York: Dover, 1959.

Barone, Michael, and Grant Ujifusa. *The Almanac of American Politics, 1986*. Washington, D.C.: National Journal, 1985.

Baxter, Sandra, and Marjorie Lansing. *Women and Politics: The Invisible Majority*. Ann Arbor: University of Michigan Press, 1980.

Beard, Mary. "The Legislative Influence of Unenfranchised Women." *Annals of the American Academy of Political and Social Science* 56 (November 1914): 54–61.

Beckwith, Karen L. "Structural Barriers to Women's Access to Office: The Case of France, Italy, and the United States." Paper presented at the meeting of the American Political Science Association, Washington, D.C., September 1984.

Benze, James, and Eugene Declercq. "The Importance of Gender in Congressional and Statewide Elections." *Social Science Quarterly* 66 (December 1985): 954–963.

Bernick, Lee. "Legislative Reform and Legislative Turnover." Paper presented at the meeting of the American Political Science Association, Washington, D.C., August 1977.

Bernstein, Robert. "Why Are There So Few Women in the House?" *Western Political Quarterly* 39 (March 1986): 155–164.

Bers, Trudy. "Local Political Elites: Men and Women on Boards of Education." *Western Political Quarterly* 31 (September 1978): 381–391.

Beyer, Hans. *Die Frau in der politischen Entscheidung: Eine Untersuchung über das Frauenwahlrecht in Deutschland.* Stuttgart: F. Enke, 1933.

Bledsoe, Timothy, and Susan Welch. "The Effect of Political Structures on the Socioeconomic Characteristics of Urban City Council Members." *American Politics Quarterly* 13 (October 1985): 467–484.

Bogdanor, V. "Conclusion: Electoral Systems and Party Systems." In V. Bogdanor and David Butler, eds., *Democracy and Elections.* Cambridge: Cambridge University Press, 1983.

Boles, Janet. "Building Support for the ERA: A Case of Too Much, Too Late." *PS* 15 (Fall 1982): 572–577.

———. *The Politics of the Equal Rights Amendment.* White Plains, N.Y.: Longman, 1979.

Breckinridge, Sophonisba P. *Women in the Twentieth Century.* New York: McGraw-Hill, 1933.

Bristow, Stephen. "Women Councillors: An Explanation of the Underrepresentation of Women in Local Government." *Local Government Studies* 6 (May-June 1980): 73–90.

Brodie, Janine. *Point of Entry: The Election of Women in Canada.* Montreal: McGill–Queen's University Press, 1984.

Brown, Robert E., and Katherine Brown. *Virginia, 1705–1786: Democracy or Aristocracy?* East Lansing: Michigan State University Press, 1964.

Browning, Rufus, Dale R. Marshall, and David Tabb. *Protest Is Not Enough: The Struggle of Blacks and Hispanics for Equality in Urban Politics.* Berkeley: University of California Press, 1984.

Bullock, Charles, and Patricia Heys. "Recruitment of Women for Congress: A Research Note." *Western Political Quarterly* 25 (September 1972): 416–423.

Bullock, Charles, and Loch Johnson. "Sex and the Second Primary." *Social Science Quarterly* 66 (December 1985): 933–944.

Burns, James MacGregor. *The Vineyard of Liberty.* New York: Knopf, 1981.

Burrell, Barbara. "Women's and Men's Campaigns for the U.S. House of Representatives, 1972–1982: A Finance Gap?" *American Politics Quarterly* 13 (July 1985): 251–272.

Bush, G. W. A. "Voters in a Multi-member Constituency: The 1977 Auckland Election." *Electoral Studies* 4 (December 1985): 241–254.

Butler, David, and M. Pinto-Duschinsky. "The Conservative Elite, 1918–1978: Does Unrepresentativeness Matter?" In Z. Layton-Henry, ed., *Conservative Party Politics.* Atlantic Highlands, N.J.: Humanities Press, 1980.

Butler, Melissa. "Early Liberal Roots of Liberal Feminism: John Locke and the Attack on Patriarchy." *American Political Science Review* 72 (March 1978): 135–150.

Byrne, Gary, and J. Kristian Pueschel. "But Who Should I Vote for for County Coroner?" *Journal of Politics* 36 (August 1974): 778–784.

Cain, Bruce E. "Assessing the Partisan Effects of Redistricting." *American Political Science Review* 79 (June 1985): 320–333.

Campbell, Angus, Philip Converse, Warren Miller, and Donald Stokes. *The American Voter.* New York: Wiley, 1960.
――――. *Elections and the Political Order.* New York: Wiley, 1966.
Carroll, Kathleen. "The Age Difference between Men and Women Politicians." *Social Science Quarterly* 63 (June 1982): 332–339.
Carroll, Kenneth. *Quakerism on the Eastern Shore.* Baltimore: Maryland Historical Society, 1970.
Carroll, Susan. "Women Candidates and State Legislative Elections, 1976: Limitations on the Political Opportunity Structure and Their Effects on Electoral Participation and Success." Paper presented at the meeting of the American Political Science Association, Washington, D.C., September 1977.
――――. "Women Candidates and Support for Women's Issues: Closet Feminists." *Western Political Quarterly* 37 (June 1984): 307–323.
――――, and Wendy Strimling. *Women's Routes to Elective Office.* New Brunswick, N.J.: Eagleton Institute, 1983.
Carver, Joan. "Women in Florida." *Journal of Politics* 41 (August 1979): 941–955.
Castles, Francis. "Female Legislative Representation and the Electoral System." *Politics* 1 (April 1981): 21–26.
Center for the American Woman and Politics. *Women in Elective Office, 1975–1980: Fact Sheet.* New Brunswick, N.J., 1984.
Charlot, Monica. "Women in Politics in France." In Howard R. Penniman, ed., *The French National Assembly Elections of 1978.* Washington, D.C.: American Enterprise Institute, 1980, 189–190.
Chou, Bir-Er, and Janet Clark. "Women Legislators in Taiwan: Barriers to Women's Participation in a Modernizing State." In *Working Papers on Women in Development.* East Lansing: Michigan State University, 1986.
Chrisman, Sarah B., Marilyn Johnson, Kathy Stanwick, Susan Vogel, Christine Li, Pauline Shoback, Patricia DeCamdia, Geraldine DiCicco, Karen Keiler, and Barbara Sigmund. *Women in Public Office: A Biographical Directory and Statistical Analysis.* New York: R. R. Bowker, 1976.
Clark, Janet. "Party Leaders and Women's Entry into the Political Elites." Paper presented at the meeting of the Southwestern Political Science Association, Fort Worth, April 1979.
――――, R. Darcy, Susan Welch, and Margery Ambrosius. "Women as Legislative Candidates in Six States." In Flammang, *Political Women,* 141–155.
Converse, Philip. "The Structure of Belief Systems in Mass Publics." In David Apter, ed., *Ideology and Discontent.* New York: Free Press, 1964, 206–261.
Cook, Beverly Blair. "Will Women Judges Make a Difference in Women's Legal Rights?" In Margherita Rendel, ed., *Women, Power and Political Systems.* London: Croon Helm, 1981, 216–239.
Cook, Edward M. *The Fathers of the Towns: Leadership and Community Structure in Eighteenth Century New England.* Baltimore: Johns Hopkins University Press, 1976.
Cope, Esther. "Some Women's Thoughts about War in Early Stuart England." Paper presented at the North American Conference on British Studies, Houston, November 1985.
――――. "Women from the Nobility and Gentry in Politics." Unpublished paper, Department of History, University of Nebraska, 1985.

Costantini, Edmond, and Kenneth H. Craik. "Women as Politicians: The Social Background, Personality, and Political Careers of Female Party Leaders." In Githens and Prestage, *Portrait of Marginality,* 221-240.

Council of State Governments. *State Elective Officials and the Legislatures, 1981-1982.* Lexington, Ky., 1981.

———. *State Elective Officials and the Legislatures, 1983-1984.* Lexington, Ky., 1983.

Countryman, Edward. *A people in Revolution: The American Revolution and Political Society in New York, 1760-1790.* Baltimore: Johns Hopkins University Press. 1981.

Cover, Albert. "One Good Term Deserves Another: The Advantage of Incumbency in Congressional Elections." *American Journal of Political Science* 21 (August 1977): 523-542.

Culley, L. "Women in Politics." In L. Robins, ed., *Updating British Politics.* London: Politics Association, 1984.

Curran, Barbara. *Lawyers' Statistical Report.* Chicago: American Bar Foundation, 1985.

Currey, Virginia. "Campaign Theory and Practice: The Gender Variable." In Githens and Prestage, *Portrait of Marginality,* 150-171.

Daniels, Mark, and R. Darcy. "As Time Goes By: The Arrested Diffusion of the Equal Rights Amendment." *Publius* 15 (Fall 1985): 51-60.

———. "Notes on the Use and Interpretation of Discriminant Analysis." *American Journal of Political Science* 27 (May 1983): 359-381.

———, and Joseph Westphal. "The ERA Won—At Least in the Opinion Polls." *PS* 15 (Fall 1982): 578-584.

Darcy, R. "Position Effects with Party Column Ballots." *Western Political Quarterly* 39 (December 1986).

———, Margaret Brewer, and Judy Clay. "Women in the Oklahoma Political System: State Legislative Elections." *Social Science Journal* 21 (January 1984): 67-78.

Darcy, R., and James R. Choike. "A Formal Analysis of Legislative Turnover: Women Candidates and Legislative Representation." *American Journal of Political Science* 30 (February 1986): 237-255.

Darcy, R., Charles D. Hadley, and Janet Clark. "The Changing Role of Southern Women in State Party Politics." Paper presented at the Citadel Symposium on Southern Politics, Charleston, S.C., March 1986.

Darcy, R., and Sarah Slavin Schramm. "When Women Run against Men." *Public Opinion Quarterly* 41 (Spring 1977): 1-12.

Darcy, R., and Sunhee Song. "Men and Women in the Korean National Assembly: Social Barriers to Representational Roles." *Asian Survey* 26 (June 1986): 670-687.

Davidson, Chandler, ed. *Minority Vote Dilution.* Washington, D.C.: Howard University Press, 1984.

Dawson, Paul, and James Zinser. "Broadcast Expenditures and Electoral Outcomes in the 1970 Congressional Elections." *Public Opinion Quarterly* 35 (Fall 1971): 398-402.

Deber, Raisa. "'The Fault, Dear Brutus': Women as Congressional Candidates in Pennsylvania." *Journal of Politics* 44 (May 1982): 463-479.

Declercq, Eugene, James Benze, and Elisa Ritchie. "Macha Women and Macho Men: The Role of Gender in Campaigns Involving Women." Paper presented at the meeting of the American Political Science Association, Chicago, September 1983.

Dexter, Elisabeth Anthony. *Colonial Women of Affairs: Women in Business and the Professions in America before 1776.* Boston: Houghton Mifflin, 1931.

Diamond, Irene. *Sex Roles in the State House.* New Haven, Conn.: Yale University Press, 1977.

———, and Nancy Hartstock. "Beyond Interests in Politics: A Comment on Virginia Sapiro's 'When Are Interests Interesting? The Problem of Political Representation of Women.'" *American Political Science Review* 75 (September 1981): 717–721.

Dinkin, Robert J. *Voting in Provincial America: A Study of Elections in the Thirteen Colonies, 1689–1776.* Westport, Conn.: Greenwood, 1977.

———. *Voting in Revolutionary America.* Westport, Conn.: Greenwood, 1982.

Dodge, Mrs. Arthur. "Women's Suffrage Opposed to Woman's Rights." *Annals of the American Academy of Political and Social Science* 56 (November 1914): 99–104.

Duncan, Otis D. "Inheritance of Poverty or Inheritance of Race?" In Daniel P. Moynihan, ed., *Understanding Poverty.* New York: Basic Books, 1969.

Duverger, Maurice. *Political Parties.* London: Methuen, 1954.

———. *The Political Role of Women.* Paris: UNESCO, 1955.

Eckert, Fred W. "Effects of Woman's Suffrage on the Political Situation in the City of Chicago." *Political Science Quarterly* 31 (March 1916): 105–121.

Eduards, Maud. *Kvinnor och Politik: Fakta och Forklaringar.* Stockholm: Liber Forlag, 1977.

———. "Sweden," in Lovenduski and Hills, *Politics of the Second Electorate,* 208–227.

Eisenstein, Zillah R. *The Radical Future of Liberal Feminism.* White Plains, N.Y.: Longman, 1981.

Elazar, Daniel J. *American Federalism: A View from the States.* New York: Crowell, 1966.

Elshtain, Jean Bethke. *Public Man, Private Woman.* Princeton, N.J.: Princeton University Press, 1981.

Engstrom, Richard, and Michael McDonald. "The Election of Blacks to City Councils: Clarifying the Impact of Electoral Arrangements on the Seats/Population Relationship." *American Political Science Review* 75 (June 1981): 344–354.

———, and Bir-Er Chou. "The Election of Women to Central City Councils in the United States: A Note on the Desirability and Compatibility Explanations." Paper presented at the meeting of the International Society of Political Psychology, Toronto, June 1984.

Epstein, Cynthia Fuchs. *Woman's Place.* Berkeley: University of California Press, 1970.

Epstein, Leon. *Political Parties in Western Democracies,* rev. ed. New Brunswick, N.J.: Transaction Books, 1980.

Erikson, Robert. "Malapportionment, Gerrymandering, and Party Fortunes in Congressional Elections." *American Political Science Review* 66 (December 1972): 1234–1245.

Eulau, Heinz, and John Sprague. *Lawyers in Politics: A Study of Professional Convergence.* Indianapolis: Bobbs-Merrill, 1961.

Fiedler, Maureen. "Congressional Ambitions of Female Political Elites." Paper presented at the meeting of the Capitol Area Political Science Association, Washington, D.C., April 1975.

Fiorina, Morris P. *Congress: The Keystone of the Washington Establishment.* New Haven, Conn.: Yale University Press, 1977.

Fishel, Jeff. *Party and Opposition: Congressional Challengers in American Politics.* New York: McKay, 1973.

Fisichella, Domenico. "The Double-Ballot System as a Weapon against Anti-system Parties." In Lijphart and Grofman, *Choosing an Electoral System,* 181–190.

Flammang, Janet. "Female Officials in the Feminist Capital: The Case of Santa Clara County." *Western Political Quarterly* 38 (March 1985): 94–118.

―――. "Filling the Party Vacuum: Women at the Grassroots Level in Local Politics." In Flammang, *Political Women,* 87–113.

―――, ed. *Political Women: Current Roles in State and Local Government.* Beverly Hills, Calif.: Sage, 1984.

Flexner, Eleanor. *Century of Struggle: The Woman's Rights Movement in the United States,* rev. ed. Cambridge, Mass.: Harvard University Press, 1975.

Fowlkes, Diane, Jerry Perkins, and Sue Tolleson Rinehart. "Gender Roles and Party Roles." *American Political Science Review* 73 (September 1979): 772–780.

Fraser, Antonia. *The Weaker Vessel.* New York: Random House, 1985.

Frost, J. William. *The Quaker Family in Colonial America: A Portrait of the Society of Friends.* New York: Saint Martin's Press, 1973.

Gallup, George. *The Gallup Poll: Public Opinion, 1935–1971.* New York: Random House, 1971.

Gelb, Joyce, and Marian Lief Palley. *Women and Public Policies.* Princeton, N.J.: Princeton University Press, 1982.

Gertzog, Irwin. "Changing Patterns of Female Recruitment to the U.S. House of Representatives." *Legislative Studies Quarterly* 4 (August 1979): 429–445.

―――. *Congressional Women: Their Recruitment, Treatment, and Behavior.* New York: Praeger, 1984.

―――, and M. Michele Simard. "Women and 'Hopeless' Congressional Candidacies: Nomination Frequency, 1916–1978." *American Politics Quarterly* 9 (October 1981): 449–466.

Githens, Marianne. "The Elusive Paradigm: Gender, Politicals and Political Behavior." In Ada Finifter, ed., *Political Science: The State of the Discipline.* Washington, D.C.: American Political Science Association, 1983.

―――, and Jewell Prestage, eds. *A Portrait of Marginality: The Political Behavior of the American Woman.* New York: McKay, 1977.

Goldenberg, Edie, and Michael Traugott. "Congressional Campaign Effects on Candidate Recognition and Evaluation." *Political Behavior* 2 (Spring 1980): 61–90.

Groeneman, Sid. "Candidate Sex and Delegate Voting in a Preprimary Party Endorsement Election." *Women and Politics* 3 (Spring 1983): 39–56.

Gruhl, John, Cassia Spohn, and Susan Welch. "Women as Policymakers: The Case of Trial Judges." *American Journal of Political Science* 25 (May 1981): 308–322.

Haavio-Mannila, Elina. "Changes in Sex Roles in Politics as an Indicator of Structural Change in Society." *International Journal of Sociology* 8 (Spring 1978): 56–85.

―――, Drude Dahlerup, Maude Eduards, Esther Gudmundsdottir, Beatrice Halsaa, Helga Maria Hernes, Eva Hanninen-Salmelin, Bergthora Sigmundsdottir, Sirkka Sinkkonen, and Torild Skard. *Det Uferdige Demokratiet: Kvinner i Nordisk Politikk.* Oslo: Nordisk Ministerrad, 1983.

Hall, Jane. "West Germany." In Lovenduski and Hills, *Politics of the Second Electorate,* 153–181.

Hallett, George. "Proportional Representation with the Single Transferable Vote: A Basic Requirement for Legislative Elections." In Lijphart and Grofman, *Choosing an Electoral System*, 113–125.

Hanson, Bertil. "Oklahoma's Experiment with Direct Legislation." *Southwestern Social Science Quarterly* 27 (December 1966): 262–273.

Hibbing, John R. *Choosing to Leave: Voluntary Retirement from the U.S. House of Representatives.* Washington, D.C.: University Press of America, 1982.

Hill, David. "Female State Senators as Cue Givers: ERA Roll-Call Voting, 1972–1979." In Flammang, *Political Women*, 177–190.

——. "Political Culture and Female Political Representation." *Journal of Politics* 43 (February 1981): 159–168.

——. "A Time Series Analysis of Female Representation in the Legislatures." Paper presented at the meeting of the Midwest Political Science Association, Chicago, April 1980.

——. "Women State Legislators and Party Voting on the ERA." *Social Science Quarterly* 63 (June 1982): 318–326.

Hinckley, Barbara. *Congressional Elections.* Washington, D.C.: Congressional Quarterly Press, 1981.

——. "Interpreting House Midterm Elections." *American Political Science Review* 70 (September 1976): 694–700.

——, Richard Hofstetter, and John Kessel. "Issues, Information Costs, and Congressional Elections." *American Politics Quarterly* 2 (April 1974): 131–152.

Huckshorn, Robert, and Robert Spencer. *The Politics of Defeat: Campaigning for Congress.* Boston: University of Massachusetts Press, 1971.

Illik, Joseph. *Colonial Pennsylvania: A History.* New York: Scribner, 1976.

Jacquette, Jane, ed. *Women in Politics.* New York: Wiley, 1974.

Jacobson, Gary. "The Impact of Broadcast Journalism on Electoral Outcomes." *Journal of Politics* 37 (August 1975): 769–793.

——. *Money in Congressional Elections.* New Haven, Conn.: Yale University Press, 1980.

——, and Samuel Kernell. *Strategy and Choice in Congressional Elections.* New Haven, Conn.: Yale University Press, 1981.

James, Sidney. *Colonial Rhode Island: A History.* New York: Scribner, 1975.

Jennings, M. Kent, and Norman Thomas. "Men and Women in Party Elites: Social Roles and Political Resources." *Midwest Journal of Political Science* 12 (November 1966): 462–492.

Jewell, Malcolm, and Samuel Patterson. *The Legislative Process in the United States.* New York: Random House, 1973.

Johansen, Elaine. *Comparable Worth.* Boulder, Colo.: Westview, 1984.

Johnson, Charles. "Political Culture in American States: Elazar's Formulation Examined." *American Journal of Political Science* 20 (August 1976): 491–509.

Johnson, Marilyn, and Susan Carroll. "Statistical Report: Profile of Women Holding Public Office, 1977." In Kathy Stanwick and Marilyn Johnson, eds., *Women in Public Office: A Biographical Directory and Statistical Analysis.* Metuchen, N.J.: Scarecrow, 1978.

Jones, Woodrow, and Albert Nelson. "Correlates of Women's Representation in Lower State Legislative Chambers." *Social Behavior and Personality* 9 (1981): 9–15.

Kammen, Michael K. *Colonial New York: A History.* New York: Scribner, 1975.

Karnig, Albert, and B. Oliver Walter. "Election of Women to City Councils." *Social Science Quarterly* 56 (March 1976): 605–613.

Karnig, Albert, and Susan Welch. *Black Representation and Urban Policy.* Chicago: University of Chicago Press, 1980.

——. "Sex and Ethnicity in Municipal Representation." *Social Science Quarterly* 60 (December 1979): 465–481.

Kazee, Thomas, and Mary Thornberry. "Can We Throw the Rascals Out? Recruiting Challengers in Competitive Districts." Paper presented at the meeting of the American Political Science Association, Chicago, September 1983.

Kelley, Jonathan, and Ian McAllister. "Ballot Paper Cues and the Vote in Australia and Britain: Alphabetic Voting, Sex, and Title." *Public Opinion Quarterly* 48 (Summer 1984): 452–466.

Kelley, Joseph J. *Pennsylvania: The Colonial Years, 1681-1776.* Garden City, N.Y.: Doubleday, 1980.

Kerber, Linda K. *Women of the Republic: Intellect and Ideology in Revolutionary America.* Chapel Hill: University of North Carolina Press, 1980.

Key, V. O., and Winston W. Crouch. *The Initiative and Referendum in California.* Berkeley: University of California Press, 1939.

Kiewiet, Roderick. *The Rationality of Candidates Who Challenge Incumbents in Congressional Elections,* Social Science Working Paper No. 436. Pasadena: Division of Humanities and Social Sciences, California Institute of Technology, 1982.

Kincaid, Diane. "Over His Dead Body: A Positive Perspective on Widows in the U.S. Congress." *Western Political Quarterly* 31 (March 1978): 96–104.

King, Elizabeth. "Women in Iowa Legislative Politics." In Githens and Prestage, *Portrait of Marginality,* 284–303.

Kirkpatrick, Jeane. *Political Woman.* New York: Basic Books, 1974.

Kleeman, Katherine E. *Women's PACs.* New Brunswick, N.J.: Eagleton Institute of Politics, 1983.

Kohn, Walter. *Women in National Legislatures.* New York: Praeger, 1980.

Kraditor, Aileen. *The Ideas of the Woman Suffrage Movement, 1890-1920.* New York: Norton, 1981.

Kritzer, Herbert, and Thomas Uhlman. "Sisterhood in the Courtroom: Sex of the Judge and Defendant in Criminal Case Disposition." *Social Science Journal* 14 (April 1977): 77–88.

Lakeman, Enid. "Electoral Systems and Women in Parliament." *Parliamentarian* 56 (July 1976): 159–162.

——. *How Democracies Vote.* London: Faber & Faber, 1970.

Lamson, Peggy. *Few Are Chosen.* Boston: Houghton Mifflin, 1968.

Lane, Robert. *Political Life: Why People Get Involved in Politics.* Glencoe, Ill.: Free Press, 1959.

Leader, Shelah Gilbert. "The Policy Impact of Elected Women Officials." In Louis Maisel and Joseph Cooper, eds., *The Impact of the Electoral Process.* Beverly Hills, Calif.: Sage, 1977.

Lee, Marcia Manning. "Why So Few Women Hold Public Office: Democracy and Sex Roles." *Political Science Quarterly* 91 (Summer 1976): 297–314.

Lefler, Hugh, and William Powell. *Colonial North Carolina: A History.* New York: Scribner, 1973.

Lemons, J. Stanley. *The Woman Citizen: Social Feminism in the 1920's.* Urbana: University of Illinois Press, 1973.

Lerner, Gerda. "The Lady and the Mill Girl: Changes in the Status of Women in the Age of Jackson." *Midcontinent American Studies Journal* 10 (Spring 1969): 5–14.

Lijphart, Arend. *Democracies: Patterns of Majoritarian and Consensus Government in Twenty-one Countries.* New Haven, Conn.: Yale University Press, 1984.

———, and Bernard Grofman, eds. *Choosing an Electoral System: Issues and Alternatives.* New York: Praeger, 1984.

Lipman-Blumen, Jean. "Role De-differentiation as a System Response to Crisis: Occupational and Political Roles of Women." *Sociological Inquiry* 43 (1973): 105–129.

Locke, John. *The Second Treatise of Government.* Indianapolis: Bobbs-Merrill, 1952.

Lockridge, Kenneth A. *A New England Town, the First Hundred Years: Dedham, Massachusetts, 1636–1736.* New York: Norton, 1970.

Lovenduski, Joni, and Jill Hills. "Conclusions." In Lovenduski and Hills, *Politics of the Second Electorate,* 320–328.

———, eds. *The Politics of the Second Electorate: Women and Public Participation.* London: Routledge & Kegan Paul, 1981.

Lynn, Naomi. "Women and American Politics: An Overview." In Jo Freeman, ed., *Women: A Feminist Perspective.* Palo Alto, Calif.: Mayfield, 1975, 264–285.

Mackerras, Malcolm. "Do Women Candidates Lose Votes? Further Evidence." *Australian Quarterly* 52 (1980): 450–455.

MacManus, Susan. "Determinants of the Equitability of Female Representation on 243 City Councils." Paper presented at the meeting of the American Political Science Association, Chicago, August 1976.

Madison, James. "Factions: Their Cause and Control." In Alexander Hamilton, John Jay, and James Madison, *The Federalist Papers,* selected and edited by Andrew Hacker. New York: Pocket Books, 1964, 16–24.

Main, Eleanor C., Gerard Gryski, and Beth Schapiro. "Different Perspectives: Southern State Legislators' Attitudes about Women in Politics." *Social Science Journal* 21 (January 1984): 21–28.

Maisel, Louis. *From Obscurity to Oblivion: Running in the Congressional Primary.* Knoxville: University of Tennessee Press, 1982.

Mandel, Ruth. *In the Running: The New Woman Candidate.* New York: Ticknor & Fields, 1981.

Mann, Thomas. *Unsafe at Any Margin: Interpreting Congressional Elections.* Washington, D.C.: American Enterprise Institute, 1978.

Margolis, Diane. "The Invisible Hands: Sex Roles and the Division of Labor in Two Local Political Parties." In Stewart, *Women in Local Politics,* 22–41.

Martin, Marion. "Fair Play in Maine: Down East Women Legislators Given Equal Footing." *State Government* 10 (October 1937): 212–213.

———, and Bernice van de Vries. "Women in State Capitols." *State Government* 10 (October 1937): 213–215.

Matthews, Donald R. "Legislative Recruitment and Legislative Careers." *Legislative Studies Quarterly* 9 (November 1984): 547–585.

Mayhew, David. *Congress: The Electoral Connection.* New Haven, Conn.: Yale University Press, 1974.

McDonald, Jean Graves, and Vickey Howell Pierson. "Female County Party Leaders and the Perception of Discrimination: A Test of the Male Conspiracy Theory." *Social Science Journal* 21 (January 1984): 13–20.

McGlen, Nancy E., and Karen O'Connor. *Women's Rights: The Struggle for Equality in the 19th and 20th Centuries.* New York: Praeger, 1983.

McPherson, Mary. "Sex, Race, and Political Participation." Unpublished paper, Department of Sociology, University of Nebraska, 1975.

Means, Ingunn. "Political Recruitment of Women in Norway." *Western Political Quarterly* 25 (September 1972): 491–521.

———. *Kvinner i Norsk Politikk.* Oslo: Cappelen, 1973.

Meier, Kenneth J. "Representative Bureaucracy: An Empirical Analysis." *American Political Science Review* 69 (June 1975): 526–542.

Merritt, Sharyne. "Recruitment of Women to Suburban City Councils: *Higgins* v. *Chevalier.*" In Stewart, *Women in Local Politics,* 86–105.

———. "Sex Differences in Role Behavior and Policy Orientations of Suburban Officeholders: The Effect of Women's Employment." In Stewart, *Women in Local Politics,* 115–129.

———. "Winners and Losers: Sex Differences in Municipal Elections." *American Journal of Political Science* 21 (November 1977): 731–744.

Mezey, Susan Gluck. "Does Sex Make a Difference? A Case Study of Women in Politics." *Western Political Quarterly* 31 (December 1978): 492–501.

———. "The Effect of Sex of Recruitment: Connecticut Local Offices." In Stewart, *Women in Local Politics,* 61–85.

———. "Support for Women's Rights Policy: An Analysis of Local Politicians." *American Politics Quarterly* 6 (October 1978): 485–497.

Mill, John Stuart. *Collected Works,* vol. 21, *Essays on Equality, Law, and Education.* Toronto: University of Toronto Press, 1984.

Miller, Lawrence. "Political Recruitment and Electoral Success: A Look at Sex Differences in Municipal Elections." Paper presented at the meeting of the Southwestern Political Science Association, Fort Worth, April 1984.

———. "Winners and Losers: Another Look at Sex Differences in Municipal Elections." Paper presented at the meeting of the Southern Political Science Association, Memphis, November 1981.

———, and Lillian Noyes. "Winners and Losers: Women Candidates for Municipal Elections Revisited." Paper presented at the meeting of the Midwest Political Science Association, Chicago, April 1980.

Moncure, Dorothy. "Women in Political Life." *Current History* 29 (January 1929): 639–643.

Monroe, Kristen, ed. *The Political Process and Economic Change.* New York: Agathon Press, 1983.

Mossuz-Lavau, Janine, and Mariette Sineau. "France." In Lovenduski and Hills, *Politics of the Second Electorate,* 112–133.

Mueller, John E. "Choosing among 133 Candidates." *Public Opinion Quarterly* 34 (Fall 1970): 395–402.

Munroe, John A. *Colonial Delaware.* Millwood, N.Y.: KTO Press, 1978.

National League of Women Voters. *A Survey of Women in Public Office.* Washington, D.C., 1937.

National Women's Political Caucus. *National Directory of Women Elected Officials, 1981.* Washington, D.C., 1981.

———. *National Directory of Women Elected Officials, 1983.* Washington, D.C., 1983.

———. *National Directory of Women Elected Officials, 1985.* Washington, D.C., 1985.

Nechemias, Carol. "Geographic Mobility and Women's Access to State Legislatures." *Western Political Quarterly* 38 (March 1985): 119–131.

———. "Women's Success in Capturing State Legislative Seats: Stability and Instability of Empirical Relationships over Time." Paper presented at the meeting of the Midwest Political Science Association, Chicago, April 1985.

Newman, Jody, Carrie Costantin, Julie Goetz, and Amy Glosser. *Perception and Reality: A Study of Women Candidates and Fund-Raising.* Washington, D.C.: Women's Campaign Research Fund, 1984.

Nohlen, Dieter. "Two Incompatible Principles of Representation." In Lijphart and Grofman, *Choosing an Electoral System,* 83–89.

"Norway's New Parliament: One Third Women." *News of Norway,* October 15, 1985, 58.

Nurmi, Hannu. "Voting Procedures: A Summary Analysis." *British Journal of Political Science* 13 (April 1983): 181–208.

O'Connor, Robert. "Parties, PACs, and Political Recruitment: The Freshman Class of the Pennsylvania House of Representatives." Paper presented at the meeting of the Midwest Political Science Association, Chicago, April 1984.

———. "Party and Political Recruitment: Access to the Pennsylvania House of Representatives." Paper presented at the meeting of the Midwest Political Science Association, Chicago, April 1985.

Ogburn, William F., and Inez Goltra. "How Women Vote: A Study of an Election in Portland, Oregon." *Political Science Quarterly* 34 (September 1919): 413–433.

Okin, Susan Moller. *Women in Western Political Thought.* Princeton, N.J.: Princeton University Press, 1979.

Ostrogorski, Moisei. *The Rights of Women: A Comparative Study in History and Legislation.* London: Swan Sonnenschein, 1893.

———. "Woman Suffrage in Local Self-government." *Political Science Quarterly* 6 (December 1891): 677–710.

Payne, James. "Career Intentions and Electoral Performance of Members of the U.S. House." *Legislative Studies Quarterly* 7 (February 1982): 93–99.

———. "The Personal Electoral Advantage of House Incumbents." *American Politics Quarterly* 8 (October 1980): 465–482.

Perkins, Jerry, and Diane Fowlkes. "Opinion Representation versus Social Representation: Or Why Women Can't Run as Women and Win." *American Political Science Review* 74 (March 1980): 92–103.

Peters, John, and Susan Welch. "The Effects of Charges of Corruption on Voting Behavior in Congressional Elections." *American Political Science Review* 74 (September 1980): 697–708.

Phillips, M. *The Divided House.* London: Sidgewick & Jackson, 1980.

Pitkin, Hanna Fenichel. *The Concept of Representation.* Berkeley: University of California Press, 1967.

———. *Fortune Is a Woman: Gender and Politics in the Thought of Niccolò Machiavelli.* Berkeley: University of California Press, 1984.

Porritt, Edward. *The Unreformed House of Commons: Parliamentary Representation before 1832,* vol. 1. Cambridge: Cambridge University Press, 1903.

Porter, Mary C., and Ann B. Matasar. "The Role and Status of Women in the Daley Organization." In Jaquette, *Women in Politics,* 85–109.

Powell, Sumner Chilton. *Puritan Village: The Formation of a New England Town.* Middletown, Conn.: Wesleyan University Press, 1963.

Ragsdale, Lyn. "Incumbent Popularity, Challenger Invisibility, and Congressional Voters." *Legislative Studies Quarterly* 6 (May 1981): 201–218.

Randall, Vicky. *Women and Politics.* New York: St. Martin's Press, 1982.

Ranney, Austin. "Parties in State Politics." In Herbert Jacob and Kenneth Vines, eds., *Politics in the American States: A Comparative Analysis,* 3d ed. Boston: Little, Brown, 1976, 51–92.

Rasmussen, Jorgen. "The Electoral Costs of Being a Woman in the 1979 British General Election." *Comparative Politics* 15 (July 1983): 461–475.

———. "The Role of Women in British Parliamentary Elections." *Journal of Politics* 39 (November 1977): 1044–1054.

Robson, Anne P. "The Founding of the National Society for Women's Suffrage." *Canadian Journal of History* 8 (March 1983): 1–22.

Rose, Richard. "Electoral Systems: A Question of Degree or of Principle?" In Lijphart and Grofman, *Choosing an Electoral System,* 73–81.

Rosenthal, Alan. *Legislative Life.* New York: Harper & Row, 1981.

Rule, Wilma. "Twenty-three Democracies and Women's Parliamentary Representation." Paper presented at the meeting of the International Political Science Association, Paris, July 1985.

———. "Why Women Don't Run: The Critical Contextual Factors in Women's Legislative Recruitment." *Western Political Quarterly* 34 (March 1981): 60–77.

Ryan, Mary P. *Womanhood in America: From Colonial Times to the Present,* 3d ed. New York: Franklin Watts, 1983.

Sainsbury, Diane. "Women's Routes to National Legislatures: A Comparison of Eligibility and Nomination in the United States, Britain, and Sweden." Paper presented at the ECPR Workshop on Candidate Selection in Comparative Perspective, Barcelona, March 1985.

Saltzstein, Grace. "Female Mayors and Women in Municipal Jobs." *American Journal of Political Science* 30 (February 1986): 140–164.

Sapiro, Virginia. "Research Frontier Essay: When Are Interests Interesting? The Problem of Political Representation of Women." *American Political Science Review* 75 (September 1981): 701–716.

Sawyer, Marian. "Women and Women's Issues in the 1980 Federal Election." *Politics* 16 (1981): 243–249.

Saxonhouse, Arlene W. *Women in the History of Political Thought: Ancient Greece to Machiavelli.* New York: Praeger, 1985.

Schlesinger, Joseph. *Ambition and Politics: Political Careers in the United States.* Chicago: Rand McNally, 1966.

Schramm, Sarah Slavin. "Women and Representation: Self-government and Role Change." *Western Political Quarterly* 34 (March 1981): 46–59.

Schwemle, Barbara. *Women in the United States Congress.* Washington, D.C., Congressional Research Service, 1983.

Seligman, Lester. "Political Recruitment and Party Structures: A Case Study." *American Political Science Review* 60 (March 1961): 77–86.

———, Chong Lim Kim, and Roland Smith. *Patterns of Recruitment.* Chicago: Rand McNally, 1974.

Shaw, Anna Howard. "Equal Suffrage: A Problem of Political Justice." *Annals of the American Academy of Political and Social Science* 56 (November 1914): 93–98.

Sigelman, Lee. "The Curious Case of Women in State and Local Government." *Social Science Quarterly* 57 (March 1976): 591–604.

———, and Susan Welch. "Race, Gender, and Opinion toward Black and Female Presidential Candidates." *Public Opinion Quarterly* 48 (Summer 1984): 467–475.

Skard, Torild. *Utvalgt till Stortinget*. Oslo: Gyldendal, 1980.

———, and Elina Haavio-Mannila. "Equality between the Sexes: Myth or Reality in Norden?" *Daedalus* 113 (Winter 1984): 141–167.

Slater, Philip E. *The Glory of Hera*. Boston: Beacon Press, 1968.

Sorauf, Frank. *Party and Representation: Legislative Politics in Pennsylvania*. New York: Atherton, 1963.

Spruill, Julia Cherry. *Women's Life and Work in the Southern Colonies*. New York: Norton, 1972.

Stanton, Elizabeth Cady, Susan B. Anthony, and Matilda Gage, eds., *History of Woman Suffrage*, 2 vols. Rochester, N.Y.: Charles Mann, 1887.

Staveley, E. S. *Greek and Roman Voting and Elections*. Ithaca, N.Y.: Cornell University Press, 1972.

Stewart, Debra, ed. *Women in Local Politics*. Metuchen, N.J.: Scarecrow, 1980.

Stewart, Ella Seass. "Woman Suffrage and the Liquor Traffic." *Annals of the American Academy of Political and Social Science* 56 (November 1914): 134–152.

Stokes, Donald, and Warren Miller. "Party Government and the Salience of Congress." *Public Opinion Quarterly* 26 (Winter 1966): 531–546.

Stone, Clarence, Robert Whelan, and William Murin. *Urban Policy and Politics in a Bureaucratic Age*. Englewood Cliffs, N.J.: Prentice-Hall, 1979.

Stoper, Emily. "Wife and Politician: Role Strain among Women in Public Office." In Githens and Prestage, *Portrait of Marginality*, 320–337.

Straffin, Philip. *Topics in the Theory of Voting*. Boston: Birkhauser, 1980.

Sumner, Helen L. *Equal Suffrage*. New York: Harper, 1909.

Tolchin, Susan, and Martin Tolchin. *Clout: Womanpower and Politics*. New York: Coward, McCann & Geoghegan, 1973.

Tully, Alan. *William Penn's Legacy: Politics and Social Structure in Provincial Pennsylvania, 1726–1755*. Baltimore: Johns Hopkins University Press, 1977.

Uhlaner, Carole, and Kay Schlozman. "Candidate Gender and Congressional Campaign Receipts." *Journal of Politics* 48 (February 1986): 30–50.

U.S. Commission on Civil Rights. *Social Indicators of Equality for Minorities and Women*. Washington, D.C.: Government Printing Office, 1978.

Valen, Henry. "The Storting Election of September 1985: The Welfare State under Pressure." *Scandinavian Political Studies* (forthcoming).

Vallance, Elizabeth. "Where the Power Is, Women Are Not." *Parliamentary Affairs* 35 (Spring 1982): 218–219.

———. *Women in the House: A Study of Women Members of Parliament*. London: Athlone, 1979.

Van der Ros, Janneke. "Women and Politics in the Nordic Countries: A Complex Picture." In Howard Penniman, ed., *Women at the Polls*. Washington, D.C.: American Enterprise Institute, unpublished manuscript.

Van de Vries, Bernice. "Housekeeping in the Legislature." *State Government 21* (June 1948): 127–128.

Van Hightower, Nicki. "The Recruitment of Women for Public Office." *American Politics Quarterly* 5 (July 1977): 301–314.

Volgy, Thomas J., James E. Schwarz, and Hildy Gottlieb. "Female Representation and the Quest for Resources: Feminist Activism and Electoral Success." *Social Science Quarterly* 67 (March 1986): 156–168.

Walker, Thomas, and Deborah J. Barrow. "The Diversification of the Federal Bench: Policy and Process Ramifications." *Journal of Politics* 47 (May 1985): 596–617.

Wang, Alice Ai-Fen, and Helen Hsieh-chin Yeh. "Women's Contributions to National Development of the Republic of China." *Proceedings of Asian Woman Parliamentarian's Seminar* (Seoul, 1982: 37–50.

Weaver, Leon. "Semi-proportional Representation Systems in the United States." In Lijphart and Grofman, *Choosing an Electoral System,* 191–206.

Webb, Stephen Saunders. *1676: The End of American Independence.* Cambridge, Mass.: Harvard University Press, 1985.

Weis, S., and Yael Yishai. "Women's Representation in Israeli Political Elites." *Jewish Social Studies* 42 (Spring 1980): 165–176.

Welch, Susan. "Are Women More Liberal than Men in the U.S. Congress?" *Legislative Studies Quarterly* 10 (February 1984): 125–134.

————. "Recruitment of Women to Public Office." *Western Political Quarterly* 31 (September 1978): 372–380.

————, Margery Ambrosius, Janet Clark, and R. Darcy. "The Effect of Candidate Gender on Election Outcomes in State Legislative Races." *Western Political Quarterly* 38 (September 1985): 464–475.

Welch, Susan, and Timothy Bledsoe. "Differences in Campaign Support for Male and Female Candidates." In Glenna Spitze and Gwen Moore, eds., *Research in Politics and Society.* Greenwich, Conn.: JAI Press, 1985.

Welch, Susan, and Albert Karnig. "Correlates of Female Office Holding in City Politics." *Journal of Politics* 41 (May 1979): 478–491.

————. "Sex and Ethnic Differences in Municipal Representation." *Social Science Quarterly* 60 (December 1979): 465–481.

Welch, Susan, and Lee Sigelman. "Changes in Public Attitudes toward Women in Politics." *Social Science Quarterly* 63 (June 1982): 312–322.

Welch, Susan, and Donley T. Studlar. "British Public Opinion toward Women in Politics: A Comparative Perspective." *Western Political Quarterly* 39 (March 1986): 138–154.

Werner, Emily, and Louise Bachtold. "Personality Characteristics of Women in American Politics." In Jaquette, *Women in Politics,* 75–84.

Werner, Emmy. "Women in Congress, 1917–1964." *Western Political Quarterly* 19 (March 1966): 16–30.

————. "Women in the State Legislatures." *Western Political Quarterly* 21 (March 1968): 40–50.

Williamson, Chilton. *American Suffrage from Property to Democracy, 1760-1860.* Princeton, N.J.: Princeton University Press, 1960.

Wolchik, Sharon. "Eastern Europe." In Lovenduski and Hills, *Politics of the Second Electorate,* 252–277.

INDEX